Considering AMERICAN Government
A READER

Edited by
Lydia M. Andrade
James W. Riddlesperger, Jr.

Kendall Hunt
publishing company

Cover image © Shutterstock.com

Kendall Hunt
publishing company

www.kendallhunt.com
Send all inquiries to:
4050 Westmark Drive
Dubuque, IA 52004-1840

Copyright © 2017 by Kendall Hunt Publishing Company

ISBN: 978-1-5249-4184-0

All rights reserved. No part of this publication may be reproduced, stored in a retrieval system, or transmitted, in any form or by any means, electronic, mechanical, photocopying, recording, or otherwise, without the prior written permission of the copyright owner.

Published in the United States of America

TABLE OF CONTENTS

INTRODUCTION   v

CHAPTER 1   Graduating From The Electoral College By Lydia Andrade   1

CHAPTER 2   When They Say the Issue Is Federalism, It Isn't By James W. Riddlesperger, Jr.   17

CHAPTER 3   Who's That Charming Stranger With the Check? By Samuel H. Fisher III   33

CHAPTER 4   "But They Didn't Call Me!": Why Polling Works By Adam J. Schiffer   53

CHAPTER 5   Americans Don't Agree; So What? By James F. Sheffield Jr.   67

CHAPTER 6   Not Even A Good Scandal? The Power of Incumbency in Congressional Elections By Jeff Fine   83

CHAPTER 7   How Do You Know Ugly When You See It? Standards and Strategies for Redistricting By Richard N. Engstrom   97

CHAPTER 8   The Speech of a Lifetime By Richard W. Waterman   111

CHAPTER 9   Don't Know Much About the Judiciary By Joseph Stewart, Jr.   129

CHAPTER 10   The Progress Problem In Congress: The Gender Gap In Congressional Female Political Representation By Jennifer Horan   137

CHAPTER 11   Who Gets To Have a Say In Policy-Making? A Look At Health Care Policy By Juan Carlos Huerta And Jo Marie Rios   149

CHAPTER 12   The Supreme's Greatest Hits By Dr. Lydia Andrade   163

INTRODUCTION

The political arena provides a forum for people who disagree on policy to work through their differences to create the laws, regulations, and systems that guide our nation. The U.S. Constitution illustrates how a political system can structure debate. It created a structure for competition between state and national governments and among the three branches of government. In that constitutional plan, the founders established what has often been called "an invitation to struggle." Moreover, struggle began almost immediately. The founders argued about many critical issues, with Alexander Hamilton and Thomas Jefferson, both members of George Washington's initial cabinet, becoming protagonists in the struggle. Hamilton favored federal power as preferable to state power, arguing that the national government should assume the debt run up by states during the Revolutionary War. Jefferson felt the states should be responsible for managing that debt. Hamilton advocated business interests as more important for economic growth as compared to the "yeoman farmers" supported by Jefferson. Moreover, Hamilton argued that England was America's natural ally even though they had been our enemy during the Revolution. Jefferson saw France as the nation's primary ally. These issues and the struggles they represent were every bit as contentious in their day as health care or climate change issues are in our times.

The Hamilton–Jefferson debate led to the development of political parties even though most of the founders thought parties to be unhealthy for American democracy. In fact, Jefferson famously wrote that

> I am not a Federalist, because I never submitted the whole system of my opinions to the creed of any party of men whatever in religion, in philosophy, in politics, or in anything else where I was capable of thinking for myself. Such an addiction is the last degradation of a free and moral agent. If I could not go to heaven but with a party, I would not go there at all. Therefore I protest to you I am not of the party of federalists. But I am much farther from that of the Antifederalists. I approved from the first moment, of the great mass of what is in the new constitution, the consolidation of the government, the organisation into Executive, legislative and judiciary, the subdivision of the legislative, the happy compromise of interests between the great and little states by the different manner of voting in the different houses, the voting by persons instead of states, the qualified negative on laws given to the Executive which however I should have liked better if associated with the judiciary also as in New York, and the power of taxation.[1]

In short, Jefferson, like most of the founders, thought the new Constitution would serve to mediate among interests in the United States in a far better way than would political parties, (which had the names "Federalist" and "Anti-Federalist" in those years).

During the first Congress, the Bill of Rights was added to the Constitution, and it created yet another protection to frame conflict in the United States: The protection in the First Amendment that noted the "right of the people peaceably to assemble, and to petition the Government for a redress of grievances." This simple statement suggested that government need to allow frustrated citizens to gather in ways that allowed them to seek government programs that benefitted their groups or, alternatively, just to blow off steam. However, that provision anticipated the development of organized interests that could pressure government in issues of public policy.

The founders thought that educated elites could rise above faction to make policy in the interests of the nation as a whole and thus parties were unnecessary. However, the struggle over policy led to Hamilton and Jefferson founding the nation's first two parties, and party organization has been a characteristic of political conflict ever since. The creation of the Constitution, and its structured conflicts between the states and the national government and among the three branches of government, the anticipation of organized interests, and the establishment of political parties have structured conflict in the United States for two and a quarter centuries. This book attempts to place struggle and competition in a contemporary context.

Modern America is divided just as meaningfully as it was in the days of Hamilton and Jefferson, and the "polarization" within modern America often leads to feelings of desperation regarding the outcome of policy debates. The election of 2016 was one of the most contentious in U.S. history. Supporters of the two major party candidates for the presidency remain deeply divided. It used to be said that elections were about pointing out the differences among Americans while governing was about trying to discover basic values that united the nation. In modern America, while elections may still serve to point out differences, the task of governing often seems incapable of finding common ground.

If politics is an invitation to struggle, it is made significant mostly because unlike private activities, public activities can be binding on behavior. Therefore, while Bill Gates and Microsoft might have dominated the software market in the United States over the last 25 years, they cannot require citizens to use their products and there are no negative consequences for choosing a competing product. In contrast, when government levies a tax, all citizens must pay or be subject to harsh punishment. Moreover, unlike the choices citizens make about spending money in the private sector, government taxes extract resources in ways and for purposes that may or may not be popular with taxpayers. Indeed, government engages in authoritative decision-making all the time; its decisions are binding on those within a nation's borders. In order to have those decisions made in a productive way, the system must ever be changing to reflect generational differences and technological development.

American politics usefully can be seen as an organic political system, as political scientist David Easton pointed out many years ago.[2] Being organic, it changes in ways to reflect contemporary values that often challenge norms that have defined American politics, sometimes for generations. As a system, there are four key elements that interact with one another to help the system be self-sustaining. The first is the political environment, which sets the basic underpinnings for governance, including building society on shared values that both define and limit decisions. Of course, the environment is constantly changing and it means that politics is constantly adapting to that change. For example, the United States is a largely capitalistic society, meaning that most decisions entered into by government will begin by assessing their impact on the American private economic sector while solutions to problems must be consistent with values of capitalism. However, the role of government in the economy is quite different than it was a generation ago, and that means that policies must continually adapt as the public demands change.

Two basic elements of the political environment found in the Constitution are considered in this text—the system in place to select the president of the United States, an awkward contrivance known as the Electoral College and the idea of federalism, an overlapping and duplicative system stemming from the fact that the Constitution had to deal with existing conditions at the time of its writing. Andrade's Chapter 1, *Graduating from the Electoral College* examines the foundational elements of presidential selection while highlighting the shared influence of the states, political parties, and the public. The chapter demonstrates that the Electoral College itself operates in a manner far different than the founders expected when they penned the Constitution at a time when there were no political parties and no formal system for nominating presidential candidates. The Electoral College was merely a political design to solve the problem of how to choose presidents and has many unresolved issues yet remaining. Of course, the fact that it might select as president a person who did not win the popular vote, a bow to the federal nature of the United States, is a case in point, as the 2016 election demonstrated. Clearly, as with other elements of the Constitution, the Electoral College structures conflict between candidates for the presidency.

Riddlesperger's Chapter 2, *When They Say the Issue Is Federalism, It Isn't* details how claims of federalism questions concerning the proper balance of power between the national and state governments have often been used as excuses for promotion of specific policy preferences. Indeed, since most Americans care about policy outcomes far more than they care about which level of government has responsibility for governance, federalism is often merely a way to displace real policy debates. Moreover, when policy debates take place, if one side sees advantage in devolving power from the national government to the states, it will do so without reference to basic preferences for national or state power.

A second element in the political system involves elements of institutions that connect Americans with their government. In a republic such as the United States, where government action is done through elected representatives, those representatives must have continuing input in order to make government policy comport with the shared values of the electorate. In the United States, these institutions that link the people to the government include public opinion, political parties and elections, and interest groups. In Chapter 3, *Who's That Charming Stranger with the Check?*, Fisher considers campaign contributions as expressions of political speech and signals to decision makers of the public's wishes. In a nation where equality is a basic value in the political environment, the inegalitarian nature of campaign contributions challenges basic notions of fairness and raises questions of the fairness of competition for well-heeled candidates who can seemingly defeat their opponents simply because they have more resources at hand. Schiffer's Chapter 4 *But They Didn't Call Me!: Why Polling Works*, explains modern polling techniques as avenues to understanding public opinion. It demonstrates that while polls can sometimes be wrong in predicting the outcome of elections and often seem mysterious in the way they are conducted, when understood properly they can come closer than other techniques to putting a finger on the pulse of American political preferences. Polls are so ubiquitous in America that they too provide evidence of the struggle between competing ideas. The ramifications of diverse public opinions are explored in Chapter 5, Sheffield's *Americans Don't Agree, So What?* While the divisiveness of the current political climate is clear, leading to extreme polarization in decision-making, division cannot be attributed to strong ideological differences in the American public, which remains relatively free from ideology. But, if ideology does not necessarily define American conflict, political parties do.

The institutions of government are necessary to convert the desires of the public into public policy. Perhaps the invitation to struggle is most profound here. The Constitution creates a system of separation of powers among the three branches—the legislative, the executive, and the judicial—that also serves to make each of the three "check" the other two to make certain that no single branch or actor becomes too powerful. Policy-making in government then becomes inordinately difficult, with the system preferring inaction over dominance by one branch of government. Assessment of political institutions in the United States would seem elemental for an educated electorate, yet recent public opinion polls suggest that barely more than a third of Americans can even name the three branches of government, much less understand how they interact with one another.[3]

A deep dive into assessing the political institutions is clearly required. Accordingly, Chapter 6, *Not Even a Good Scandal?: The Power of Incumbency in Congressional Elections* by Fine explores the role of incumbency advantage in explaining Congressional tenure. The lack of competition in Congressional elections challenges the notion that elections are proper reflections of the will of the people. This may explain why as a matter of course, Congress is the least popular of the branches of government, most recently hovering in the vicinity of 20% approval ratings.[4]

Representation in the United States has always represented a struggle—with the Connecticut Compromise in the Constitution giving us one chamber of Congress representing the states equally (The Senate) and one representing states proportional to their population (The House of Representatives). Because the House was based upon population, the Constitution required a counting of the population each 10 years, a process that gave us the U.S. Census. In Chapter 7, *How Do You Know Ugly When You See It?: Standards and Strategies for Redistricting*, Engstrom examines the process of reapportioning and redistricting of Congress, a process that has led to contentious partisan battles. Parties have become so adept at controlling the redistricting process that most districts in the House are no longer competitive between the two parties. In fact, *The Cook Political Report* demonstrates that while as recently as 1997, there were 164 competitive House seats, by 2017, there are only 72 competitive seats.[5] A major part of the decline in competition stems from the redistricting issues Engstrom addresses. Redistricting politics are perhaps the most purely partisan battles in politics, with the control of Congress potentially determined by who wins in the drawing of district lines.

Congressional politics are one form of institutional struggle, but presidential leadership often frames issue conflict in America. In Chapter 8, *The Speech of a Lifetime*, Richard Waterman considers presidential rhetoric as public leadership. It demonstrates compellingly that while speeches are often important for presidents to convey their messages and can set the stage for political success, the media often overinterprets their meaning as they are being delivered. Great speeches can alter the outcome of policy struggles. Presidents who manage their messaging most effectively are often the most successful leaders.

In Chapter 9, *"Don't Know Much about the Judiciary*, Stewart details how media coverage, both in the news and in entertainment, skews the understanding that Americans have of the judicial branch of government. The judicial process does involve differences in judicial philosophies, but those differences are on relatively narrow grounds with large areas of agreement about what the law is. Moreover, media portrayals of the norms of having contentious trails belies the fact that most cases, criminal and civil alike, are settled long before a trial occurs.

Finally, the political system entails the making of public policy. Of course, if government was not involved in public policy, there would be little reason to study it at all. Policy is the "stuff" of politics. It involves spending our money, regulating our behavior, providing services and in the case of military members or first responders, risking one's own safety for the survival of the system. Which issues we decide are worthy of societal action, how we decide to deal them and the policies we create in response have tremendous importance and are rarely if ever universally agreed upon. In Chapter 10, *The Progress Problem in Congress: The Gender Gap in Congressional Female Political Representation*, Horan considers the history and possibly explanations for the gender inequity in representation found in the United States. The United States continues to have significantly fewer women elected to national office than many other modern democracies. The implications for our democracy raised by such underrepresentation are significant. Studies have continually demonstrated that gender diversity can lead to very different outcomes in group decision-making. Whether they will be addressed remains a question.

The importance of the various institutional and noninstutional policy-making participants is examined in Chapter 11, *Who Gets to Have a Say in Policy-Making: A Look at Health Care Policy*, by Huerta and Rios. Probably the most contentious policy of our time—the Affordable Care Act—demonstrates the key to successful policy-making is the inclusion of numerous interests and significant compromise. Only with the inclusion of hospitals, medical care providers, organized labor, senior citizens, and insurance companies in the 13-month negotiation was the policy-making process successful. Finally, some of the most important policy determining Supreme Court cases are detailed in Chapter 12, *The Supreme's Greatest Hits* by Andrade. Of course, it is a bit unrealistic to think that any short list of cases captures the essence of the Supreme Court. However, a careful reading of the case summaries shows both that judges are guided by some commonly held principles of judicial decision-making and that court decisions can have the impact of law. Judges are more than "politicians in black robes," but their responsibilities often lead them to make decisions that have long-term political consequences.

Governing is a difficult activity. It was not meant to be easy. As James Madison pointed out in Federalist Paper number 51: "If men were angels, no government would be necessary. If angels were to govern men, neither external nor internal controls on government would be necessary."[6] But, because the human condition does not involve perfection, Madison goes on, a government must be created to allow the public interest to be served through the "rough and tumble" of a complex political system. Accordingly, he argued that "Ambition must be made to counteract ambition. The interest of the man must be connected with the constitutional rights of the place. It may be a reflection on human nature, that such devices should be necessary to control the abuses of government."[7] In a nutshell,

Madison states the point. Governing is exceedingly difficult. Moreover, in the American republic, the struggle to find common ground is a perennial challenge. Not just in 2017.

Notes

1. Letter from Thomas Jefferson to Francis Hopkinson, March 13, 1789; https://founders.archives.gov/documents/Jefferson/01-14-02-0402.
2. David Easton, *The Political System. An Inquiry into the State of Political Science*, (New York: Knopf, 1953).
3. Reid Wilson, "Only 36 percent of Americans can name the three branches of government," *Washington Post*, September 18, 2014.
4. Support was at 19% on May 25, 2017 according to the Monmouth Poll.
5. David Wasserman, "Introducing the 2017 Cook Political Report Partisan Voter Index," April 7, 2017, http://cookpolitical.com/file/Cook_Political_Report_Partisan_Voter_Index_.pdf.
6. James Madison, Federalist Paper #51.
7. Ibid.

GRADUATING FROM THE ELECTORAL COLLEGE

BY LYDIA ANDRADE
The University of the Incarnate Word

LEARNING OBJECTIVES

Students should be able to:

1. Explain how the population size of a state is reflected in the Electoral College makeup and how this influences presidential campaigns.
2. Explain the role of political parties in the Electoral College selection process and how this empowers the two-party system.
3. Explain why critics claim the Electoral College may be undemocratic and how it may select a president that the plurality of the U.S. public does not want.
4. Explain the various suggested reforms to the Electoral College and evaluate the likelihood of them being implemented.

On January 20, 2017, Donald J. Trump was sworn in as president of the United States despite having lost the popular vote by more than three million votes.[1] His election set off protests across the United States[2] and the day after his inauguration saw one of the largest political marches in U.S. history.[3] Trump beat his opponent, Hillary Clinton, by attaining 306 Electoral College votes to her 232, but the majority of Americans did not vote for him.[4] In 2001, George W. Bush was also sworn in as president of the United States having won 271 Electoral College votes (one more than the minimum for election) and having *lost* the popular vote by over 540,000 votes.[5] Additionally, the public perception of the Bush "win" was that it was only given to him due to the interference of the Supreme Court. Before these two cases, the last time the winner of the popular vote and Electoral College majority differed was the election of 1876.[6]

How could this happen? How can the Electoral College give us a president that we (the people) did not select? And what role does the Supreme Court play in the process? Clearly, the questions of what this thing called the Electoral College is and how it works are important to understanding our political system.

The Electoral College is quite simply the group of people who select the president of the United States. But who are they and how are they selected? How do they decide for whom to cast their electoral ballots? If they pick the president and they have the ability to select someone other than who the voters chose, we had better understand the institution and who controls it!

Let's start at the beginning.

TIME SCHEDULE

The Electoral College presidential selection process takes place over several weeks as follows.

- Election Day (every four years): In early November, the Electoral College electors are chosen by each state. We call this Election Day. The citizens of the United States go to the polls and there is much discussion about voting for the president. In reality, we are not voting for the president, we are voting for the list of potential Electoral College members associated with a presidential candidate. All the news programs that evening will report who the next president will be. This however is simply a guess based on which electors were selected and based on the assumption that all the electors will vote the way they are supposed to—but we will get to that question later.
- The presidential candidate who wins a state's **popular vote** on Election Day sends his or her electors to the Electoral College.
- Electoral College Votes: Mid-December—The first Monday after the second Wednesday in December, the **electors** meet in their home states and cast ballots for president and vice president. They will cast separate votes for president and vice president.
- The votes are counted: January 6th—The Electoral College votes are opened and counted before a joint session of Congress.
- Inauguration Day: January 20th—The president-elect and vice president-elect are sworn into office.

How are Electors Selected?

To become president, a candidate must win a simple majority of the 538 Electoral College votes. Each state is allocated a number of electors based on the size of their population. As a result, the minimum number of electors given to any state is three—the same as the smallest congressional delegations. The allocation of electors based on state size explains why some states seem to be so much more important to candidates than others. Presidential candidates will be most interested in winning those states with the largest numbers of Electoral College votes in order to get that majority in the Electoral College.

The U.S. Constitution requires that electors are chosen by popular vote within each state but leaves it up to the states to decide whether this is done on a statewide or district basis. The electors can be chosen by general ticket or winner-take-all system where the candidate who wins the most votes will collect all the state's electors. In 48 of the 50 states, this means that a presidential candidate only has to win a **plurality** of a state's popular vote to control all of the Electoral College seats.[7] (Only Nebraska and Maine use a different system for selecting their electors.) Quite simply, in a plurality system, the candidate who wins one more popular vote than the others in a state will have his or her list of Electoral College members seated for that state. So if a state has 10 Electoral College positions and a candidate wins a plurality of the popular vote in that state, all 10 electors will be those associated with this candidate. This becomes very important in the large population states with lots of electors and we will see candidates focus all their efforts on gaining that plurality. (See Table 1 for a list of states and their Electoral College allocations.) But it also means candidates don't have to actually win a majority of the votes to control a state's electors! Imagine a scenario where there are three candidates: Abigail, Benjamin, and Carlos.

Table 1. Electoral Vote Allocation by State, 2010–2020

State	Votes	State	Votes	State	Votes
Alabama	9	Kentucky	8	North Dakota	3
Alaska	3	Louisiana	8	Ohio	18
Arizona	11	Maine	4	Oklahoma	7
Arkansas	6	Maryland	10	Oregon	7
California	55	Massachusetts	11	Pennsylvania	20
Colorado	9	Michigan	16	Rhode Island	4
Connecticut	7	Minnesota	10	South Carolina	9
Delaware	3	Mississippi	6	South Dakota	3
District of Columbia	3	Missouri	10	Tennessee	11
Florida	29	Montana	3	Texas	38
Georgia	16	Nebraska	5	Utah	6
Hawaii	4	Nevada	6	Vermont	3
Idaho	4	New Hampshire	4	Virginia	13
Illinois	20	New Jersey	14	Washington	12
Indiana	11	New Mexico	5	West Virginia	5
Iowa	6	New York	29	Wisconsin	10
Kansas	6	North Carolina	15	Wyoming	3

Source: "Distribution of Electoral Votes" National Archives. 2015. http://www.archives.gov/federal-register/electoral-college/allocation.html

If Abigail wins 40% of the popular vote and Benjamin and Carlos each win 30%, no one has won a majority. Abigail with a plurality will control all of the electors from that state despite the fact that 60% of the public voted for someone else. This scenario played out in a number of states as recently as 1992 when Democrat Bill Clinton won only a plurality in many states even though Republican George H.W. Bush and Independent candidate H. Ross Perot together received more votes.

RESOLUTION OF DISPUTED APPOINTMENTS

The Constitution requires that all disputes concerning appointment of electors have to be resolved by the states themselves. So, if there is a question in any state about who should be sent to the Electoral College or the process used to select the Electoral College members—it should be settled at the state level. Why then did the U.S. Supreme Court, a national government institution, end up hearing *Bush v. Gore* in 2001? Well, the issue in Florida had to do with a recounting of disputed ballots in several counties. The election was so close that the counting and recounting of the ballots might have been decisive in who would win. The U.S. Supreme Court agreed to hear the case based on the logic that when the Florida Supreme Court ruled that the disputed vote recount could continue—despite the fact that the Electoral College electors had been certified by Florida Secretary of State Kathleen Harris—the Florida court had violated the Constitutional requirement that state *legislatures* be permitted to determine the method by which electors are chosen. Harris had been assigned this task by the legislature. The U.S. Supreme Court stopped the vote recount, and per the Florida legislature's instruction to allow the secretary of state to certify the election, gave Mr. Bush the electoral votes from Florida. It was these disputed electors that gave Bush the majority of Electoral College votes necessary to become president despite having fewer total votes nationally than his opponent Al Gore.

HOW DO STATES APPOINT THEIR ELECTORS?

Anyone can serve as an elector except for members of Congress and other government officials. So how does someone end up on the ballot as a potential elector? Well, it depends on the state.

Remember when voters cast ballots in November, they select a list of electors associated with one political party's candidate. So, if voters live in a state with three Electoral College seats, they will in essence be voting for the three Republican Electoral College nominees **OR** the three Democratic nominees (or the nominees of whatever candidate they vote for). Voters cannot mix and match from the two lists—they must select the entire list from one party/candidate.

> *So, how do the candidates for the Electoral College electors get selected to represent their party or candidate on the ballot?*

The answer to this is determined by state law. Each state can decide who selects the nominees for the Electoral College as well as how they may do so. This means that not only will there be multiple ways potential electors are chosen across the United States, but also that the process is subject to change. All a state has to do to change the process of nominating Electoral College nominees is to change its law. Regardless of the method chosen, all states have their Electoral College nominees selected using a mechanism involving the political parties. So, the political parties are instrumental in selecting the people who end up on the list of electors.

Currently, 35 states have their potential electors nominated at the state party conventions. So, for example, when the Texas Republican party meets at its state convention (usually in the summer preceding the presidential election) one of the things they do is select the electors the Republicans will send to the Electoral College if their candidate wins a plurality of the popular vote. The Democrats do the same at their convention. Six states (this includes the District of Columbia) have the potential electors chosen by the state party's central committee. The remaining states use a variety of methods. The key point is that in every state selecting Electoral College candidates is a political party function.[8]

> *How come I have never heard of any of these Electoral College people or—are their names on the ballot?*

Some states list the names of the Electoral College nominees on the ballot with the name of the candidate with whom they are associated. This is referred to as a **long ballot**. The states that do this tend to be those with just a few Electoral College positions.

Overwhelming, however, most states use a **short ballot** and do not list the nominees.[9] They assume that voters know when they are voting for the presidential candidate that they are really selecting the list of potential electors associated with that candidate.

Short versus Long Ballots

What did the 2016 presidential ballot look like in the State of Arizona?

IF Arizona used a short presidential ballot:

Select one candidate for president of the United States

☐ **Clinton**
☐ **Trump**

IF Arizona used a long presidential ballot:

Select one candidate for president of the United States

☐ **Clinton**
1. Electoral College nominee name here
2. Electoral College nominee name here
3. Electoral College nominee name here
4. Electoral College nominee name here
5. Electoral College nominee name here
6. Electoral College nominee name here
7. Electoral College nominee name here
8. Electoral College nominee name here
9. Electoral College nominee name here
10. Electoral College nominee name here
11. Electoral College nominee name here

☐ **Trump**
1. Electoral College nominee name here
2. Electoral College nominee name here
3. Electoral College nominee name here
4. Electoral College nominee name here
5. Electoral College nominee name here
6. Electoral College nominee name here
7. Electoral College nominee name here
8. Electoral College nominee name here
9. Electoral College nominee name here
10. Electoral College nominee name here
11. Electoral College nominee name here

NOTE: As of 2016, Arizona had 11 Electoral College positions therefore 11 potential electors are associated with each candidate.

NOTE: As of 2016, Arizona prints the names of the potential electors on the ballot.[10]

This is one major source of confusion for the public—they think they are actually voting for the president because the candidate's name is all they see on the ballot, when in reality their votes are actually cast for the Electoral College nominees pledged to the candidate whose name they mark.

Are these electors required to vote for the candidate who won the popular election?

There is no Constitutional or Federal law requiring electors to vote for the candidate who won their state's popular election and with whom they are associated. However, states have the choice to require their electors to vote for the candidate with whom they are associated through state law or political party rule. Laws or rules that require an elector to vote for their party's candidate are called **binding requirements**. Currently, 20 states have no such requirements. That means the electors may vote for whomever they like with no *legal* repercussions.[11] Even with binding requirements, electors can vote for whomever they want and the vote still counts. It is only after the fact that there are any ramifications. States can impose fines for an elector not voting as directed, though these fines tend to be modest (less than $1000).[12]

The binding requirements give us a way of discussing elector's behaviors. The electors can be classified as:

1. **Faithful electors**—bound by state law or party rule to vote for their party's presidential and vice presidential candidate and does so.
2. **Faithless electors**—bound by state law or party rule to vote for their party's presidential and vice presidential candidate and does NOT do so.
3. **Unpledged electors**—electors from a state with no binding requirement.

We do not use the term "unfaithful" to describe electors' voting behavior.

Although electors can be faithless, they rarely are. Up until 2016, there had only been eight since the beginning of the twentieth century and in none of the elections was there more than one faithless elector.[13] In the 2016 election, however, there were seven electors who did not vote for their party's candidate.[14] Of these seven, five Democratic electors voted for someone other than Hillary Clinton and two Republican electors voted for someone other than Donald Trump.[15] Five of the seven electors were from states with no binding requirements, so technically they were not faithless.[16] In none of these cases (in 2016 or previous elections), however, did the "faithless" vote change the outcome of an election.

Understanding how these folks got selected to be electors explains why they are unlikely to be faithless. They are party animals! They are almost always lifelong party activists who were recognized by their political party to be in the Electoral College to select the president. Therefore, the chance that they will not vote for their party's candidate is slim.

The way Electoral College potential electors are selected for independent or minor party presidential candidates (i.e., Ross Perotin 1992 and 1996, Ralph Nader in 2000, or Evan McMullin in 2016) varies by state. Most commonly, the names of the potential electors are submitted when the candidate goes through the process of getting his or her name on the ballot. This means that independent candidates normally control their own Electoral College list.

How are the Ballots Cast?

Election Day is in early November, and the Constitution requires that electors meet on the Monday after the second Wednesday in December after the election, in their own states. They cast separate ballots for president and vice president, a change from the original Constitution passed as the Twelfth Amendment after the election of 1800. The Constitution prohibits their voting for two candidates from their own state. So, the electors from any state cannot vote for both a presidential and vice presidential candidate from their own state. The votes are recorded on a state certificate, which is sealed and sent to the president of the U.S. Senate.

How are the Electoral College Votes Counted?

The ballots are opened and counted before a joint session of Congress on January 6th in the year following the election. Congress may set a different day for the vote count—especially if the 6th falls on a Sunday.[17] A **simple majority** of the Electoral College vote is required for a candidate to be selected the president- or vice president-elect. A simple majority means one more than 50%. Since there are 538 electors, 50% +1 = 270. Ballots are opened and read alphabetically by state. Any state combination can be used to yield the required 270 votes. Therefore, it is possible for a candidate to win a *plurality* of the popular vote in the 11 highest population states and thus control the Electoral College and be selected as president of the United States. Or another way to think about this: theoretically, the majority of the people in 39 states can vote against the winning candidate. Take a look at Table 1 and see which states you would focus on if you were running for president.

The president of the Senate opens and reads the state certificates before a joint session of Congress. He or she then asks for objections. If there are objections, they must be submitted in writing and signed by at least one member of the House and one member of the Senate. If at least one member from each chamber does not sign on to the objection, the objection dies. In 2000, as votes were being counted for the disputed election of George W. Bush (Republican), multiple members of the House of Representatives filed objections concerning the Florida Electoral College ballots. However, no member of the Republican-controlled Senate would sign on so the objections died on the floor.[18]

If however an objection is registered by members from both chambers, the objections will be filed, and each chamber will individually consider the validity of the charges. Meetings concerning the objections are limited to 2 hours after which a vote is held in each chamber to accept or decline the objection. The House and Senate then reconvene in joint session to announce their votes. If both chambers agree to the objection then the Electoral College vote (or votes) in question are not included in the final count. If however the two chambers are not in agreement or do not accept the objection, then the disputed votes are counted.[19] This is what happened after the election in 2004 when objections were raised and heard concerning the electoral vote from Ohio. Both chambers considered the objections but in the end the objections were rejected and the electoral votes from Ohio were counted.[20]

What If No One has a Majority?

If there is no clear winner in the Electoral College vote count (no one wins a majority), then the newly elected House of Representatives will decide who the next president will be. (Remember: The entire House of Representatives was up for reelection in the November election in which we also selected the members of the Electoral College.) The House must select a president from the top three candidates (top in terms of the number of EC votes obtained). The votes in the House are taken by states, with each state having one vote. House rules determine the procedure for casting of votes.[21]

If there is no clear winner for vice president, the Senate chooses the vice president. Unlike the House, each senator may cast an individual vote but the Senate is required to choose from the top two vote getters.[22]

If there is a clear winner for president but not vice president (or the other way around) then only the designated chamber will meet and have business to do.

What If there is No Winner by Inauguration Day?

If the House has not selected a president by inauguration day (January 20th) then the new Vice president (assuming one has been selected) would be sworn in and then temporarily bumped up to president until the situation can be resolved.[23]

Since the Twelfth Amendment (which deals with presidential selection) does not address the possibility of Congress failing to select both a president and vice president, it is unclear what would happen if neither chamber could decide. If there were no clear winner for president or vice president, then we would *most likely* swear in the Speaker of the House (he or she is next in line of succession); although, Congress has the right to declare by law who may serve as president or vice president if neither has been chosen prior to Inauguration Day.[24] The outgoing president cannot simply stay in office until the problem is resolved because his or her term has expired.

What If the Major Party Candidate Dies or Resigns Sometime in the Selection Process?

In a nutshell, it depends on when they die or resign. But, remember that before their formal selection at the joint session of Congress, candidates are political party representatives only. Voters selected the Electoral College members, the Electoral College members cast ballots for president and vice president, and the election is not final until Congress certifies the election.

If the candidate dies or resigns *before* the November election, then it is simply a question of the state law or party rules on how to fill the vacancy. There is no federal law stating how electors would be selected in this circumstance.[25] Most likely, the party national committee would simply select a new candidate. If there were sufficient time, the party's new candidate's name would be listed on the ballot (along with the names of the potential electors in a long ballot state). Even if there was no time to change the ballot to include the new candidate's name, recall that voters really just vote for the Electoral College members in the election. If a party nominee had died or resigned before the election, voters would go ahead and select the Electoral College members they prefer and then it would be up to electors to vote for the new candidate or not and deal with any binding requirements they might have in their states.

The procedure for handling the situation of the candidate dying or resigning after the November election but prior to the electors' meet is less clear as it is not addressed in the

Constitution or law.[26] Some argue that in this scenario, the parties would simply select a replacement candidate and given that the electors are party loyalists they would simply vote for the new candidate. Other scholars contend that the binding requirements would require the electors to cast their votes for the dead candidate. If that were the case and the deceased candidate received a majority of the Electoral College votes, then the selection of the next president (or vice president) would be turned over to the House of Representatives (or Senate).

Finally, if the candidate dies or resigns after the Electoral College has met and before the opening of ballots before a joint session of Congress, selection would most likely be left to the House (if it is a presidential candidate) or Senate (if it is the vice president candidate). The ballots would be opened and a dead person would have been chosen, so the House or Senate would have to meet to make a new selection.[27]

So Why Does this Matter or Why Should I Care?

Quite simply, we need to understand the workings of the Electoral College in order to fully comprehend the dynamics of presidential elections and candidate behavior. Since the requirement for winning the White House is a simple majority of the Electoral College vote and the electors are most often faithful, candidates will focus their campaign efforts on the largest states—those with the greatest number of Electoral College votes. Additionally, since the state's electors are chosen in a winner-take-all manner, presidential candidates will campaign most actively in those states where no single candidate has a wide lead. Candidates do not need to spend time or money in states where one candidate has a significant advantage. Instead, the candidates will focus on those states where the margin of winning is tighter and the impact of additional campaign dollars and efforts will have the potential for a greater payoff.

So, if one lives in a state where the presidential candidates are spending a great deal of time and effort or in a state the candidates seem to have forgotten, the way the Electoral College works is probably the explanation for such candidate behavior.

Possibility of Reform

Some people argue that the Electoral College is undemocratic and, particularly after the elections of 2000 and 2016, there is too much of a chance that the Electoral College will not select the candidate who wins the popular vote. Critics argue that the winner-take-all mechanism for determining electors in a state exaggerates the electoral success of presidential candidates who may have barely won a plurality of the popular vote. In doing so, it gives that candidate an artificial advantage in reaching the 270 Electoral College votes necessary to win office and devalues the wishes of the populace who may have voted in the minority. Additionally, voters in small states or those living in large states that are considered "safe" for one candidate or the other may be safely ignored by the candidates.

In response to these criticisms, there are some who call for the reform or even the elimination of the Electoral College. The most common reforms include the district plan, the proportional plan, the automatic plan, and the national popular vote plan.

District Plan

In this plan, a state's Electoral College positions would be distributed to candidates on both a statewide basis and using districts that represent subdivisions of the state. Two of the state's electors would be selected based on the results of the statewide vote and the remaining electors would be determined based on the results in districts. A state could simply utilize their existing congressional districts to delineate the Electoral College districts or they could choose to draw distinct districts for this purpose only. Each voter would cast one vote for president and one for vice president in the determination of Electoral College electors (just like they do in the current system). These votes would then be used in two ways. First, the votes would be counted on a statewide basis and the candidate who wins a plurality of the votes would control the statewide electors. The votes would then be tallied once again in each district to determine which candidate would control the individual district electors. This is the system that two states—Maine (four Electoral College votes) and Nebraska (five Electoral College votes) have selected to use. In the 2016 election, Republican Donald Trump won a single electoral vote from Maine by winning the rural northern congressional district while Democrat Hillary Clinton won the other district as well as the statewide popular vote, thus receiving the balance (three) of the electoral votes in Maine.[28]

Proponents of this plan argue that such a system does not leave those who voted for the losing candidate unrepresented as is the case in the winner-take-all system used in most states. Additionally, this plan takes into consideration the geographical nuances of a state. You can imagine a state in which 51% of the population live in one or two large urban areas and the remaining 49% are distributed across the rest of a generally rural state. These two groups of people may have significantly different political interests. Under the district plan, the regional or geographical variations in the state's voting preferences are reflected in the allocation of electors.

Proportional Plan

Another commonly suggested modification for the Electoral College is the proportional plan. In this system, all the state's electors are allocated based on the proportion of the popular vote won by a candidate statewide. So, if a candidate receives 30% of the vote across the state, he or she will be given 30% of the state's electors.

Realistically, the chance that the election results are ever as simple as 30% of the population voting one way and the other 70% voting another is slim. Proponents of the proportional plan suggest two possible ways of dealing with electoral splits. The *strict* proportional plan would allocate the electors down to the thousandth, which will cause the splitting of Electoral College votes. The *rounded* proportional plan would utilize some form of mathematical rounding of the vote totals such that only whole Electoral College votes are generated. So, in a state with 10 Electoral College electors, if one candidate gets 58.989% of the statewide vote and the other candidate gets 41.011%, the first candidate would receive six electors and the other would receive four.

Supporters of this plan argue that it is the most fair as it most accurately reflects the electoral desires of all the voters. Additionally, new or third political parties would have a greater opportunity to win at least a few electors and thus demonstrate the electoral success necessary to attract future voters.

Opponents of both the proportional and district plans argue that any mechanism that splits a state's electors across multiple candidates increases the chance that a deadlock occurs in the Electoral College and no candidate receives a clear majority. If this were to happen, then the presidential and vice presidential selection would be left to Congress.

Automatic Plan

One additional suggestion for reforming the presidential selection system is the automatic plan. This plan comes closest to the current winner-take-all system of all the reforms. This plan would directly or automatically assign Electoral College votes to the candidate who wins a plurality of the popular vote. In doing so, the position of Electoral College elector is eliminated. While this would resolve the issue of potential faithless electors, it does nothing to address the question of the inflation of the winning margin of candidates winning a plurality.

National Popular Vote Plan

In recent years, there has been a movement to simply allow the national popular vote to select the winner. One way to have this happen would be a Constitutional Amendment, which like with the other plans, is highly unlikely. Another route to accomplish the same task would be to have a number of states enter into an agreement to cast all of their electoral votes for the national popular vote winner. If enough states, particularly states that potentially have close elections, agreed to this "Interstate Compact" idea, their votes would assure the popular vote winner would win nationally. Such a plan could be adopted by individual states and would not require a Constitutional Amendment.[29]

States are free to determine the means of allocating their Electoral College electors, so any one of them could adopt the district, proportional, or national popular vote plan at any time. The automatic plan, or adopting any of the other systems nationally, on the other hand, would require amending the Constitution. Whether it be a change in a state law or state or national constitution, the process required to change the presidential selection process according to any of these plans would be quite difficult, time consuming, and require significant public support. Therefore, chance that these changes are made any time soon is small. So, in the meantime, it remains vital that we understand how the Electoral College and current system works.

Prospects for reforming the Electoral College system are remote, though the national popular vote plan has fewer barriers than others would have because it would only require actions of a few key states. On the one hand, the Electoral College has not yielded anything like a "worst case scenario" throughout American history, and except for the elections in 2000 and 2016, has elected the national popular vote winner in each election since 1888. On the other hand, with so many states not being competitive in presidential elections, including the two largest states of California and Texas, many voters feel as if their votes don't count. A reform that might give voters a greater sense of ownership in their democracy might yield positive effects, both in giving them greater incentives to vote and in making them regain some of their lost respect for those who govern.

Key Terms

Binding requirement—state law or political party rule that requires electors to cast their ballots for the presidential and vice presidential candidates from the political party with whom they are associated.

Elector—a member of the Electoral College, responsible for voting to select the president and vice president of the United States.

Faithful elector—a member of the Electoral College who is bound by state law or party rule to vote for their party's candidate for president and does so.

Faithless elector—a member of the Electoral College who is bound by state law or party rule to vote for their party's candidate for president and does not do so.

Long ballot—a ballot used in the presidential election that lists the names of the Electoral College nominees associated with each political party's presidential candidate.

Pluralities—criteria for winning election that simply entails obtaining more votes than any other candidate.

Popular vote—the expression of electoral preferences by the public.

Proportional allocation—the allotment of Electoral College electors based on the percentage of the popular vote obtained by a given presidential candidate.

Short ballot—a ballot used in the presidential election that does not list the names of the Electoral College nominees associated with each political party's presidential candidate.

Simple majority—criteria for winning election that entails obtaining 50% +1 of the votes.

Unpledged elector—a member of the elector college who is not bound by state law or party rule to vote for a specific party's candidate for president.

Multiple Choice Questions

1. In most states, a presidential candidate ends up controlling the Electoral College electors by:
    a. winning a plurality of the popular vote.
    b. winning a majority of the popular vote.
    c. winning a majority of the Electoral College vote.
    d. winning a plurality of the Electoral College vote.
    e. winning both the popular and Electoral College vote by a majority.
Answer: A

Chapter 1: Graduating from the Electoral College   13

2. The mechanisms states use to nominate the potential Electoral College members include:
   a. they are selected by the state party central committee.
   b. the determination is left to the political parties and not determined by state law.
   c. they are chosen at the state party convention.
   d. they are selected by the candidate themselves.
   e. They may include all of the above.

Answer: E

3. Voters are more likely to know who their state Electoral College electors are if:
   a. they live in a short ballot state.
   b. they live in a long ballot state.
   c. they read the newspaper regularly.
   d. they actively follow presidential politics.
   e. they are comfortable with the dynamics of presidential politics.

Answer: B

4. An elector who is bound by state law or party rule to vote for a specific presidential candidate and actually does so, is known as:
   a. a faithless elector.
   b. an unpledged elector.
   c. a responsible elector.
   d. a faithful elector.
   e. a legitimate elector.

Answer: D

5. In order for an objection to the Electoral College ballots to be considered in Congress:
   a. it must be submitted in writing.
   b. it must be signed be one member of each chamber.
   c. each chamber considers the charges separately.
   d. Congress considers the charges for only 2 hours.
   e. All of the above statements about the objection process must be used.

Answer: E

Discussion Questions

1. There are several stages to the work of the Electoral College.
   a. Identify the criteria for "winning" control of the electors from each state as well that for winning the Electoral College.
   b. Explain how the criteria for winning influences the type of campaign a presidential candidate will run.
2. Presidents do not focus equally on all states during a campaign. Explain how the allocation of electors to each state will influence where presidential candidates spend their time during the campaign.

3. Political Parties play a key role in the implementation of the Electoral College. Explain and discuss how the Electoral College process empowers political parties.
4. Critics have long suggested that the presidential selection mechanism imbedded in the Electoral College causes the preferences of voters who are in the minority in their states to be ignored. Explain and discuss the basis for this criticism and the suggested reforms that would address these claims.

Notes

1. N.A. "2016 Election Results." Accessed February 14, 2017, http://www.cnn.com/election/results.
2. Mele, Christopher and Annie Correal. "Not Our President: Protests Spread after Donald Trump's Election." November 16, 2016. Accessed February 14, 2017, https://www.nytimes.com/2016/11/10/trump-election-protests.html.
3. Chenoweth, Erica and Jeremy Pressman. "This Is What We Learned by Counting the Women's Marches." February 7, 2017. Accessed February 14, 2017, https://www.washingtonpost.com/news/monkey-cage/wp/2017/02/07/this-is-what-welearned.html.
4. N.A. "2016 Election Results." accessed February 14, 2017, http://www.cnn.com/election/results.
5. N.A. "2000 Presidential Election Popular Vote Totals." Accessed February 13, 2015, http://www.archives.gov/federal-register/electoral-college/2000/popular_vote.html.
6. Congressional Research Service. "The Electoral College: How It Works in Contemporary Presidential Elections." RL 32611, 2012.
7. N.A. "What is the Electoral College?" Accessed February 13, 2015, http://www.archives.gov/federal-register/electoral-college/about.html.
8. National Association of Secretaries of State. "Summary: State Laws Regarding Presidential Electors." 2016. https://www.nass.org/component/documan/task=doc_download&grid=1864&Itemid=391.
9. Congressional Research Service. "The Electoral College: How It Works in Contemporary Presidential Elections." RL 32611, 2016.
10. Arizona Revised Statutes. 2017. Title 16, Article 6, Section 16-502.
11. National Conference of State Legislatures. "The Electoral College." 2016. http://www.ncsl.org/research/elections-and-campaigns/the-electoral-college.aspx.
12. National Association of Secretaries of State. "Summary: State Laws Regarding Presidential Electors." 2016. www.nass.org/component/documen/task=doc_download&grid=1864&Itemid=391
13. Congressional Research Service. "The Electoral College: How It Works in Contemporary Presidential Elections." RL 32611, 2016.
14. Boccagno, Julia. "Which Candidates Did the Seven 'Faithless' Electors Support?" December 21, 2016. http://www.cbsnews.com/news/which-candidates-did-the-seven-faithless-electors-support.

15 Boccagno, Julia. "Which Candidates Did the Seven 'Faithless' Electors Support?" December 21, 2016. http://www.cbsnews.com/news/which-candidates-did-the-seven-faithless-electors-support.
16 National Association of Secretaries of State. "Summary: State Laws Regarding Presidential Electors." 2016. www.nass.org/component/documen/task=doc_download&grid=1864&Itemid=391.
17 Congressional Research Service. "The Electoral College: How It Works in Contemporary Presidential Elections." RL 32611, 2016.
18 Mitchell, Alison. http://www.nytimes.com/2001/01/07/us/over-some-objections-congress-certifies-electoral-vote.html
19 Congressional Research Service. "The Electoral College: How It Works in Contemporary Presidential Elections." RL 32611, 2016.
20 Congressional Research Service. "The Electoral College: How It Works in Contemporary Presidential Elections." RL 32611, 2016.
21 Congressional Research Service. "The Electoral College: How It Works in Contemporary Presidential Elections." RL 32611, 2016.
22 Congressional Research Service. "The Electoral College: How It Works in Contemporary Presidential Elections." RL 32611, 2016.
23 Congressional Research Service. "The Electoral College: How It Works in Contemporary Presidential Elections." RL 32611, 2016.
24 Congressional Research Service. "The Electoral College: How It Works in Contemporary Presidential Elections." RL 32611, 2016.
25 N.A. "What Happens if the President-Elect Fails to Qualify before Inauguration?" 2017. Accessed February 24, 2017. http://www.archives.gov/federal-register/electoral-college/faq.html.
26 N.A. "What Happens if the President-Elect Fails to Qualify before Inauguration?" 2017. Accessed February 14, 2017. http://www.archives.gov/federal-register/electoral-college/faq.html.
27 N.A. "What Happens if a Candidate Dies or Becomes Incapacitated?" 2015. Accessed February 13, 2017. http://www.archives.gov/federal-register/electoral-college/faq.html.
28 N.A. "2016 Election Results." 2016. Accessed February 14, 2017. http://www.cnn.com/election/results.
29 Congressional Research Service. "The Electoral College: How It Works in Contemporary Presidential Elections." RL 32611, 2016.

WHEN THEY SAY THE ISSUE IS FEDERALISM, IT ISN'T

BY JAMES W. RIDDLESPERGER, JR.
Texas Christian University

Learning Objectives

Students should be able to:

1. Understand how the creation of federalism was a necessary convenience in drafting the U.S. Constitution.
2. Understand that politicians rarely care about whether power is located at the national or state levels except as they affect policy outcomes.
3. Understand that in the arena of civil rights, federalism was often used to displace real debates about policy.
4. Understand that the U.S. Supreme Court has had different interpretations of the powers of national and state governments over time.

In May 2017, President Donald Trump announced a budget proposal that would slash more than $600 billion in Medicaid funding for the poor from federal government assistance to the states. In devolving responsibility to the states, Trump's budget director Mick Mulvaney promised that the cuts would create efficiency by allowing states to tailor their spending to meet the individual needs of the states. In contrast, during April of 2017, President Trump announced an executive order taking from states and cities the right to provide safe sanctuary for undocumented residents of the nation, saying that "sanctuary cities" violate federal law. These two Trump initiatives both involve federalism, but in one instance involve enhancing national power and in the other, devolving responsibility away from the national government to the states.

Why is the president on both sides of the argument about whether states or the federal government should have primary responsibility for regulating the rights of American residents? Because he wants to accomplish policy goals unrelated to federalism. He wants to create an environment where undocumented residents will feel uncomfortable in the United States and perhaps return to their countries of origin to fulfill his campaign promise of deporting undocumented residents. And he wants to cut federal spending on health care to accomplish other economic goals such as increasing spending on national defense and provide tax relief for taxpayers.[1]

Similarly, President Trump's predecessor in office, Barack Obama, was often criticized by his political opponents for being schizophrenic on the issue of federalism: "He'll let the states have their way when their policies please blue team sensibilities and he'll call in the feds when they don't. Thus, he'll grant California a waiver to allow it to raise auto emissions standards, but he'll bring the hammer down when the state tries to cut payments to unionized health care workers."[2] This correct assertion from the conservative Cato Institute points to a constant theme in American political history. Rarely does anyone in national politics really care about whether power resides at the state or national level. Instead, they care about the effects of policies, and will advocate for the level of government most likely to help them achieve their policy goals.

One of the basic features of American government is the division of powers between national and state governments, an organizational feature known, as if intended to bore generations of students, as federalism. Often discussions of federalism focus on mundane issues such as different interpretations of how power should be divided or differing kinds of fiscal programs that can describe the relationship between the state and national governments. But in truth, federalism can also be a topic to study the essence of politics, for since the creation of the Constitution, it has often been at the center of political controversy.

Over the course of this essay, we will discuss why federalism came about in the first place, what its advantages and disadvantages are, and why this chapter got its title: "When They Say the Issue Is Federalism, It Isn't." Undertaking this task should help students understand that federalism is not a disembodied concept, with nothing more to it than dividing power as in a "layer cake" or as in a "marble cake," or distributing power as in a picket fence (who has picket fences anymore anyway?), but that it becomes a part of the discussion to *displace* real issues. Because of that, federalism is really not a boring concept, but a concept that helps us understand why so many people are fascinated by politics.

THE ORIGINS OF FEDERALISM

As with most topics in American politics, scholars often begin the discussion with a consideration of what the Founding Fathers were thinking. Of course, like us, they were mostly thinking about things other than politics! But when they thought about politics, they thought of ways to make the system work better. The first Constitution of the United States was called the Articles of Confederation. It was called that, not surprisingly, because it set up a **confederate** form of government. That is, almost all of the political power was held by state governments, and the national government could not do much of anything unless it had the unanimous consent of all 13 states. The Continental Congress could not even directly tax citizens of the country, but rather relied on the states' generosity to conduct business. And the states were not very generous. As a result, the national government under the Articles was weak and unable to help orchestrate the development of a national economy or the raising of an army. Perhaps that latter shortcoming was most significant in the timing of the passage of the Constitution, because when a band of former revolutionary war soldiers began a violent protest in what became known as **Shays's Rebellion**, the national government could not even muster enough troops to put that mini-insurrection down. They even discussed sending George Washington up there on his white horse hoping one old man with a good name could dissuade the rebellion.

Yet, the founders who wrote the Articles had organized governmental power in that manner for a reason: people in America feared a strong central government. Remember that the Declaration of Independence had voiced a concern that the reason for a revolution was the "tyranny" of power exercised by the English government. The Articles had been a reaction to that fear. Over time, most national leaders came to consider it an overreaction.

As a result, the challenge facing James Madison as he prepared for the Constitutional Convention was to figure out a way to give the national government "proper energy" without raising the fears of those who wanted a limited government. He could not propose a **unitary** system, where the national government would have all of the political power, for two reasons. First, the states were already organized and they would not ever agree to give up their political power. Second, to propose such a change would enkindle the fears of those "anti-federalists" who thought a strong national government might bring about the kind of tyranny that had caused the revolution only a little more than a decade earlier.

Madison devised the federal system as a useful compromise between the confederate and the unitary designs. It was not designed for its elegance or for its efficiency. Indeed, federal governments are, by their very nature, inelegant and inefficient. Rather, it was designed as a system that both advocates of a strong central government and those who feared strong central government could endorse. And that is how it worked out.

Still, the sales job necessary to have the Constitution ratified by the states was monumental. In a series of articles called *The Federalist*, Madison, along with Alexander Hamilton and John Jay, wrote to assure citizens that the new document struck a proper balance between confederation and unitary forms. Consider the writing of Hamilton, using the arcane language of the eighteenth century. He assures readers that the new Constitution, in shifting away from a confederacy, still preserves state powers: "The proposed Constitution, so far from implying an abolition of the State governments, makes them constituent parts of the national sovereignty, by allowing them a direct representation in the Senate, and leaves in their possession certain exclusive and very important portions of sovereign power. This fully corresponds, in every rational import of the terms, with the idea of a federal government."[3] Or, more famously, Madison writes in Federalist 10: "it clearly appears, that the same advantage which a republic has over a democracy, in controlling the effects of faction, is enjoyed by a large over a small republic—is enjoyed by the Union over the States composing it . . . The influence of factious leaders may kindle a flame within their particular States, but will be unable to spread a general conflagration through the other States."[4]

From the very beginning, there was disagreement about what the term "federalism" meant in practical application. From the very beginning, these fights were usually not about federalism, but rather about policy. The most famous early example of this came in 1830 when a famous exchange took place between President Andrew Jackson and his Vice-President, John C. Calhoun. Jackson proposed a toast declaring "Our Federal Union: It must be preserved." Calhoun replied with a toast arguing exactly the opposite position: "The Union, next to our Liberty, most dear." For Calhoun, that meant that states, rather than the national government, should be the center of power.

A little elaboration of this story illustrates how this conflict occurred. Calhoun was from South Carolina and had initially been a strong nationalist. But, he also was from a

Southern family that saw no contradiction between liberty and slavery. His family had been rewarded by the economic system that exploited slaves, and he believed it to be a beneficial system for both races. Additionally, he was opposed to high tariffs on imported British woolen clothing because though that tariff protected the manufacturing industries of the Northern states its "protectionism" made it difficult for producers of raw materials in the South. In retaliation to the protective tariff, other nations put tariffs on American goods, thereby making it difficult for Southerners to sell their goods in Europe. In other words, he saw the policies of the nation as being detrimental to the economy of the South.

In his desire to come up with a way to make public policy favorable to the South, he developed a theory called "interposition." Essentially, this theory argued that the states "interposed" between the people and the national government and that as a result, states should have a right to decide for their citizens whether federal law should apply in their state. As a result, Calhoun argued that states had the right to **nullify**, or declare null and void, national laws within their borders. Calhoun's argument about the nature of federalism was begun, in other words, not because he had a long cherished notion that states should be superior to the national government, but because he opposed the inexorable movement at the national level to prefer abolition over slavery and Northern manufacturers over Southern planters.

The Civil War (or what the Southern states called "the war between the states") has often been portrayed as a conflict over the issue of federalism. In fact, though, a careful look at the issues surrounding the conflict suggests that federalism was not the real issue; slavery was. When the states of the South passed articles of secession from the union, their language was cast normally in the context of **"states' rights,"** or the notion that the proper place for most of the domestic power in the nation should rest with the state governments. However, a closer reading of each of those articles tells the real story. It was a fear of abolition of slavery, along with the economic impact that abolition would have on the economy of the South, that justified secession. Consider this wording from the secession article of Calhoun's home state of South Carolina, complaining that the Northern states were not cooperating in returning fugitive slaves to the South: "Thus the constituted compact has been deliberately broken and disregarded by the non-slaveholding States, and the consequence follows that South Carolina is released from her obligation."[5]

Since the beginning, then, when someone has argued that they merely want to protect the power of the states over the national government or that they want to give states power because the state government is "closer to the people," if one looks behind the claim, federalism is not the issue. I will discuss three different applications of the concept of federalism and illustrate in each that federalism is not the issue.

Federalism and Civil Rights

Indeed, the whole history of opposition to civil rights in the period from the end of Reconstruction following the Civil War until after the passage of the Civil Rights Act of 1964 was a series of claims by those opposed to civil rights that all they cared about was preserving the rights of the states. The famous examples of Governor Ross Barnett opposing the desegregation of the University of Mississippi and Governor George Wallace standing in the doorway of the University of Alabama illustrate the point.

An African-American student named James Meredith applied for admission to the University of Mississippi in early 1961 and received a telegram almost immediately denying his admission. On May 31, 1961, Meredith, with the assistance of the NAACP Legal Defense and Educational Fund, filed suit in the U.S. District Court alleging that Meredith had been rejected solely because of his race. In September of 1962, Supreme Court handed down its decision upholding Meredith's right to admission at the University of Mississippi. In an address to the citizens of Mississippi, Governor Ross Barnett argued that under the federalism of the Tenth Amendment of the Constitution, the national government had no right to force its will on Mississippi: "In the absence of constitutional authority and without legislative action, an ambitious federal government, employing naked and arbitrary power, has decided to deny us the right of self-determination in the conduct of the affairs of our sovereign state. Having long since failed in their efforts to conquer the indomitable spirit of the people of Mississippi and their unshakable will to preserve the sovereignty and majesty of our commonwealth, they now seek to break us physically with the power of force."[6] The rest of the story is that Meredith was admitted and eventually graduated. But the lesson for federalism is equally clear. Whenever someone claims that federalism is an issue, they are making a suspicious argument. In this case, Barnett was not really arguing about the power of the national government, he was, instead, opposed to integration of the University of Mississippi.

One year later, a similar confrontation emerged at the University of Alabama. Governor George C. Wallace had won election in 1962 and in his inaugural address, he promised to maintain "Segregation now, segregation tomorrow, segregation forever." As a result, when two African-American students, Vivian Malone and James Hood, tried to enter the university, Wallace stood in the doorway to the building to keep them from enrolling at the school. His justification: not the avowal that he had made at his inauguration, but rather a statement about the proper powers of the state and national governments: "The unwelcomed, unwanted, unwarranted and force-induced intrusion upon the campus of the University of Alabama today of the might of the Central Government offers frightful example of the oppression of the rights, privileges and sovereignty of this State by officers of the Federal Government. This intrusion results solely from force, or threat of force, undignified by any reasonable application of the principle of law, reason and justice. It is important that the people of this State and nation understand that this action is in violation of rights reserved to the State by the Constitution of the United States and the Constitution of the State of Alabama. While some few may applaud these acts, millions of Americans will gaze in sorrow upon the situation existing at this great institution of learning."[7]

Both of these examples illustrate the point dramatically. Here, Southern governors who owed their political success to the segregationist policies of the South, stood publicly to make the argument that the issue in civil rights was federalism. In both cases, that argument was used to hide the real issue—opposition to integration of their state universities.

Stages of the Commerce Clause

The Constitution has not changed much at all over the more than two centuries since it was written, yet the Supreme Court has had different understandings of what federalism has meant over that time. The key point to understand here is not that the meaning of the word federalism has changed over that time, but that political agendas have changed. Those changing agendas have been reflected in decisions of the Supreme Court. The two sides in the long-running debate can be called by different names. On the one side is the **"federalist"** narrative and on the other is the **"states' rights"** narrative. Certainly there is nothing surprising about those names. At different points in time, the different views have been dominant. In fact, there are four distinct "stages" of understanding of federalism:

Stage I—Founding National Power—1789 through 1872

Stage II—Economic Growth and Laissez-Faire—1873 through 1936

Stage III—New Deal and the Positive State—1937 through 1986

Stage IV—The Revival of States' Rights—1987 through?

In this essay, we evaluate the last two stages, which constitute the modern era of American politics.

Stage III—New Deal and the Positive State—1937 through 1986

Three key cases can sum up this stage, which witnessed the expansion of congressional power beyond that which Chief Justice Marshall could have imagined—although still relying on his words for its foundation.

The first case, ***N.L.R.B. v. Jones & Laughlin Steel Corp.***, 301 U.S. 1 (1937), upheld the National Labor Relations Act of 1935 by a vote of 6 to 3. The statute prohibited "unfair labor practices" that obstructed "the free flow of **interstate commerce**." In upholding the act Chief Justice Hughes reverted to an expansive understanding of the power of Congress over interstate commerce by stringing a series of quotes from precedents:

The congressional authority to protect interstate commerce from burdens and obstructions is not limited to transactions which can be deemed to be an essential part of a "flow" of interstate or foreign commerce. Burdens and obstructions may be due to injurious action springing from other sources. The fundamental principle is that the power to regulate commerce is the power to enact "all appropriate legislation" for its "protection and advancement" . . . ; to adopt measures "to promote its growth and insure its safety" . . . ; "to foster, protect, control and restrain" . . . . That power is plenary and may be exerted to protect interstate commerce "no matter what the source of the dangers which threaten it" . . . . Although activities may be intrastate in character when separately considered, if they have such a close and substantial relation to interstate commerce that their control is essential or appropriate to protect that commerce from burdens and obstructions, Congress cannot be denied the power to exercise that control. . . . **Undoubtedly the scope of the power must be considered in light of our dual system of government and may not be extended so as to embrace effects upon interstate commerce so indirect and remote as to embrace them, in view of our complex society, would effectually obliterate the distinction between what is national and what is local and create a completely centralized government.** (emphasis added, pp. 36–7)

The Court abandoned the distinction between direct and indirect effects of intrastate commerce on interstate commerce that had marked the *Schechter* majority opinion. Apart from that, there was nothing much new in the language of **N.L.R.B. v. Jones & Laughlin**. It was the outcome that changed. The N.L.R.B. can be sustained by resorting to the first part of the quote above, or it can be held unconstitutional by resorting to the highlighted words. The winning side needed five votes.

In **Wickard v. Filburn**, 317 U.S. 111 (1942), however, there is a new ingredient. The Supreme Court was willing to look at the cumulative economic effect of purely local activity in order to determine its impact on interstate commerce. The second Agricultural Adjustment Act (1938) was thus upheld, even as to a farmer who had produced grain in excess of his allotment, but whose excess grain had been entirely consumed on his own farm, by his family or his livestock.

Justice Jackson began by reverting to Chief Justice Marshall's opinion in **Gibbons v. Ogden**, which, he said, "described the Federal commerce power with a breadth never yet exceeded" (p. 120). The opinion concluded that even though an individual contribution might be trivial by itself, the single contribution, taken with that of others, is far from trivial (pp. 127–28). Then Jackson discussed the economic consequences of consuming grain within the boundaries of a farm:

> It can hardly be denied that a factor of such volume and variability as home-consumed wheat would have a substantial influence on price and market conditions. This may arise because being in marketable condition such wheat overhangs the market and if induced by rising prices tends to flow into the market and check price increases. But if we assume that it is never marketed, it supplies a need of the man who grew it which would otherwise be reflected in purchases in the local market. Home-grown wheat in this sense competes with wheat in commerce. . . . This record leaves us in no doubt that Congress may properly have considered that wheat consumed on the farm where grown if wholly outside the scheme of regulation would have substantial effect in defeating and obstructing its purpose to stimulate trade therein at increased prices. (pp. 128–29)

The third case, **Katzenbach v. McClung**, 379 U.S. 294 (1964), which upheld the application of the public accommodations provision of the Civil Rights Act of 1964, applied this substantial economic effect doctrine to a single-site, locally owned barbecue business in Birmingham, Alabama against the claim that it was not engaged in interstate commerce. Ollie's Barbecue seated 220 customers, but it served African Americans only through takeouts. It was located on a state highway, 11 blocks from an interstate and farther from rail or bus stations. However, the evidence revealed that of the $150,000 of food consumed annually in the restaurant, about $70,000 of it was meat that had been in interstate commerce; thus the local business was determined to part of that commerce as well. The opinion recalled the observation from **Wickard v. Filburn** that though trivial by itself this contribution, taken with others, is far from trivial. Moreover, the court held that it ought to defer to a congressional judgment that a subject substantially affects interstate commerce, "if there is any rational basis for such a finding" (pp. 303–4). For more than 20 years such expansive interpretations of the power of Congress over interstate commerce held sway.

Cooperative Federalism and the "New Federalism"

During this generation of federal–state relations, the nature of the financial relationship between the two changed significantly. As the federal government became better able to collect taxes through the income tax and the needs of the states were growing, the relationship known as "cooperative federalism" emerged. For the history of the nation until that time, the programs of the states and national government had remained relatively independent of one another in a manner often referred to as "dual federalism." But as the two governments developed shared programs in which it seemed in their mutual self-interest to share costs and administrative responsibilities, a new era emerged. "Grants-in-aids" allowed the states to finance programs using federal dollars with strict standards in programs such as the ones to build interstate highways. Such programs led to increasing difficulty in separating the functions of the national and state governments from one another. From dual federalism, which political scientist Morton Grodzins likened to a layer cake, had emerged cooperative federalism, which he imagined to resemble a "marble cake."[8]

Over time, the relationship between the nation and states became less "cooperative" and states felt that they were the victims of a dominant national government. However, the Supreme Court upheld the power of Congress to impose conditions on the receipt of federal funds, as, for example, in requiring states to raise the legal age for consuming alcohol to 21 as a condition for receiving federal highway funds.[9]

President Richard Nixon tried to address these concerns in his version of "new federalism," a program often known by the name of its most famous component, general revenue sharing. Nixon's idea was that the national government ought to rebate monies to states and localities so that they could spend them more effectively according to local needs.[10] Revenue sharing was quite popular at the state and local level but allowed the national government little room for accountability in tracing the expenditure of federal dollars. It also led to federal contributions to wealthy cities, even cities that objectively did not need the funds. Accordingly, funding for Nixon's program waned relatively quickly and was cancelled entirely by the 1980s as federal budget deficits soared.

Instead, President Ronald Reagan proposed a new "New Federalism," this time one that would actually be "devolution," displacing some federal power and giving it to the states. Reagan's favorite tool for devolution was the use of "block grants," a form of grant dating to the administration of Lyndon Johnson but which Reagan wanted to use to replace the categorical grant (grants-in-aid) programs through which the national government was able to dominate states. Under categorical grants, the national governments could require states to implement rules they did not want by requiring such implementation as a requirement for attaining federal funds. Reagan wished to replace the many federal categorical grants with just a few block grants through which state discretion in spending would increase dramatically. Ultimately, Reagan believed that by giving states more discretion, less wasteful spending would occur and the federal contributions could diminish over time.[11] The Reagan programs had the desired effects in some ways—federal funds to the states diminished in fact in a number of areas.[12] Moreover, the Reagan vision of federal–state relationships set the stage for a redefinition of federal–state relationship in the court.

Stage IV—The Revival of States' Rights—1987 through?

The date that marks the end of Stage III and the beginning of Stage IV is imprecise. Justice O'Connor's dissent in *South Carolina v. Dole*, 107 S. Ct. 2793 (1987), spoke with wistful respect for the Stage II decision in *U.S. v. Butler* (1936), which had relied on the Tenth Amendment reservation of powers to the states—a position that was effectively repudiated in 1937 and after. That may be a part of the beginning, but three cases from 1995 to 2000 clearly establish Stage IV. All three are five-to-four decisions with Justices Breyer, Ginsburg, Souter, and Stevens as the consistent dissenters. The majority opinions were by Chief Justice Rehnquist and Justice Scalia (joined by O'Connor, Kennedy, and Thomas). These decisions held that the Gun-Free School Zones Act of 1990, the Brady Handgun Violence Prevention Act of 1993, and the Violence Against Women Act of 1994 involved unconstitutional uses of congressional power.

The Gun-Free School Zones Act of 1990 made it a federal offense knowingly to possess a firearm in a school zone. The claimed interstate commerce foundation of the legislation was that the possession of firearms in local school zones led to violent crime. Violent crime had interstate economic consequences due first to the costs of the crime itself and the need to insure against the risk of violence, second to the burden on the free flow of travel to areas known to be especially at risk of violence, and third to the impairment of the learning environment and its effects on worker productivity. In the case of *United States v. Lopez*, after reviewing the major Commerce Clause decisions, Chief Justice Rehnquist concluded that there were "three broad categories of activity that Congress may regulate under its commerce power":

1. Congress may regulate the use of the channels of interstate commerce.
2. Congress is empowered to regulate and protect the instrumentalities of interstate commerce, or persons or things in interstate commerce, even though the threat may come only from intrastate activities.
3. Congress' commerce authority includes the power to regulate those activities having a substantial relationship to interstate commerce; . . . i.e., those activities that substantially affect interstate commerce.(pp. 558–59)

The Chief Justice acknowledged that some cases required only that an activity affect interstate commerce while others required that it must substantially affect interstate commerce to come within the power of Congress to regulate. Rehnquist then made the key determination in the case:
We conclude, consistent with the great weight of our case law, that the proper test requires an analysis of whether the regulated activity "substantially affects" interstate commerce. (p. 559)
In our view, this comes very close to the old distinction between a direct and an indirect effect on interstate commerce. What troubled Rehnquist was the realization that under the government's theory of the Commerce Clause, "we are hard pressed to posit any activity by an individual that Congress is without the power to regulate." Of course, that is exactly what had happened following the court's decisions in the late 1930s and early 1940s, especially the cumulative effect position in *Wickard*. The limitations on the power of Congress over interstate commerce had become the political limitations involved in getting a bill through Congress, rather than constitutional limitations applied by the Supreme Court.

Chapter 2: When They Say the Issue Is Federalism, It Isn't

No federal statute had been held unconstitutional until the Rehnquist-led court began to have further these thoughts on the subject:

> To uphold the Government's contentions here, we would have to pile inference upon inference in a manner that would bid fair to convert congressional authority under the Commerce Clause to a general police power of the sort retained by the States. Admittedly, some of our prior cases have taken long steps down that road, giving great deference to congressional action.... The broad language in these opinions has suggested the possibility of additional expansion, but we decline here to proceed any further. To do so would require us to conclude that the Constitution's enumeration of powers does not presuppose something not enumerated..., and that there never will be a distinction between what is truly national and what is truly local.... This we are unwilling to do. (pp. 568–69)
>
> Justice Thomas in his concurring opinion was prepared to go even further:
>
> In an appropriate case, I believe that we must further reconsider our "substantial effects" test with an eye toward constructing a standard that reflects the text and history of the Commerce Clause without totally rejecting our more recent Commerce Clause jurisprudence. (p. 586)

The *Lopez* decision marked the first decision since 1936 in which the Supreme courts struck down federal legislation on the basis of the Commerce Clause.[13]

The Brady Handgun Violence Prevention Act presented a different twist in ***Printz v. U.S.***, 521 U.S. 898 (1997). The problem was that the act imposed on state "Chief Law Enforcement Officers" (CLEOs) an interim obligation to conduct background checks on prospective handgun purchasers. This was too much for Justice Scalia. The petitioners in the case objected to "being pressed into federal service," and claimed that such compelled enlistment was unprecedented until very recent years (p. 905).

> The Government points to a number of federal statutes enacted within the past few decades that require the participation of state or officials in implementing federal regulatory schemes. Some of these are connected to federal funding measures, and can perhaps be more accurately described as conditions upon the grant of federal funding than as mandates to the States; others, which require only the provision of information to the Federal Government, do not involve the precise issue before us here, which is the forced participation of the States' executive in the actual administration of a federal program.... Even assuming they represent assertion of the very same congressional power challenged here, they are of such recent vintage that they are no more probative than the statute before us of a constitutional tradition that lends meaning to the text. Their persuasive force is far outweighed by almost two centuries of apparent congressional avoidance of the practice. (pp. 917–18)
>
> ... It matters not whether policymaking is involved, and no case-by-case weighing of the burdens or benefits is necessary; such commands are fundamentally incompatible **with our constitutional system of due sovereignty.** (p. 935)

Dual sovereignty is another doctrine that was last seriously heard in 1936 in ***U.S. v. Butler***, 297 U.S. 1, which might as well have been written by Scalia:

> The expressions of the framers of the Constitution, the decisions of this court interpreting that instrument and the writings of the great commentators will be searched in vain for any suggestion that there exists in the clause under discussion or elsewhere in the Constitution, the authority whereby every provision and every fair implication from that instrument may be subverted, the independence of the individual states obliterated, and the United States converted into a central government exercising uncontrolled police power in every state of the Union, superseding all local control or regulation of the affairs or concerns of the states. (p. 77)

Finally in ***U.S. v. Morrison***, 120 S. Ct. 1740 (2000) Chief Justice Rehnquist held the Violence Against Women Act of 1994 unconstitutional, on much the same basis as in ***Lopez***. This was despite the fact that extensive congressional hearings had substantiated the serious impact of gender-motivated violence on victims and their families. The Chief Justice said that this was a criminal statute that had nothing to do with commerce or commercial activity. As to the findings of the impact on victims and their families, he concluded that "the existence of such congressional findings, coupled with a recitation of its impact on interstate commerce, is not sufficient, by itself, to sustain the constitutionality of Commerce Clause legislation." A congressional finding of fact **"does not necessarily make it so"** (citing ***Lopez*** at 557). This, of course, is a fair distance from the position in ***Wickard*** that the Supreme Court ought to defer to the congressional judgment, **"if there is any rational basis for doing so."** Instead, Rehnquist wrote that:

> Indeed, we can think of no better example of the police power, which the Founders denied the National Government and reposed in the States, than the suppression of violent crime and vindication of its victims.

Justice Sandra Day O'Connor's tendency to side with women in cases involving violence against women was not enough to override her interest in preserving the rights of the states through the Eleventh Amendment. She sided with the majority.[14]

A rhetorical question: On the basis of Rehnquist's opinions in ***Lopez*** and ***Morrison***, should the public accommodations section of the 1964 Civil Rights Act now be held unconstitutional?

CONCLUSION

One final consideration in the evolution of states' rights under the Rehnquist and Roberts courts necessarily follows from the legal and political outcomes of the 2000 presidential election and then the review of the constitutionality of the Patient Protection and Affordable Care Act of 2010 (sometimes called Obamacare). Legally, the decision to stop the recounting of the ballots in Florida and ending the election of 2000 seemed to point in a new direction regarding the court's preference for the powers of the states. The decision in ***Bush v. Gore*** **II** overturned the Florida Supreme Court's interpretation of Florida state law. Yet, the same five judges who have consistently formed the majority in developing new states' rights in other cases now ruled that the Florida Court's decision violated the "Equal Protection Clause" of the Fourteenth Amendment. The majority saw the obvious contradiction, with Rehnquist writing:

> None are more conscious of the vital limits on judicial authority than are the members of this Court, and none stand more in admiration of the Constitution's design to leave the selection of the President to the people through their legislatures and to the political sphere.[15]

However, he added, when cases come to us, "it becomes our unsought responsibility to resolve the federal and constitutional issues the judicial system has been forced to confront."

The dissenters in the case, however, were nonplussed by the conclusions of the majority. Justice Stevens:

> In the interest of finality, however, the majority effectively orders the disenfranchisement of an unknown number of voters whose ballots reveal their intent—and are therefore legal votes under *state* law but were for some reason rejected by ballot counting machines. It does so on the basis of the deadlines set forth in Title 3 of the United States Code. But, as I have already noted, those provisions merely provide rules of decision for Congress to follow when selecting among conflicting slates of electors. They do not prohibit a state from counting what the majority concedes to be legal votes until a bona fide winner is determined.

Justice Breyer:

> The Constitution and federal statutes themselves make clear that restraint is appropriate. They set forth a road map of how to resolve disputes about electors, even after an election as close as this one. That road map foresees the resolution of electoral disputes by state courts . . . But it nowhere provides for involvement by the United States Supreme Court.

Legally, then, the majority seems to be in unfamiliar territory, resolving a dispute according to federal law when it could have allowed the state law to be controlling. While the case did not involve the Commerce Clause, it seemed to go against the judicial instincts one would have ordinarily ascribed to the majority.

When the Affordable Care Act was passed in 2010, it had as one of its basic characteristics a mandate that citizens either buy health insurance or pay a tax penalty if they chose not to buy insurance. This was justified by Congress by the right of the national government to regulate interstate commerce. In the ***National Federation of Independent Business v. Sebelius***[16] case, the Supreme Court had a careful balancing act—trying to support the intent of a major piece of congressional legislation while keeping its dedication to limitation of federal authority over the states. The decision was reflective of this dilemma. In the decision, with Chief Justice John Roberts being the critical vote, the court decided that the mandate was unconstitutional as it related to interstate commerce; it was an "overreach" of federal authority. Thus, the court kept its fidelity to the principles of the states' rights narrative. But, the mandate was approved as part of the national government's taxation power in Article 1, Section 8 of the Constitution:

> The individual mandate cannot be upheld as an exercise of Congress's power under the Commerce Clause. That Clause authorizes Congress to regulate interstate commerce, not to order individuals to engage in it. In this case, however, it is reasonable to construe what Congress has done as increasing taxes on those who have a certain amount of income, but choose to go without health insurance. Such legislation is within Congress's power to tax. (p. 2608)

The case in many ways reflected the theme of this essay. Federalism is a basic characteristic of American democracy, but policy preferences drive the national debate. Critics of the Affordable Care Act saw this decision as confirming the federalist narrative because the law was declared constitutional. But states' rights narrative supporters took some consolation in the notion that the court curtailed the national right to justify far-reaching national policies under the right to regulate interstate commerce.

Politically, the impact of the decision is to enhance the potential that the narrow edge that the majority now enjoys regarding definition of the Commerce Clause will continue into the future. With President Donald Trump as the likely proponent of one or more future members of the court, the preference for states' rights is far higher than it would have been under a Gore administration.

Clearly, we have not yet seen the final word in defining the nature of the relationship between the national and state governments. Future cases and future courts will continue to require the reexamination of that relationship. For now, however, it seems clear that those who favor the states' rights perspective hold the keys and that the Stage IV definition will continue.

Key Terms

Confederate system—a manner of arranging power between a central government, such as the U.S. federal government, and component governments, such as state governments, in which the component governments have ultimate authority. The United States was governed by a confederate system under the Articles of Confederation.

Devolution—the idea that many of the responsibilities assumed by the national government in the years after the New Deal should be returned to the states.

Federalist narrative—a set of propositions that concludes that in the division of power between the national and state governments, the national government should prevail under most circumstances. This narrative primarily rests on an expanded view of the "necessary and proper" clause in the Constitution.

Interstate commerce—the flow of economic activity between two or more states. The power to regulate interstate commerce is enumerated in Article I, Section 8 of the U.S. Constitution. Contests over how broad that power is have largely defined the legal debate about federalism in the Supreme Court.

Nullify—the notion that any state should have the right to reject national laws that are contrary to the interests of the state. It was most prominently argued by John C. Calhoun in the years before the Civil War, but has found its way into modern debates about federalism as well.

Shays's Rebellion—an armed uprising in Massachusetts in 1786–87 against perceived injustices of government. The rebellion exposed the weakness of government under the Articles of Confederation and was used as a justification for writing a new document with expanded national government powers.

States' rights narrative—a set of propositions that concludes that in the division of power between the national government and the states, the two levels of government have equal sovereignty. It generally argues that the "police power" of the state limits the powers of the national government and often cites the Tenth Amendment of the Constitution as requiring curtailment of national government power.

Unitary system—a system of governance in which the central government retains all of the ultimate authority in a nation and component governments, such as state and local governments, exercise only such authority as the central government grants them.

Multiple Choice Questions

1. In a confederate form of government,
   a. the national government holds sovereign power over state governments.
   b. the national and state governments share power equally.
   c. the national government holds sovereign power over national security policy while states hold power over domestic policy.
   d. the state governments hold sovereign power over the national government.
   e. state governments allow local governments to exercise home rule authority.

Answer: D

2. The idea that individual states can decide to render national laws as unenforceable and void within their borders when they violate state interests is called
   a. federalism.
   b. nullification.
   c. unification.
   d. devolution.
   e. Shays's Rebellion.

Answer: B

3. The "federalist narrative" in American politics suggests that
   a. the supremacy clause of the U.S. Constitution always decides conflicts between the national government and the states in favor of the national government.
   b. the Tenth Amendment to the Constitution reserves most welfare issues to be handled at the state level.
   c. there is a clear line of separation between the powers of the national and state governments.
   d. the powers of the national and state governments are inherently intertwined and inseparable.
   e. the interstate Commerce Clause of the U.S. constitution allows the national government significant authority in regulating economic activity within the states.

Answer: E

4. Which Alabama governor argued that states' rights allowed him to keep the University of Alabama as a segregated institution?
   a. George Wallace.
   b. Ross Barnett.
   c. James Madison.
   d. John C. Calhoun.
   e. William Rehnquist.

Answer: A

5. In *Bush v. Gore*, the Supreme Court held that
   a. the interests of the state of Florida outweighed the requirements of the U.S. Constitution.
   b. George W. Bush was the duly elected president of the United States.
   c. despite the fact that Florida had an important role in the presidential election, the requirements of the U.S. Constitution outweighed Florida's.
   d. Vice President Gore had overstepped his authority in appealing the outcome of the 2000 election to the Supreme Court.
   e. the butterfly ballot used in some Florida counties biased the 2000 election outcome in favor of Al Gore.

Answer: C

Discussion Question

When the founding fathers decided to pursue a new Constitution in the summer of 1787, one of their core difficulties was how to both give the national government "proper energy" and keep in place the powers that states enjoyed. In your essay, explain how Madison approached the issue of federalism. Then, as the nation developed, policy issues developed that converted John C. Calhoun from being a nationalist to advocating for increased powers of states. Define the concept of nullification and explain how Calhoun's adoption of that concept reflects the idea that "when they say the issue is federalism, it isn't."

Notes

1. Mattie Quinn, "How Trump's Health Budget Would Impact States," *Governing*, May 25, 2017; David Post, "The Sanctuary Cities Executive Order: Putting the Bully Back in 'Bully Pulpit'," *Washington Post*, May 2, 2017.
2. Gene Healy, "Obama's Phony Federalism," Cato Institute, November 17, 2009.
3. James Madison, Alexander Hamilton, and John Jay, *The Federalist Papers*, (New York: Penguin Books, 1987), p. 122.
4. James Madison, Alexander Hamilton, and John Jay, *The Federalist Papers*, (New York: Penguin Books, 1987), p. 128.
5. http://www.yale.edu/lawweb/avalon/csa/scarsec.htm.
6. Governor Ross Barnett's Proclamation to the People of Mississippi, September 13, 1962, http://americanradioworks.publicradio.org/features/prestapes/barnettspeech.html.
7. Statement of Governor George C. Wallace, University of Alabama, June 11, 1963, http://www.archives.state.al.us/govs_list/schooldoor.html.
8. The American System, (Chicago: Rand McNally, 1966), pp. 8–9.
9. South Dakota v. Dole, 483 U.S. 203 (1987).
10. Richard P. Nathan and Fred C. Doolittle, et al. *Reagan and the States*, (Princeton: Princeton University Press, 1987), p. 40.
11. Ibid., pp. 57–66.
12. Ibid., p. 63.
13. Bill Swinford and Eric N. Waltenburg, "The Consistency of the U.S. Supreme Court's 'Pro-State' Bloc," *Publius* 28:2 (Spring 1998):31.
14. Carol S. Weissert and Sanford F. Schram, "The State of U.S. Federalism, 1999–2000," *Publius* 30:1–2 (Spring 2000): 16.
15. Decision of December 12, 2000 accessed at www.findlaw.com.
16. 132 S. Ct. 2566 (2012).

WHO'S THAT CHARMING STRANGER WITH THE CHECK?

BY SAMUEL H. FISHER III
University of South Alabama

LEARNING OBJECTIVES

Students should be able to:

1. Gain an understanding of campaign finance in federal campaigns by becoming familiar with data presented on the FEC website and data on Opensecrets.org.
2. Gain an understanding of different styles of representation as presented in this chapter.
3. Use data from the FEC and Opensecrets.org to compare sources and amounts of campaign funds of candidates running for the same office.
4. Be familiar with the tension between the ability to give money as a form of political speech and the ability of monetary contributions to corrupt elected officials as shown in majority and dissenting opinions in *Citizens United v. FEC* and *McCutcheon v. FEC*.

"You have 30 minutes before you fly to the coast for BBQ Grill Manufacturers Awards dinner. You have time to talk to one of two constituents waiting in the reception area," said Larry, the new summer intern.

"Did either contribute to the last election campaign?" replied Rep. Paella.

"Both did. $100 from Joe of the Air Quality Association and $2500 from Jennifer of the Beef is Best Association," mumbled Larry.
"Use your brain! I'll talk to Jennifer," exclaimed the representative.
—Hypothetical conversation.

"Under the majority's view, I suppose it may be a First Amendment problem that corporations are not permitted to vote, given that voting is, among other things, a form of speech."
—John Paul Stevens in *Citizens United v. FEC* opinion.

Without money, it is nearly impossible for an aspiring candidate to win a seat on the city council, the mayor's office, the state legislature, Congress, or the presidency. Only after a person is successfully elected can they make decisions on behalf of others. This decision-making ability is the representative function of the elected official that places

---

Contributed by Samuel H. Fischer. Copyright © Kendall Hunt Publishing Company.

them in a position of power to act for or against the interests of individuals or groups. Candidates need money to run a successful campaign and, conversely, voters see giving money as an effective means to have their concerns heard. Without the ability of individuals to give money, it can prove difficult to gain the attention of their representative. In elections, we see the nexus of representation and money. Campaign finance represents two dynamics in politics. One dynamic is a political candidate's need for large sums of money to pay for media ads, campaign consultants and workers, travel, and all the other campaign costs. The other dynamic is that of the voters being heard. Your vote is anonymous so how do you get the attention of the candidate once they are in office so that you can encourage the introduction of legislation or the amending of legislation by others for a favorable outcome? Money, lots of money, provides a way to stand out and be noticed by a political candidate. When an elected official has a choice between a citizen who contributed to the campaign and one who has not contributed, the choice is very likely to spend time, help out, or listen to the contributor. So, money is simply a form of participation.

But, the impact of money in politics can also be seen as a corrosive agent. Instead of representing the best interests of all their constitutions, political officials turn their attention to those individuals who provided the most money whether it be directly to their campaign or indirectly through activities in support of the official. The interests of the voters and contributors may or may not coincide. Voters may want increased services such as education and a cleaner environment, which requires higher spending; but contributors, especially those with higher incomes, are likely to push for lower taxes and spending by government for such programs. The political official has a dilemma. Contributions are necessary to run an effective campaign and getting out the vote requires those contributions.

The implication is that money provides leverage for effective representation for individuals and organizations. Because campaigns are so expensive, candidates are more than willing to hold their hands out. This interplay leads to the appearance of corruption, real or not. To counter the possible corrupting influence of money on politics, Congress and state legislatures passed laws limiting campaign contributions, instituting reporting requirements for those contributions, and who can contribute. It is not surprising that individuals and groups have found innovative ways to circumvent the statutory limits and reporting requirements with the underlying assumption those contributions will result in favorable representation.

REPRESENTATION

In order to understand the importance of campaign contributions in U.S. electoral politics, it is important to understand the concept of representation. The United States has a republican form of government. Instead of every citizen taking part in deciding every policy or law, representatives are elected to make those decisions for their constituents. Representation is usually characterized in two forms: **agent** or **trustee**. An elected official acting as an **agent** will represent the majority interests of the constituency. Regardless of the representative's personal opinion, the choice of the district's majority will always drive the representative's vote on policy. The assumption is that elected officials are responsive to constituent concerns when making decisions on proposed laws and public policies. Normally, we think of elected officials representing the interests of constituents in their district without regard to their own opinion or acting as an agent. A representative acting as a **trustee** acts differently. In the role of trustee, the representative will use their own judgment to determine what is best for their district and constituents. The reality is that many representatives who seek to act as agents must resort to the trustee role for votes on issues that are either unknown or irrelevant to constituents.

Defining representation can go beyond agent and trustee and does not have to be limited to legislative behavior. Representation can be described as **geographical, descriptive**, or **surrogate**. **Geographical representation** is easy to envision. Every House member and Senator is elected from districts or states that are geographically bounded. The inhabitants of that area have unique interests and concerns that the representative can then translate into action through legislative votes, the introduction of legislation, and budgeting choices. **Descriptive representation**, on the other hand, is the idea of how much do the demographic characteristics of the representative mirror the demographic characteristics of the majority of the constituents in the district or state? The closer the representative mirrors the major demographic characteristics of the district, the better the descriptive representation will be. Take for example a congressional district in which 85% of the population is African American. In order to achieve true representation, does their member of Congress need to be African American? The premise of descriptive representation is that a representative with very similar socio-economic, life experience, and racial and religious characteristics will also have similar attitudes toward issues and bills in Congress and thus provide effective representation of constituents in the district.

Surrogate representation is another type of representation that is not bound by district or state political boundaries. In this instance, a person looks to a representative or senator from outside their district or state to further his or her interests. As an example, if you live in Mobile, Alabama and you have been a fervent Democrat for years then you know full well that the likelihood of electing a Democrat to Congress from the first congressional district of Alabama is as likely as Mobile Bay totally freezing over. In this instance, you would look to Democrats from *other districts* to support and appeal to for favorable votes on issues or policies that you know will not be looked at and supported by your district's representative. Besides individuals looking to representatives outside their district, this can be especially true for corporations. They will look to representatives outside the districts in which they are headquartered to pursue favorable policies.

Ultimately, no matter which definition of representation you believe best exemplifies how members of Congress make their legislative decisions, to the voters representation is quite simply when the representative's choice on legislation is the same choice the voter would make. In any situation where a choice must be made by an elected official, there will be voters who are happy with the choice and voters who are very unhappy with the choice.

Elected officials face choices and in making those choices there are winners and losers. How those choices are made can be affected by campaign contributions. Consequently, to get what you want from elected officials, does it help to give to political campaigns? And if elected officials are responsive to monetary contributions does that mean the individuals or organizations that can contribute large sums of money are more likely to have their interests represented than the vast majority of individuals that contribute either very little or none at all?

A Brief History of Elections and Money

Elections today are much different than elections early in U.S. history primarily because of who gets to cast a vote. The Founding Fathers were not the supporters of democracy you might think based on what we are all taught in elementary school. This is clear if you look at the Constitution. At the outset, the only federal office directly elected by the people was representatives to the U.S. House. Senators were selected by state legislatures and the president, to this day, is elected by electors, where winning the popular vote does not guarantee victory in the Electoral College (just ask Hillary Clinton in the 2016 election and Al Gore in the 2000 election). In the beginning, the electorate was limited to white males who owned businesses or land and paid taxes. The Framers thought such attributes spoke to their virtue. Over the years, the electorate was expanded to include nonproperty owners, women, minorities, and people under the age of 21. This resulted in an expanded and diverse electorate that candidates had to appeal to for their votes.

Even if the pool of eligible voters was small compared to today, to get people to vote the way you hope has always required money. Money was necessary to pay for pamphlets, favorable newspaper articles, food and drink at political rallies, and printing of ballots. There were no formal restrictions on how much money could be raised, the source of the contribution, or how it could be spent. Sometimes, money went directly to encouraging voters to cast a ballot by offering free booze. Even George Washington was accused of providing free liquor to encourage favorable votes when the polls opened on Election Day. Consequently, many states passed laws banning the sale of alcohol while the polling places were open to prevent candidates from "buying" votes.

Money, or things bought by money, since our nation's inception, has been the lifeblood of electoral politics. Whether it is old-fashioned cash, dollars exchanged electronically, or Bitcoins, the possession of it in large quantities goes a long way to increasing the possibility of success. Having more money than your opponent does not guarantee victory but the lack of money assuredly makes it difficult to win.

So, what is the point of contributing to political campaigns directly or indirectly for the contributor? It buys representation and the more money that can be offered, the greater the representation will be. If money spent on campaigns through direct campaign donations to candidates, or donations to political party organizations, or money spent independently on behalf of candidates, were not an effective method of representation, then the amounts of money spent on campaigns would not be so large.

Winning reelection is the key to having power in Washington since longevity is important to acquiring institutional power in Congress. Therefore, the obvious goal is to get more votes than all the other candidates at the polls. Getting those votes costs money. However, today, campaign finance laws administered by the Federal Election Commission (FEC) dictate contribution limits to candidates and political organizations that individuals may not exceed. So, if major contributors max out the direct contribution limits to my campaign committee, I can then point them to a smorgasbord of political actions committees—PACS, Super PACS, 501(c)3, 501(c)4, 527—which will spend money in support of my campaign or in opposition to my opponent. However, there can be no coordination of spending between my campaign and these other committees.

Given a choice as a politician, who will you invite in for a friendly conversation—the disgruntled constituent who has never given a single penny to your campaign, the constituent you have never heard from, or the individual who enthusiastically wrote you a check during your campaign? The answer is obvious since the money collected and spent on the campaign, directly or indirectly, not only has the effect of encouraging votes for the preferred candidate but also discourages support for the opposition. I may have a single vote but my contribution becomes a potential vote multiplier. By contributing to a political campaign or spending money on behalf of a political campaign, I can increase the chances of my candidate winning, since money is needed to get the campaign message to the voters. Monetary contributions translate into getting the campaign message to the voters that can result in convincing voters to provide support. For the other candidate, the inability to match or surpass that ability to raise money inhibits their ability to effectively get out their campaign message. Of course, this raises the concern that wealth dictates the quality of representation. Should those with more wealth be entitled to better and more responsive representation?

There are two critical ingredients to electoral success. The first is money... I've forgotten the second.
—Mark Hanna

The 1896 election stands out as a hallmark of big money influence. William McKinley, the Republican Presidential nominee, ran against the Democratic nominee, William Jennings Bryant in a hotly contested election. These were the days when presidential campaigns were not based primarily on the visibility of the candidate. McKinley ran his campaign from his front porch while his campaign manager, Mark Hanna, went about collecting the necessary sums of money to publicize the candidate. The final figure is approximately $4 million compared to less than $1 million collected by William Jennings Bryan.[1] Adjusting for inflation, the $4 million collected in 1896 would be approximately $114 million in 2014. That is large amount but much less than the $333 million raised by President Trump's 2016 campaign and the $564 million raised by Clinton. The primary contribution sources for McKinley's campaign were large corporations and individual businessmen. They were sent a letter detailing what the expected sum should be in order to recognize the importance of putting McKinley in office, in order that their interests be protected. The money was spent on extensive advertising throughout the nation that had not been done on that scale in the past. Hanna's strategy was successful and McKinley triumphed, and the nation discovered the importance of advertising in national elections.

Hanna's recipe of directly soliciting business for campaign contributions raised concern about the possible corrupting effect of money. In the following years, Teddy Roosevelt sought legislation to take corporate wealth out of the elections by preventing direct contributions to political candidates. The Tillman Act of 1907 was designed to eliminate corporate money from federal elections; however, there was a fatal flaw in the legislation.[2] A law proscribing bad behavior is always nice but if it lacks "teeth," that is, a mechanism to enforce the law and penalize violations, then it is merely decoration. As it turns out, the Tillman Act had no provision for administrative enforcement. Candidates, banks, and corporations were free to ignore the law. Congress continued to pass laws to restrict and regulate campaign contributions for many years (Federal Corrupt Practices Act of 1925,

Hatch Act of 1939 and later amendments, and the Taft-Hartley Act of 1947) but as with the Tillman Act there was no administrative structure to enforce the acts.

Flash forward to 1971 and the passage of the Federal Election Campaign Act of 1971, the next major attempt to regulate campaign finance. This law created the FEC and gave it the ability to enforce campaign finance laws. The attempt to again place limits on corporate and individual contributions was in part a reaction to actions of President Richard Nixon. His change of heart on increasing the base payments to milk producers (something he had publically stated he was opposed to), helped lead to campaign finance reform. At the time, milk producers were guaranteed a minimum price per gallon as a way to encourage milk production and they sought an increase but Nixon's Secretary of Agriculture (with Nixon's support), opposed any increase. It would have been up to the Department of Agriculture to permit that increase and Nixon had said no. However, after the contribution of $250,000 to President Nixon's reelection committee for the 1972 presidential election (the Committee to Re-elect the President or CREEP), Nixon reversed his stand and overruled the agriculture secretary. To make this contribution less obvious, the campaign was not given money directly but rather it was funneled through several organizations. Some of these organizations had interesting names: Americans Dedicated to Better Public Administration, Volunteers Against Citizen Apathy, and Americans United for Objective Reporting (Schell 1975, 146). There were additional large sums of money funneled to CREEP from corporations seeking to influence presidential policies related to their businesses for the 1972 presidential election.

Perhaps the most notorious political scandal of the Nixon administration and in U.S. history was the Watergate scandal. This scandal, which is now something of a dim memory for many people, proved to be consequential, not only for Nixon's presidency, but for campaign finance reform. During the Watergate scandal, it came out that there was a safe in the White House containing hundreds of thousands of dollars in cash. This money was in part used to pay-off the men caught burglarizing the Democratic campaign offices in the Watergate complex (hence the scandal is known as Watergate). None of this money was publically reported and was used to fund political "dirty tricks" during the 1972 presidential campaign. The large sums of money present in the White House and the methods used to pass the money to the campaign provided a strong nudge to updating campaign finance laws.

In 1974, Congress passed an amendment to the 1971 FECA; the first substantive attempt to limit campaign contributions in federal election. However, newly amended campaign law was far from bullet proof. As always, people and organizations looked for ways to circumvent the barriers to contributing and raising money for political campaigns without finding themselves in jail. In a 1976 legal challenge to the new law, the *Sun Oil* case, the bulk of the Campaign Reform Act was left intact but in a key ruling by the Supreme Court, corporations and labor unions were able to set up political actions committees (PACs) with contributions from corporate employees and from labor union members. These PACs could then contribute to campaigns. Funds from a corporation's general treasury could not be used but there were lots of ways to encourage senior management to "voluntarily" contribute to corporate PACs and as well as getting the shop floor workers to do the same for labor PACs. The legality of such behavior had been in question until the ruling and the clarification stimulated a spectacular rise in the number of PACs after this ruling. The FEC recorded 608 PACs at the end of 1974 and by the beginning of 2014 there are over 7000 PACs registered with the FEC.[3]

A dilemma for the FEC has consistently been enforcing the rules. In 1974, Congress amended the Campaign Reform Act to give the commission the power to investigate campaign contributions and expenditures and assess monetary penalties for infractions. This however did not really solve the problem since political campaigns could run the risk of taking illegal contributions and *if caught* paying a fine after a successful election without the winner suffering any real consequences unless the violation grabs the public's attention and wrath.

Limitations were also set in place for how much individuals could contribute to political campaigns during two-year election cycles. The amount is adjusted each election cycle to reflect inflation. For the 2017–2018 election cycle the FEC states that individuals can give up to $2,700.00 to a candidate or the candidate's campaign committee per election. That means someone can give a candidate $2,700 in the primary and another $2,700 in the general election for any particular candidate in any specific race. They can also increase the amount of giving by directing money to the national, state, and local party committees, and to political action committees.

Most individuals have limited disposable income to donate to political campaigns. No doubt campaigns will take Visa, Mastercard, or American Express, but how many individuals have sufficient resources to borrow money this way in order to give to political campaigns? Well, not many. Less than 1% of the population gave $200 or more in the 2009–2010 election cycle (Center for Responsive Politics 2011).[4] If money has clout then a very small percentage of the population is actively using this for their desired policy ends. Corporations and unions through PACs have been extremely active in giving to candidates and independent of candidates. This very miniscule percentage of individual givers and organizations also look beyond their home districts and states in their giving decisions. It is not unusual for candidates to receive contributions from individual and organizations that are not resident to the candidate's congressional district or even the state. Besides giving directly to candidates, which was limited, donors gave indirectly by giving to political party campaign committees run by the national Democratic and Republican party organizations and other campaign committees, such as the Republican and Democratic congressional campaign committees, not connected to a particular campaign. These committees could then direct money to candidates or spend on activities that support or oppose a candidate. The large amounts of soft money flowing to these committees raised concerns among some politicians.

The Bipartisan Campaign Reform Act of 2002 (BCRA), sometimes referred to as the McCain-Feingold act, sought to limit the impact of soft money contributions, primarily to the national political parties, and also put restrictions on **electioneering communications**. "**Soft money**" is defined as funds that are not regulated by federal election laws while "hard money" are funds raised for political campaigns that are subject to federal election laws.[5] Prior to the passage of BCRA, political parties could raise unlimited amounts of money for federal election activities, such things as get out the vote activities, voter registration drives (within 120 days of a federal election), voter identification, public political communications via any media (TV, print, mail, telephone banks, etc.) except for the Internet.[6] There was also an attempt to prevent children making campaign contributions since in many instances it is unlikely that Dave, Jr. and young Melissa really have $2,000.00 each to give to the same political candidate as their parents each did. This portion of the BCRA was struck down by the Supreme Court in *McConnell v. FEC* (2003).

Citizens United, a nonprofit group that produced a critical documentary in 2008 on Hillary Clinton, challenged the BCRA's limits on electioneering communications. Citizens United was a nonprofit corporation that took contributions from individuals and corporations to make the documentary *Hillary: The Movie*. It was released to movie theaters and DVD; however, Citizens United also wanted to release it prior to presidential primaries as a video on demand through local cable companies. They went to court to overturn the ban on electioneering communication within 30 days of a federal election on the grounds that it was restraint of their First Amendment right of free speech. Citizens United lost in district court but appealed ultimately to the Supreme Court. The court ruled in favor of Citizens United. In the majority opinion, the court clearly held that corporations have the same free speech rights as individuals.[7] The logic of placing limits or prohibitions on expenditures for political speech is the appearance or perception of corruption. In this case, corporations have far more financial resources to fund their political speech than the vast majority of living-breathing individuals. However, corporations are considered to be individuals for legal purposes and like real people, corporations have free speech rights. The majority on the court believed that a corporation's ability to spend large amounts of money would not give the appearance of corruption.

> This Court now concludes that independent expenditures, including those made by corporations, do not give rise to corruption or the appearance of corruption. That speakers may have influence over or access to elected officials does not mean that those officials are corrupt. And the appearance of influence or access will not cause the electorate to lose faith in this democracy.

Justice Stevens in a dissent argued that corporations in these circumstances are not the same as living people. He stated that:

> . . . corporations have no consciences, no beliefs, no feelings, no thoughts, no desires. Corporations help structure and facilitate the activities of human beings, to be sure, and their "personhood" often serves as a useful legal fiction. But they are not themselves members of "We the People" by whom and for whom our Constitution was established.

Simply put, should a corporation or labor union have the same First Amendment free speech rights as individual citizens? Since corporations are considered individuals for legal purposes and previous cases have established corporations enjoy First Amendment rights, then the expenditure of funds from the corporation's treasury for political purposes is perfectly appropriate.

However, if the disposable income available for campaign contributions of corporations, such as McDonald's or AT&T, is compared to the typical individual, there is no question. Corporations have much more money to contribute than most individuals. The court held that putting restrictions on what corporations or other organizations spent on electioneering communications was an unacceptable restriction on the First Amendment right to free speech. The point of speaking out is to gain the attention of lawmakers and have them respond to the constituent's concerns. Since politicians are more likely to listen to the needs and concerns of campaign contributors, especially those that contribute

Table 1. Major Campaign Finance Acts

1867 Naval Appropriations Act	prevented candidates from requiring campaign donations from naval shipyard workers.
1883 Civil Service Reform Act (Pendleton Act)	applied rules of the 1867 act to all federal employees.
1907 Tillman Act	bans campaign contributions by banks and corporations.
1925 Corrupt Practices Act	limits congressional campaign spending and includes requirement for disclosures of contributors.
1947 Taft-Hartley Act	ban on contributions from labor unions, corporations, and interstate banks.
1971 Federal Election Campaign Act and 1974 amendments (FECA)	places limits on contributions and also creates the Federal Election Commission to enforce the act.
2002 Bipartisan Campaign Reform Act (McCain-Feingold)	eliminates unlimited contributions to political parties and prohibits use of corporate or union funds for political ads.

large sums of money, it raises the specter of corporations having better representation than individuals.

As noted earlier, campaign finance laws also set overall limits on how much any individual may contribute overall during a single election cycle. As of 2013, the law limited the total amount to $123,200.00. For well over 99% of the population this is not an issue. Only a very small percentage of individuals have the ability to make contributions in excess of that limit. However, in the aftermath of *Citizens United*, another case made its way to the Supreme Court. In *McCutcheon v. FEC*, the question before the court was the permissibility of any overall limit on political contributions. Contribution limits to specific candidates, party committees, and others as spelled out in the FEC regulations were not challenged. McCutcheon, an Alabama businessman, argued that such overall contribution limits inhibits his right of free speech.

The court majority ruled that "Congress may regulate campaign contributions to protect against corruption or the appearance of corruption."[8] But the court goes on to note that Congress " . . . may not, however, regulate contributions simply to reduce the amount of money in politics, or to restrict the political participation of some in order to enhance the relative influence of others. The court held that "the only type of corruption that Congress may target is *quid pro quo* corruption." Large contributions to political campaigns are not seen as corrupting. It must be clearly money offered to influence specific actions by an elected official. The ability to gain access to make a case is not sufficient grounds for corruption or the appearance of corruption. Limits on the aggregate amount of contributions by individuals was eliminated by the court though the per candidate limit remains in place (see Table 2 for current FEC limits).

Table 2. Contribution Limits for 2017–2018 Federal Elections

Donors	Recipients				
	Candidate Committee	PAC[1] (SSF and Nonconnected)	State, District, and Local Party Committee	National Party Committee	Additional National Party Committee Accounts[2]
Individual	$2,700* per election	$5,000 per year	$10,000 per year (combined)	$33,900* per year	$101,700* per account, per year
Candidate Committee	$2,000 per election	$5,000 per year	Unlimited Transfers	Unlimited Transfers	
PAC - Multicandidate	$5,000 per election	$5,000 per year	$5,000 per year (combined)	$15,000 per year	$45,000 per account, per year
PAC - Nonmulticandidate	$2,700* per election	$5,000 per year	$10,000 per year (combined)	$33,900* per year	$101,700* per account, per year
State, District, and Local Party Committee	$5,000 per election (combined)	$5,000 per year (combined)	Unlimited Transfers		
National Party Committee	$5,000 per election[3]	$5,000 per year			

* Indexed for inflation in odd-numbered years.

1. "PAC" here refers to a committee that makes contributions to other federal political committees. Independent-expenditure-only political committees (sometimes called "super PACs") may accept unlimited contributions, including from corporations and labor organizations.

2. The limits in this column apply to a national party committee's accounts for: (i) the presidential nominating convention; (ii) election recounts and contests and other legal proceedings; and (iii) national party headquarters buildings. A party's national committee, Senate campaign committee, and House campaign committee are each considered separate national party committees with separate limits. Only a national party committee, not the parties' national congressional campaign committees, may have an account for the presidential nominating convention.

3. Additionally, a national party committee and its Senatorial campaign committee, may contribute up to $47,400 combined per campaign to each Senate candidate.

The original overall limit on campaign contributions for the 2013–2014 election cycle was $123,200.

Dark Money

Dark money refers to donations made to organizations that are not required by law to disclose the contributor names. In the aftermath of the decision in *Citizens United* and *McCutcheon*, a wide variety of organizations have been created to spend money on political campaigns, both directly and indirectly. One such result has been the development of **Super PACs**: organizations that can raise unlimited amounts of money to spend on electioneering communications—running media ads on TV, radio, the Internet and other media outlets—as long as the activities are not coordinated with a particular political candidate. These Super PACs are often referred to by their designation in the U.S. tax code: 501(c)4 or 501(c)6. The tax code allows for the creation of nonprofit organizations to educate the public about political campaigns and to spend money on political campaigns.[9] These organizations are typically a source of dark money since they are not required to disclose who their donors are, unlike political party campaign committees and candidate campaign committees. This ability to provide anonymity provides a shield for donors who may want to mask their contributions from the public. Because of the anonymity of the donors to the public, the phrase dark money has become the descriptive term used in stories about that type of campaign contribution. It is very unlikely though that the beneficiaries, political candidates, of the campaign ads run by such groups will be unaware of individuals providing the funding.

The Koch brothers, Charles and David, of Koch Industries have become emblematic of the use of private wealth to seek better representation. The Koch brothers from Kansas are a prime example of what some see as those with money attempting to skew the political system to their advantage. Over $2 million from Koch Industries were contributed to candidates, primarily Republican, in 45 states in 2012. They also contributed through various PACs and organizations that are not required to disclose their contributors. A *Washington Post* article explored the network of organizations connected to the Koch brothers that raised approximately $407 million during the 2011–2012 election cycle.[10] This figure is a little more than raised by labor unions, with approximately 14 million members, in the same election cycle.[11] It is clear that they are trying to influence the outcomes of elections far beyond the borders of their home state of Kansas.

Conservatives have so far been more effective at raising money this way than liberals; however, the use of dark money groups to influence elections is not ideologically blind. During the 2012 election cycle, conservative groups raised $265.5 million compared to $33.6 million for liberal groups.[12] By 2014, the gap closed somewhat with conservative groups raising $128 million compared to $32.7 million for liberal groups.[13] Both liberal and conservative ideological groups have not shied away from soliciting money while assuring donors the donation sources would not be made public or reported to the FEC or IRS. The sums of monies funneled through dark money groups are very likely to increase dramatically in the next presidential election since there is not an incumbent running.

Fixing the System

Should wealth determine representation? The Founding Fathers, while wary of the masses, were also suspicious of accumulated wealth distorting government decision-making. To prevent distortion yet still allow for individuals to express their political opinions through campaign contributions, the United States could possibly follow two routes: pass a Constitutional amendment specifically overturning *Citizens United* and *McCutcheon* thus allowing the reinstitution of previous campaign contribution limitations or to press for public financing of all federal campaigns. If campaigns were publically funded, there would be no need for candidates to raise money from wealthy donors. For the foreseeable future, it is highly unlikely that public financing of elections will be a viable alternative. The Supreme Court ruled against public financing of Arizona state elections in *McComish v. Bennett* (2011). In addition, the Republican party (who has been most successful in this) controls both houses of Congress, and there is little evidence that legislation advocating public financing would even come up for a vote much less reach the president's desk for signature.

What may spur a fix to the current system is a major political scandal revolving around contributions and public policy. The court has defined corruption in very narrow terms—a specific contribution by a contributor in exchange for a specific action by recipient of the contribution—so it would take an event akin to Nixon's White House safe stuffed with cash to fund illegal activities to bring about significant change. The Watergate scandal eventually led to Nixon's resignation to avoid an impeachment by the House and trial by the Senate due to the public outcry. In subsequent years, the public has been bombarded with political scandals. At the presidential level, there has been Whitewater, Iran-Contra, Abscam, Monica Lewinsky, IRS investigation of religious groups political activities, and Benghazi, to name a few. Except for strong partisans, the public's sense of outrage now appears to be minimal and short-lived. Additionally, most scandals do not reflect incidents where there was a *quid pro quo* understanding when a donation was given. Only if there were multiple examples of representatives who were the recipients of large contributions from individuals or organizations where there was a clear subsequent vote on a policy that clearly benefited the contributors is there likely to any movement to reform campaign finance law.

There is strong evidence that money has an impact beyond Congress and state legislatures. States where money was poured into ads critical of state Supreme Court justices running for reelection claiming they were being soft on crime found a resulting increase of in rulings against criminal defendants.[14] State attorneys general are also becoming a focus of campaign contributions and lobbying with great effect.[15] Corporations seeking favorable regulatory environments have found providingcampaign contributions can result in sympathetic state attorneys general. This is similar to the intense partisan battles over the nomination and Senate confirmation of Supreme Court justices. The assumption is that supporting or opposing particular nominees will lead to a favorable legal environment. While we normally think of the potentially corrupting influence of money on the decision-making of legislators, governors, or presidents, the evidence suggests however that the legal system, especially at the state level, may also be corruptible.

CONCLUSION

In an ideal world, money would not play a factor in elections or the passage of legislation but that would be akin to getting free ice cream every day for breakfast without any unhealthy effects. The reality is that money is important for both the candidate seeking political office and for the individual, whether a living, breathing person or corporation, seeking effective and substantive representation. It is clear that the ability to contribute money to political campaigns, and moreover, the ability to donate large sums of money provides access to lawmakers. It may be difficult to prove *quid pro quo* corruption as a consequence, but it is not difficult to believe that those that can contribute are afforded more responsive representation than those that are unable to afford to offer a significant monetary contribution. Over the years there have been multiple attempts, some successful and some not, to place restraints on the role of money. Such efforts have been dented by legal challenges and by the proliferation of alternative campaign finance channels. Despite the notion that the provision of money is a legitimate exercise of free speech, it is difficult to keep a straight face and state that my $1,000 contribution to a political official does not hold anymore sway than your $10 contribution to the same person.

In an era of growing income and wealth inequality among the American public, the corrupting influence of campaign contributions or independent expenditures is expected to increase. Super PACs continue to spend unlimited amounts of money in support or opposition to particular candidates. Even though donors may remain anonymous, it is highly unlikely that the beneficiaries of those donations, the candidates, are or ever will be ignorant of the source. The Koch brothers and others do not spend millions of dollars without an expectation of a tangible and concrete reciprocation in the form of favorable legislation or favorable changes in regulatory policies.

Another problem with the loosening of campaign contribution restrictions is the transition of representation based on geographical or descriptive characteristics to one based on campaign contributions from across the country may lead to elected officials paying less attention to local issues. In the past, the common saying was that "all politics are local." It now may be the case that "all politics are national." An article in *The New York Times* about the changing nature of Louisiana politics and elections highlighted this apparent trend.[16] The uniqueness and quirkiness of Louisiana politics, not known for high ethics but well known for high interest, is being subsumed by a flow of outside money in support of national issues. As the focus turns from the concrete concerns of local residents—providing funding for new bridges or roads, providing tax breaks for local businesses and local agriculture, preventing a local military base from closing—to that of national groups with specific national agendas. These national policies such as deficit and tax reduction, military base closure/realignments, and reduced infrastructure spending will result in policies that may or may not benefit the local communities.

An alternative to the present system is public funding for political campaigns. Money and political campaigns are inseparable under any circumstance. To run campaign ads, hire experts to organize and run political campaigns, find transportation, feed volunteers, buy bumper stickers and yard signs, and the myriad of other activities connected to political campaigns requires a source of money—a lot of money. For quite some time there has been some limited public financing of presidential campaigns.[17] Presidential candidates that choose to receive public funding have limits on how much can be spent in each state during the nomination phase and for the general election. However, if a presidential candidate chooses not to accept public funding then they are free to spend as much as they can raise with no limits. George W. Bush chose not to accept matching funds for the 2000 primary season and in 2008 Barack Obama turned down matching funds for the general election. However, the public funding does not extend to House and Senate candidates. In the near future, it is unlikely that a Republican Congress would extend public funding. Recent Supreme Court rulings also point to the poor chances of finding ways to limit the amount and sources of campaign contributions. If anything, present restrictions are more likely to be removed or further relaxed. As long as campaign contributions are seen as a form of political speech for individuals, corporations, labor unions, and other organizations there is little likelihood of change. Only a constitutional amendment that specifically removes the First Amendment protections for monetary contributions will open the door for campaign finance regulation.

ACTIVITIES

1. Which style of representation, trustee or agent, would you use if you were a congressman for the congressional district where you currently live? Explain the reasons why you chose that style.
2. Do you think contributing money to a political campaign is a valid form of free speech? Explain why or why not.
3. Read the syllabus portion (pp. 1–7) of the *Citizens United v. FEC* decision (the URL for the decision is found in the Resources section) for a summary of the court's decision and then read Justice Steven's dissenting opinion (pp. 1–3 and p. 89). Which side, the majority or minority, do you agree with? Explain why.
4. Randomly pick two current congressional representatives. Go to OpenSecrets.org and compare the sources and amounts of contributions of the two officials. Do the contribution sources reflect the economic and social interests of their respective districts? Do their committee assignments have any connection to the sources of campaign contributions?

Appendix: Resources

The Internet has several good resources on campaign finance for federal campaigns. There are sources for state-level campaigns but the information is not consistent from state to state.

The Federal Election Commission (http://fec.gov) website presents a wealth of detailed data in raw format for individuals and organizations that have the ability to convert the data into a useable form. The site also has detailed information about campaign finance laws for potential political candidates and for individuals considering the creation of an organization to raise funds for political campaigns.

OpenSecrets (http://opensecrets.org) uses data from the FEC site and puts it into a more useable form for individuals curious about particular candidates, elections, interest groups, and other political organizations. In addition to information about the current election cycle, users can view campaign finances for election cycles going back to 1990. It is also possible to find individual contributions at the local level so that you can see who in your Zip code are major givers to political campaigns.

Supreme Court opinions on campaign finance can be found online at http://www.supremecourt.gov/opinions/opinions.aspx. The *Citizens United v. FEC* opinion is found at http://www.supremecourt.gov/opinions/09pdf/08-205.pdf. The *McCutcheon v. FEC* opinion can be found at http://www.supremecourt.gov/opinions/13pdf/12-536_e1pf.pdf.

Key Terms

Agent—a style of representation where the representative makes choices on how to vote or writes legislation based on the preferences of district constituents and not the preferences of the representative.

Dark money—contributions to organizations that are not required by law to disclose donor names.

Electioneering communications—communication that is broadcast electronically (over the air, cable, or satellite) shortly before a federal election, which refers to specific candidates and is focused on an electorate that may vote in that election.

Geographical representation—representation of constituent interests within a specific geographically limited area.

Hard money—money donated directly to a candidate's political campaign.

Soft money—money donated to noncandidate organizations, which can be used to fund activities in support or opposition of a political candidate. These activities may not be coordinated with any political candidate.

Surrogate representation—the interests of individuals or groups represented by representatives located in another district or state.

Trustee—a style of representation where the representative makes choices on how to vote or writes legislation based on his or her preferences instead of those of the district's constituents.

Multiple Choice Questions

1. Members of Congress are elected by voters in their district but once in Congress may represent the interests of people who do not reside in the member's district. This is an example of:
   a. surrogate representation.
   b. actual representation.
   c. agent representation.
   d. trustee representation.
   e. delegate representation.

Answer: A

2. A congressman who makes his or her decisions on how to vote on legislation based solely on his or her constituents' opinions is acting as _____ while a congressman who relies solely on his or her own judgment is acting as _____.
   a. an agent; a trustee
   b. an agent: a surrogate
   c. a trustee; an agent
   d. a surrogate; a trustee
   e. a trustee; a surrogate

Answer: A

3. The Supreme Court ruled in _____ that there can be limits on the level of contributions to individual candidates and organizations by an individual but there cannot be an overall limit on total amount of political contributions.
   a. *McCutcheon v. FEC*
   b. *McConnell v. FEC*
   c. *Citizens United v. FEC*
   d. *McCain v. FEC*
   e. *Sun Oil v. FEC*

Answer: A

4. Super PACs are able to raise money from individuals and are not necessarily required to disclose the names and amounts that individuals gave. This is commonly known as _____.
   a. Soft money
   b. Dark money
   c. Hard money
   d. Anonymous money
   e. Fuzzy money

Answer: B

5. Early campaign finance regulations allowed corporations and labor unions to solicit donations for their PACs but prevented the use of corporate operational funds or labor union operational funds. The decision in _____ freed corporations and labor unions to use their own funds for political purposes.
   a. *McConnell v. FEC*
   b. *McCutcheon v. FEC*
   c. *Citizens United v. FEC*
   d. *McCain v. FEC*
   e. *Sun Oil v. FEC*

Answer: C

6. If I gave $1000 to a senatorial candidate to vote yes on a specific legislative bill and the candidate ultimately does vote yes is an example of *quid pro quo*. In *Citizens United v. FEC* the majority saw that as
   a. a friendly gesture.
   b. a donation to a like-minded candidate.
   c. a corrupt act.
   d. a donation of no policy consequence.
   e. a donation for long-term support.

Answer: C

7. The *Citizens United* case in part involved an issue of _____.
   a. overall campaign contributions
   b. hard money contributions
   c. minor PACs
   d. electioneering communication
   e. individual campaign contributions

Answer: D

8. Campaign contributions normally referred to as _____ are given directly to the political candidate.
   a. hard money
   b. soft money
   c. dark money
   d. anonymous money
   e. fuzzy money

Answer: A

9. Giving money directly or indirectly to a political candidate is an example of:
   a. political free speech.
   b. commercial free speech.
   c. political corruption.
   d. private free speech.
   e. civic duty.

Answer: A

10. Money that is not given directly to a political candidate but is used to support or oppose a candidate through political ads on TV, radio, print, or the Internet is commonly called:
    a. hard money.
    b. dark money.
    c. anonymous money.
    d. fuzzy money.
    e. soft money.

Answer: E

Discussion Questions

1. What are two examples of campaign finance laws? In each case, what was one major regulation on campaign contributions imposed by the law? Were those regulations successful? Explain why or why not.
2. Analyze the following table of campaign contributions by different groups in the 2015–2016 election cycle to Democrats and Republicans. What are three conclusions that can be drawn from this table? Provide at least one reason for each conclusion.

Contributions, 2015–2016 Election Cycle (figures in millions)

	Democrats	Republicans
Business	$1123.1	$1161.4
Labor	$51.9	$8.0
Ideological	$178.4	$93.0
Other	$1353.4	$1262.4

Source: OpenSecrets: https://www.opensecrets.org/overview/blio.php

Notes

1. The amount raised for McKinley varies from $4 million to $7 million depending upon the source.
2. Nationally chartered banks were also banned from making campaign contributions. In light of the Great Recession, it is not surprising that banks would have a vested interest in who holds the key chair positions in Congress.
3. http://www.fec.gov/press/summaries/2014/tables/pac/PAC1_2014_18m.pdf
4. Source: http://www.opensecrets.org/overview/DonorDemographics.php?Cycle=2010&filter=A
5. Source: http://www.fec.gov/press/bkgnd/bcra_overview.shtml

6 Source: http://www.fec.gov/press/bkgnd/bcra_definitions.shtml#Federal Election Activity
7 http://www.supremecourt.gov/opinions/09pdf/08-205.pdf
8 http://www.fec.gov/law/litigation/McCutcheon.shtml
9 https://www.opensecrets.org/outsidespending/nonprof_summ.php
10 http://www.washingtonpost.com/politics/koch-backed-political-network-built-to-shield-donors-raised-400-million-in-2012-elections/2014/01/05/9e7cfd9a-719b-11e3-9cdark money389-09ef9944065e_story.html
11 http://www.bls.gov/news.release/union2.nr0.htm
12 http://www.opensecrets.org/outsidespending/summ.php?cycle=2012&chrt=V&disp=O&type=U
13 http://www.opensecrets.org/outsidespending/summ.php?cycle=2014&chrt=V&disp=O&type=U
14 http://www.nytimes.com/2014/10/22/upshot/soft-on-crime-tv-ads-affect-judges-decisions-not-just-elections.html?src=xps and http://www.nytimes.com/2014/10/28/opinion/joe-nocera-are-our-courts-for-sale.html?src=xps
15 http://www.nytimes.com/2014/10/29/us/lobbyists-bearing-gifts-pursue-attorneys-general.html?src=xps
16 http://www.nytimes.com/2014/10/30/us/politics/national-concerns-drain-color-from-politics-in-louisiana.html?module=Search&mabReward=relbias%3Aw%2C%7B%221%22%3A%22RI%3A6%22%7D
17 http://www.fec.gov/ans/answers_public_funding.shtml

"BUT THEY DIDN'T CALL ME!" WHY POLLING WORKS

BY ADAM J. SCHIFFER
Texas Christian University

LEARNING OBJECTIVES

Students should be able to:

1. Demonstrate how understanding of the importance of knowledge of population characteristics can facilitate poll evaluation.
2. Demonstrate understanding of the role of competing considerations and ambivalence in public opinion.
3. Demonstrate an understanding of the sources of polling bias.

Opinion polls are everywhere. The frequency and variety of political polls has exploded recently in the United States; and, for better or worse, they have become central to many aspects of politics and governance.

A representative democracy works best when citizens and government officials are able to gauge public sentiment on the hot issues and controversies of the day. Before scientific polling was invented, politicians merely had to guess at public opinion – and the guesses were often colored by which citizens had the initiative and resources to make their voices heard. By contrast, scientific opinion polling provides a feasible way to estimate the opinion of all 200 million adult eligible voters. Although members of Congress do not always vote with the majority preferences of their districts or states, they definitely pay careful attention to polls and shape their behavior and even their speeches–down to the word–around what the polls tell them about public opinion. Poll results also affect the national conversation. For instance, candidates for elected office who are leading in polls can expect more favorable media coverage and better fundraising than those who are behind. It is thus crucial for informed citizens to understand the strengths and limitations of the polling enterprise.

If you want to know whether the science of polling is reliable, the last person you should ask is a candidate for office, a politically active citizen, or an opinionated talk show host. To them, the accuracy of a poll depends on what the poll says about their side. If a new poll shows a candidate leading, then the candidate will tout the results in a press release, and his or her supporters on cable news networks and blogs will spread the word. On the other hand, candidates and activists on the wrong end of polling results often

Contributed by Adam J. Schiffer. Copyright © Kendall Hunt Publishing Company.

dismiss them by attacking the whole enterprise of polling. The phrase "the only poll that matters is on election day" is so common that it works its way into the public remarks of nearly every major political campaign that finds itself down in a poll. Citizen supporters of such candidates resort to all varieties of rationalization for their dismissal of polls, including the ever popular "it can't be accurate—*they didn't call me!*"

Though this sentiment is common, it is ultimately misguided. They don't need to call you in order to gain an accurate snapshot of the American electorate.

Still, this skepticism toward polling is understandable, and far more widespread than just partisans on the losing side of an election. It is difficult to grasp intuitively how calling a randomly selected group of 1000 citizens – less than .0005% of U.S. eligible voters – can yield a reliable snapshot of such a large, diverse nation.

It turns out that such a poll can indeed be accurate. There are many threats to the validity of polls, several of which will be discussed later in this chapter – but the seemingly small size of a typical commercial or academic poll sample simply is not one of them. A quick tour through some basic statistical reasoning will illustrate this point.

SAMPLING: THE NON-THREAT TO POLLING VALIDITY

First, to be clear, we can never be certain that any poll accurately reflects the whole **population**. The only way to tap the opinions of 200 million American adults with total accuracy is to poll all of them, and only the Federal Government's decennial Census has the resources to attempt that (and they still miss some people). Uncertainty is unavoidable in the science of polling. However, using statistics, we can quantify this uncertainty, and estimate with a high degree of likelihood how closely a 1000-person poll comes to the "true population" value, which could only be derived from an ideal-but-impossible poll of all 200 million adults.

Because skepticism of this process is so pervasive, it is worthwhile to understand the statistical logic behind polling, beginning with a simple example. Imagine a hypothetical nation with eight residents, preparing for a presidential election. The nation's best-known pollster has a limited budget and can call only four people. The pollster therefore must draw a random **sample** of four from the population of eight. He puts the phone numbers of the eight residents in a hat and draws four randomly, hoping that, just by chance, he will draw a sample that accurately mirrors the opinion of the whole population. As it turns out, four of the residents (persons A, B, C, D) plan to vote for the Democratic candidate, and the other four (persons E, F, G, H) will vote for the Republican – but the pollster does not know that, just as a real pollster will never know the true opinion of the entire U.S. population.

To illustrate what might happen, Figure 1 shows all possible samples of four from a population of eight. The 70 possibilities are arranged on the chart by their outcome, with 100% Democratic on the left, 100% Republican on the right, and a 50/50 split in the middle. This array of all possible samples from a given population is called a **sampling distribution**. If the random sampling is done properly, all 70 combinations of voters have an equal likelihood of being drawn.

Notice first, the tallest part of the curve which shows that 36 out of the 70 samples will draw two Democrats and two Republicans. Thus, in this simple example, the pollster has a greater than 50% chance of drawing a sample that perfectly mirrors the population. Unfortunately, the other 34 possible samples will give a biased result. Thirty-two of them will include three citizens of the same party, thus showing either 25% for the Democrat or 25% for the Republican. The remaining two samples would terribly misrepresent the population's preferences by drawing four citizens of the same party – but fortunately there is only a 2 in 70 chance of that happening.

Though the real world of polling is more complicated, the basic logic of the example holds. *If you know the characteristics of every possible sample that could be taken from a given population, you can estimate how accurate your sample is likely to be.* So how many samples of 1000 can be taken from the pool of 200 million eligible adult voters? The number is unspeakably large. To put it into perspective, think of a typical lottery. For a weekly drawing game that picks 6 numbers out of a possible 50, there are 15.9 million different combinations of numbers (most people think it's much lower, which is why lotteries are so popular). How about choosing a sample of 50 from a university with 20,000 students? Remarkably, there are about 3.5×10^{150} possibilities, a number far larger than the number of atoms in the known universe. And that is just 50 students from a medium-sized state university! As you can imagine, the number of possible 1000-person samples in the United States is beyond human comprehension.

Fortunately, thanks to the principles of statistical inference, we do not need a list of all possible samples in the sampling distribution to calculate the poll's reliability. Notice that the shape of the sampling distribution in Figure 1 roughly resembles a bell curve (also known as a normal curve). According to a powerful statistical principle called the central

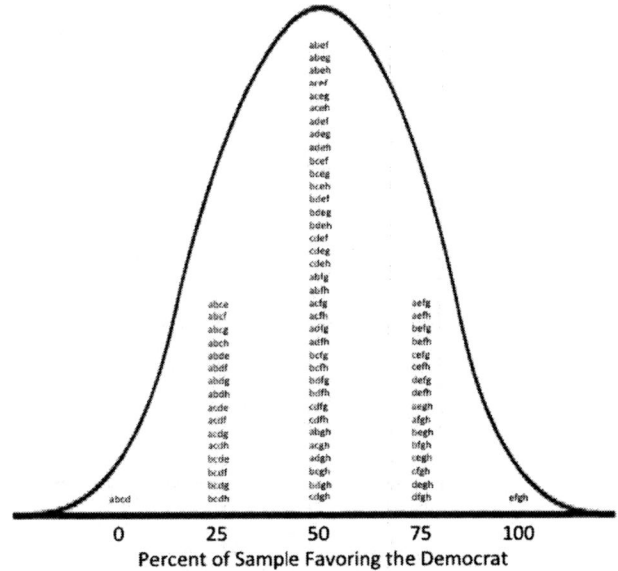

Figure 1. Sampling Distribution

limit theorem, if your sample is large enough – and all professional poll samples are – the sampling distribution takes the exact shape of a normal curve. Importantly, all normal curves have consistent, well-understood properties.

Figure 2 illustrates those properties. Imagine that the bell curve in Figure 2 is actually an array of all possible samples of 1000 American adults. Though the number of samples under the curve is far too large to wrap our brains around, we know several things about the distribution. First, just as in Figure 1, the peak of the curve corresponds to the true population value, which is the unknowable opinion of all 200 million adult eligible voters that we are trying to estimate. If, for example, 52% of all adults wanted the Democrat to win the next presidential election, then 52% Democratic would be at the peak of any sampling distribution for that population. Next, around 68% of all possible samples fall within one standard error (explained below) above or below the true population value. Slightly more than 95% of all samples fall within two standard errors above or below the true population value. The other 5% of samples would be in the "tails" of the curve, more than two standard errors away from the true value.

The standard error is a measure of how widely dispersed the possible samples are around the true population value. A low standard error indicates that the samples are relatively close to the true value, meaning most samples taken for a poll are likely to be fairly accurate. A higher standard error, however, means that the samples are spread out more widely – thus, just by chance, a pollster could draw a sample that badly misrepresents the population. The standard error is inversely related to sample size: the larger the sample, the smaller the standard error, and thus the more confidence we can have that any given sample is within a certain range of the true population value.

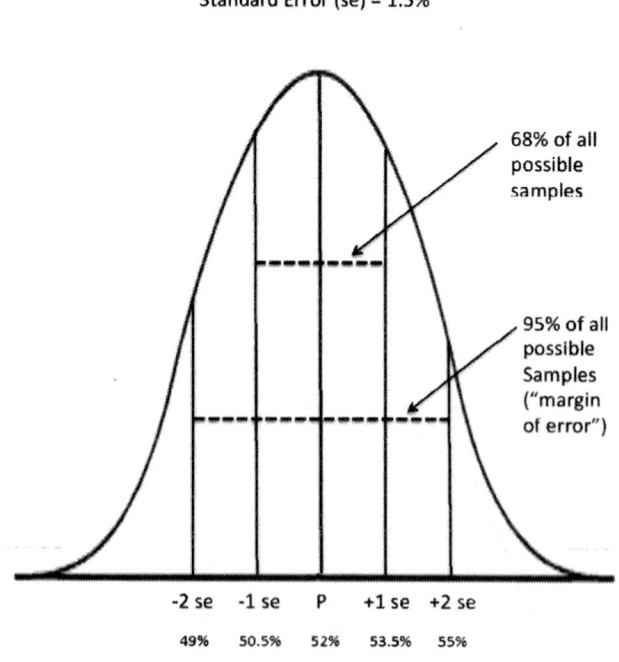

Figure 2. Sampling Distribution for a poll of 1000 citizens

The standard error of a poll with 500 respondents is approximately 2.2%, whereas increasing the sample size to 1000 lowers the standard error to about 1.5%. Thus, doubling the size of a poll from 500 to 1000 gives us more confidence that its results are closer to the true population value.

Figure 2 shows that, if a random sample of 1000 is drawn from a large population, about 68% of all possible samples fall within 1.5% (one standard error) of the true population value. In other words, returning to our example of a presidential election in which 52% of the electorate plans to vote for the Democrat, there is a 68% chance that any given random sample of 1000 will show somewhere between 50.5% and 53.5% favoring the Democrat. Though that itself is impressive, pollsters and political scientists want to be more than 68% sure that their results fall within a certain margin. In fact, the norm in professional polling is to be 95% sure. This is where the familiar concept of a **margin of error** comes in, which is a number that most news outlets report along with a poll's result.

The margin of error for a poll is typically expressed as "plus or minus X percent." This means that 95% of all possible samples of that size will fall within X percentage points of the true population value. To encompass 95% of all samples, the margin of error must extend nearly two standard errors in each direction (1.96, to be exact). Thus, the margin of error, expressed as "plus or minus X percent," simply means "plus or minus 1.96 standard errors." Putting it all together, if a news story reports a new poll showing the president with a 56% approval rating and a margin of error of +/- 3, this means that, if all other aspects of the poll are valid, there is a 95% chance that the president's actual approval, if we were to poll all 200 million adult eligible voters, would fall between 53 and 59%.

Whether you find that degree of accuracy impressive is a matter of opinion, of course. A poll that misstates the candidates' standing by three points in a close election might predict the wrong winner. However, skeptics who automatically dismiss polls because they sample such a tiny proportion of the population are clearly off base.

Furthermore, the most important political contests feature multiple polls taken within a short period of time, which improves the confidence of the prediction. Although a single poll will, just by chance, fall outside the margin of error of the true population value 5% of the time, the odds of two consecutive otherwise-valid polls being that far off is .25% (5% of 5%), and for three consecutive polls there is only about a one-in-ten-thousand chance. Also, though polls can be biased for a number of reasons, many of which are discussed below, the bias due to sampling error is equally likely to fall above or below the true population value. Hence, if you average a large number of polls together that ask the same question during the same time period, the overestimates and underestimates obtained through random error cancel each other out, and the average is highly likely to be accurate.

This is an upside of the massive proliferation of polls during the last few election cycles: it enables us to compute averages of frequently polled questions, such as presidential approval or which candidate is leading a presidential race, that are far more accurate than any single poll could be. Recent presidential elections saw hundreds of publicly released polls from more than a dozen media and commercial polling firms. Several analysts, including news website Real Clear Politics (RCP) and the polling blog Pollster, calculated averages of the polls throughout the campaign season, culminating with final predictions.[1] Even though any given poll is subject to error – for example, Gallup's final poll overestimated

Obama's 2008 victory margin by four points – the average-based predictions were remarkably accurate. Pollster and RCP each came within one percentage point of Obama's actual victory margin.[2] Blogger Nate Silver, using sophisticated statistical analysis of all available polls supplemented with demographic information, correctly predicted the presidential winner in 49 of the 50 states, and predicted every single Senate election winner.[3] In 2012, he predicted all 50 states correctly. The bottom line is that, when the ever-more-frequent polls are combined with expert analysis of them, they have performed quite well over recent election cycles. Even in 2016 – a year widely thought to be a "miss" for the polling industry – the polls mostly performed up to expectations, at least according to those who held them to realistic expectations. This will be discussed in detail in the last section.

The Real Threats to Polling Validity

The statistical properties underpinning the sampling discussion assume that all other aspects of the poll are valid. However, pollsters face many serious challenges while attempting to construct usable polls. As a result, polls vary widely in their quality, and informed consumers of opinion polling must understand the real threats to its validity, and which types of polls are better at minimizing the threats.

First, the statistical logic of sampling only holds if the sample was truly random, meaning every citizen in the target population had the same chance of being selected. If it were possible to put every adult eligible voters' name in a hat and pull out 1000 of them – or, more realistically, put them in a spreadsheet and have a computer algorithm randomly select 1000 – then the sample would be truly random, subject only to the statistical variation described in the previous section. Unfortunately, it is never that simple in the real world.

There is no perfect method for sampling randomly from the entire adult population; and once you have picked your sample, there is no perfect way to reach all of them or to assure that they are willing to talk to you. This becomes a problem if your actual sample – those who you are able to reach and who are willing to complete the survey – differs in systematic, politically relevant ways from your target population. For example, if you randomly call households at 2 p.m. on a weekday, you will only reach folks such as stay-at-home moms and dads, the retired, the disabled, and night-shift workers. Even the most common polling time, early evening, will miss certain workers. This is why the best polls call their selected respondents repeatedly, at different times of the day, trying to maximize the chance that they will catch the person at home.

In a telephone poll, the sampling itself is easy – computers randomly dial phone numbers from all of the assigned area codes. The challenge is that most people are not willing to participate in a poll. Because there is no way to verify whether the unreachable households are politically similar to your respondents, you must obtain as high a response rate as possible. Unfortunately, due to Americans' busy schedules, the advent of caller ID and voicemail, and the proliferation of unsolicited nuisance calls during dinner, the percentage of citizens willing to speak to pollsters is far lower than ideal. For example, the respected Pew Research Center reported in 2012 that their **response rate** for a typical phone poll was 9%, down from 36% in the 1990s.[4] Door-to-door surveys yield the highest response rate. However, they are so expensive that only the most prestigious (and infrequent) academic polls like the quadrennial American National Election Studies can afford to conduct them. While polls conducted via the Internet hold considerable promise for the future, broadband access is not widespread enough to enable full representative samples of the U.S. population.

Election polling has an additional hurdle to overcome. If the goal of an election poll is to predict the outcome, then only voters should be included in the sample. However, there is no foolproof technique for figuring out whether a citizen plans to vote. Pollsters cannot merely ask whether a respondent intends to vote – a certain proportion of voters will lie about it, while others might genuinely intend to vote but end up staying home. Pollsters thus must rely on what are called likely voter screens, which are typically a battery of questions – designed to gauge a respondent's voting history and enthusiasm for the current election – that in tandem produce a probability that s/he will actually end up voting.

Other challenges facing polling stem not from the limitations of technology or of the capabilities of pollsters, but rather from the unavoidable fact that any measure of "public opinion" is only as solid as the opinions it attempts to tap, and only as current as the moment the question is asked.

A brief discussion of the psychology of attitude formation will shed light on these challenges. Many people assume that, for any given political issue, most citizens have either a solid opinion on the issue or no opinion at all. On a hot-button issue such as the death penalty, each person is thought to have a solid attitude – meaning one which is well-informed and unlikely to change – in his or her head either for or against it, which would be expressed as an opinion when prompted by a pollster.

However, this is simply not how most political brains operate. Instead of one solid attitude, citizens hold a set of **considerations**, which are individual tidbits of information – a fact, an experience, a memorable argument – that might help sway someone to one side of an issue.[5] Figure 3 illustrates this process. Importantly, citizens often hold considerations with conflicting implications for a particular issue. While there is nothing inherently contradictory about any of the considerations in the figure – a reasonable person could believe that her religion condemns the death penalty, while also believing that it brings closure to victims' families – a person simultaneously holding these considerations would feel ambivalence toward the death penalty, being pulled in both directions. In fact, studies show a tremendous amount of ambivalence toward even the most emotional, contentious issues such as abortion and gay rights.[6]

Because of competing considerations, answering a poll question is not simply a matter of verbalizing an attitude. Rather, citizens answer questions by tapping the considerations about which they have thought most recently (those "at the top of their heads").[7] Considerations move to the top of someone's head though a process called **priming**, which can take many forms. Going to church could prime the "my religion prohibits the death penalty" consideration. Alternately, watching a news report about a gruesome murder could prime the "victims' families" consideration. But here is the problem: the wording of poll questions will often prime considerations. Though this is not the case for all citizens – the most politically active folks tend to have firmer opinions on issues – it is true for enough of the citizenry to produce substantially different results from small, seemingly arbitrary changes in question wording.

Pollsters can inadvertently bias poll questions in many ways. First, responses to a question can be affected by previous questions on the poll. Often the most widely discussed question on a commercial poll is presidential approval, so it is crucial that pollsters get it

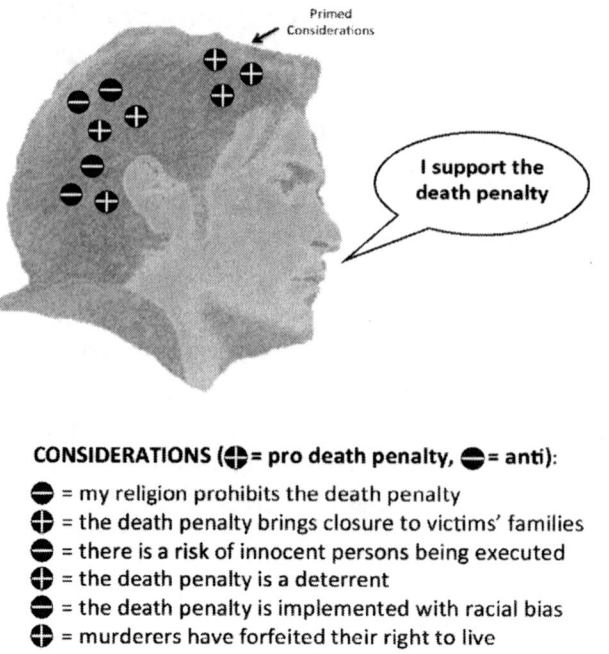

Figure 3. Competing Considerations and Opinion Poll Response

right. However, many citizens – particularly those in the middle of the ideological spectrum – are ambivalent toward any president, with a mix of positive and negative considerations. For example, someone might have been ambivalent toward President Donald Trump early in his presidency, approving of his swift actions to cut corporate regulations but wary of his stance toward Russia. If the survey asks for an opinion on Russia, even if it does not mention Trump, it might prime the "Russia" consideration, thus causing the respondent to disapprove of the president. Important questions, or those most susceptible to priming, should therefore come early in the survey.

For any given question, pollsters must take great care to use neutral language that does not sway the respondent toward one side of the issue. This is more difficult than it sounds. On the one hand, it is relatively easy to avoid obviously biased questions. The voluntary-response Internet polls run by news channels and websites, in addition to being worthless from a sampling perspective, are also notorious for using terrible questions. Lou Dobbs, the former CNN opinion-show host, was particularly adept at slanting questions to achieve his desired outcome. He once asked, "Are you outraged that the cash-strapped District of Columbia is using $500,000 in taxpayer money to build a day labor center?" Not surprisingly, 97% of respondents said "yes," which, in our polarized political environment in which you cannot get 97% of voters to agree on anything, is a sure sign of a bad poll.[8]

Unfortunately, bias need not be so obvious to have an effect. Consider the following question, asked several times in 2009 by CNN/Opinion Research Corporation: "From everything you have heard or read so far, do you favor or oppose Barack Obama's plan to reform health care?"[9] If the task is to tap the public's opinion of the health care reform measures under consideration at the time, then calling it "Barack Obama's plan" distracts from the question by priming the respondent's opinion of the president. This was particularly inappropriate because, during much of the timeframe in which this question was asked, President Obama had not formally taken a stand on any of the proposals floating through Congress – in other words, there was no Obama plan.

Pollsters also need to take great care not to adopt the preferred language of one side of an issue. Not only do Democrats and Republicans disagree on policy outcomes, they often disagree on the terminology used to describe such policies. For example, Republicans refer to proposals for lowering tax rates as "tax relief," an ingenuous phrase designed to increase support for tax cuts. After all, who could oppose relief? It is also constructed to turn citizens against taxation in general, as "relief" is only associated with inherently bad things like sunburns, hurricanes, and hemorrhoids. Accordingly, that phrase should never work its way into a poll question.

Is Professional Polling in Trouble?

Starting in the early 2000s, politicians, pundits, and activists – particularly those on the losing side of a poll – expended considerable energy predicting the demise of polling accuracy. The ticking time bomb threatening to explode the whole enterprise, they argued, was the shrinking response rate.

This argument resonated loudly among Republicans in their tough 2008 election cycle, and in turn reached a fever pitch among Democratic activists during the 2010 congressional elections. In 2010, liberal bloggers, commentators, and campaign staff could be heard coast-to-coast dismissing polls that predicted large Democratic losses. And, given that every commercial poll made such predictions, the skeptics essentially dismissed the entire enterprise of polling. Their main argument – in addition to the occasional lament that "they didn't call me" – was that the groups who tended not to respond to polls, including younger voters and racial minorities, were more likely to vote Democratic. Indeed, younger citizens and Hispanics went 2-1 for Barack Obama in 2008, while 95% of African Americans voted for him. Any poll that under-sampled those groups would seem to run the risk of overstating potential Republican gains. It turns out, though, that the polls were every bit as accurate as they had been in the previous two midterm election cycles, with the final polls in statewide races having an average error of only 2.1%.[10]

The 2012 presidential election brought an even bigger attack on polling credibility. Many supporters of Republican candidate Mitt Romney – including bloggers, conservative cable news pundits, and Republican officeholders – insisted that the polls showing Romney losing were "skewed" because the formulas pollsters used to correct for bias were too favorable to Democrats. But alas, the polling averages were accurate, the critics were embarrassed, and Romney himself – who reportedly believed the arguments about biased polling – was "shell-shocked" when he lost.[11]

The contentious 2016 general election yielded perhaps the biggest polling controversy yet. Nearly every national poll – as well as polls in several crucial states – predicted a win for Democrat Hillary Clinton. After Trump's surprising Electoral College victory, many folks declared polling dead, or at least critically wounded. However, a careful examination reveals that the polls performed reasonably well, subject to their usual limitations. The problem came when citizens and pundits failed to recognize those limitations.

According to analysts at Silver's website FiveThirtyEight, the final average of national polls had Clinton leading Trump by 3.9%.[12] RCP's average put Clinton up by 3.2%.[13]

To evaluate the polls' accuracy, it is important to remember that Clinton won the popular vote, which is what national polls attempt to predict. In fact, she won by 2.1%, putting the polls within a point or two of the result, depending on which averaging algorithm is used. According to FiveThirtyEight's calculations, the polls performed slightly better than usual in 2016. The mean error of the final averages between 1968–2012 was 2.0%, while the 2016 difference was 1.8%.[14]

The state polls were more varied, but that too is normal. State polls often have smaller sample sizes than national polls and are seldom done by the most experienced national firms. Also, they are conducted far less frequently than national polls, even in the hottest battleground states. This sparsity is a crucial limitation, as the reliability of polling averages depends on the number of polls included in them.

Some state polling did well. Polling averages in the battleground states of Virginia, Nevada, Colorado, and Florida all came within 2% of the result. However, the states that ended up swinging the election to Trump – Wisconsin, Pennsylvania, and Michigan – showed wider polling discrepancies (6.4%, 4.9%, and 4.3%, respectively), and the polls also missed badly in Ohio, Iowa, and Minnesota.[15] This regional skew is no coincidence, as a leading theory of the polling errors is that the likely voter screens failed to pick up the enthusiasm for Trump among the upper-Midwestern white voters without college degrees who were key to his victory.[16]

While pollsters obviously hope to avoid such high-profile misses, astute students of polling need to put these results in proper perspective. One of the last articles published on FiveThirtyEight prior to the election was titled, "Trump Is Just a Normal Polling Error Behind Clinton." And sure enough he was. The polls performed within their known limitations – in this case, by slightly underestimating Trump's standing. Of course, many Clinton fans pushed back against FiveThirtyEight's prediction, accusing Silver and colleagues of exaggerating the uncertainty to generate traffic to the website. They chose instead to rest their hopes on the analysis of Princeton University brain scientist Sam Wang, who had been dabbling in political prediction using extremely sophisticated mathematical models. He argued, in an authoritative and convincing fashion, that Clinton had a greater than 99% chance of winning the election.[17] In fact, he was so confident that he promised to eat a bug on live TV if Trump won. A few days after the election, he kept his word and ate a cricket on a CNN talk show.

Wang's mistake, and that of so many other pundits and candidate supporters, was more philosophical than mathematical. It was a failure to acknowledge the limitations of what polls can tell us about the future. In fact, FiveThirtyEight's "Trump Is Just a Normal Polling Error Behind Clinton" headline aptly summarizes a key point that so many analysts miss: polling errors are "normal," an inevitable consequence of both sampling science and the limitations of predicting human behavior. A modest amount of polling error does not equate to "failure" any more than a student who misses three test questions out of 100 fails the test. The failure was in the interpretation of an imperfect but useful enterprise, not in the enterprise itself.

Looking toward the future, the low-response problem may indeed be a ticking time bomb. After all, if only 9% of the people you call are willing to talk to you, then surely that 9% differs in important ways from the other 91%. However, the bomb has not yet detonated, and there is still time to defuse it. While it is indeed true that polls tend to under-sample certain groups, it is easy for pollsters to calculate the degree of bias and to correct for it statistically. If 22% of the U.S. adult population is 18–29 years old, but only 8% of a sample fits that age range, then the pollster simply gives extra weight to the 8% of the sample so that it contributes 22% to the population's opinion estimate.[18] There are obvious limitations to this, such as the assumption that the young citizens who could be reached are politically similar to those who were excluded from the sample. Even so, polls continued to perform well in recent elections.

Let's be clear about it: if people become even less willing to speak to pollsters, the science of polling will need to change in order to survive, perhaps more fundamentally than at any time since phone polling was perfected several decades ago. Fortunately, commercial and academic pollsters devote a considerable amount of brainpower and resources to solving the problem before it damages their work. For example, big breakthroughs in the accuracy of internet-based polling have been made in the last few years.

Polling is hardly the only industry forced to adapt to rapidly changing circumstances. In fact, compared to other industries, the challenges facing polling are relatively manageable – take, for example, the issues facing a professional musician in an era in which consumers increasingly view music as something that does not need to be paid for. As long as there is sufficient demand for accurately gauging the opinions of the electorate – backed up by a willingness to pay for it – someone will figure out how to do so. And, for better or for worse, such demand is at an all-time high. Thus, the next poll you see from a respected academic or commercial pollster is likely to be reasonably accurate, **even if they didn't call you.**

Key Terms

Considerations in Public Opinion—Pieces of information known to an individual that may influence their opinion on certain topics.

Margin of Error—The percentage of the points the true population value may be from that found in a sample.

Population—The entire group one seeks to understand and from which a sample is taken to do a poll.

Priming—The process through which opinion considerations are brought to the forefront of an individuals thinking.

Response Rate—The percentage of people who respond to a poll in relation to how many were contacted.

Sample—The sub-group of the sample who are surveyed in order to understand a larger population.

Multiple Choice Questions

1. Individuals who hold conflicting considerations on a topic and have not developed solid opinions often demonstrate:
    a. Ambivalence
    b. Apathy
    c. Low voter turnout
    d. Inconsistent voting
    e. All of the above

   Answer: A

2. The measure of how widely dispersed possible samples are around the true population value is known as:
    a. The standard deviation
    b. The margin of error
    c. The standard error
    d. The bias rate
    e. The distribution

   Answer: C

3. The percentage of people a pollster gets to answer a poll out of the total population is referred to as:
    a. The final poll numbers
    b. The adjusted sample
    c. The survey population
    d. The response rate
    e. The percentage acceptance rate

   Answer: D

4. The series of questions used by pollsters to determine if a respondent is likely to vote is known as:
    a. Likely voter screens
    b. Filter questions
    c. Voter history questions
    d. Electoral participation screens
    e. Respondent filters

   Answer: A

Discussion Question

1. Describe and explain the sources of polling bias.

References

"2008 National Presidential General Election: McCain vs. Obama." Pollster: <http://www.pollster.com/polls/us/08-us-pres-ge-mvo.php?nr=1> Accessed May 2011.

"Assessing the Representativeness of Public Opinion Surveys." 2012. Pew Research Center for the People & the Press, 15 May: <http://www.people-press.org/2012/05/15/assessing-the-representativeness-of-public-opinion-surveys/> Accessed October 2014.

Bialik, Carl. 2016. "The Polls Missed Trump. We Asked Pollsters Why." FiveThirtyEight, 9 November: <https://fivethirtyeight.com/features/the-polls-missed-trump-we-asked-pollsters-why> Accessed March 2017.

Blumenthal, Mark. 2011. "Poll Accuracy Held Steady in 2010." Huffpost Pollster, 14 February: <http://www.huffingtonpost.com/2011/02/14/poll-accuracy-held-steady-in-2010_n_823181.html> Accessed May 2011.

"Election 2008 National Head-to-Head Polls." Real Clear Politics: <http://www.realclearpolitics.com/epolls/2008/president/national.html> Accessed May 2011.

Enten, Harry. 2016. "Trump Is Just a Normal Polling Error Behind Clinton." FiveThirtyEight, 4 November: <https://fivethirtyeight.com/features/trump-is-just-a-normal-polling-error-behind-clinton> Accessed March 2017.

Fiorina, Morris P., Samuel J. Abrams, and Jeremy C. Pope. 2006. Culture War? The Myth of a Polarized America. New York: Pearson Longman.

"General Election: Trump vs. Clinton." RealClearPolitics: <http://www.realclearpolitics.com/epolls/2016/president/us/general_election_trump_vs_clinton-5491.html> Accessed March 2017.

"Health Policy." Polling Report: <http://pollingreport.com/health4.htm> Accessed May 2011.

Keeter, Scott. 2011. "Public Opinion Polling and Its Problems," in Goidel, Kirby, Political Polling in the Digital Age: The Challenge of Measuring and Understanding Public Opinion. Baton Rouge: Louisiana State University Press.

"National Polls." FiveThirtyEight: <https://projects.fivethirtyeight.com/2016-election-forecast/national-polls> Accessed March 2017.

Reeve, Elspeth. 2012. "The Whole Romney Ticket Believed in Unskewed Polls?" *The Wire*, 8 November. <http://www.thewire.com/politics/2012/11/whole-romney-ticket-believed-unskewed-polls/58852> Accessed October 2014.

Silver, Nate. 2016. "Pollsters Probably Didn't Talk to Enough White Voters Without College Degrees." FiveThirtyEight, 1 December: <https://fivethirtyeight.com/features/pollsters-probably-didnt-talk-to-enough-white-voters-without-college-degrees> Accessed March 2017.

"Today's Polls and Final Election Projection: Obama 349, McCain 189." FiveThirtyEight: <http://www.fivethirtyeight.com/2008/11/todays-polls-and-final-election.html> Accessed May 2011.

Wang, Sam. Princeton Election Consortium. <http://election.princeton.edu/>

Zaller, John R. 1992. The Nature and Origins of Mass Opinion. Cambridge: Cambridge University Press.

Notes

1. Real Clear Politics is <www.realclearpolitics.com>. During the 2008 election, Pollster was <www.pollster.com>; but was bought by the Huffington Post website and is now found at <http://www.huffingtonpost.com/news/pollster>.
2. Pollster: <http://www.pollster.com/polls/us/08-us-pres-ge-mvo.php?nr=1>, RCP: <http://www.realclearpolitics.com/epolls/2008/president/national.html>.
3. <http://www.fivethirtyeight.com/2008/11/todays-polls-and-final-election.html>
4. Pew, "Assessing the Representativeness of Public Opinion Surveys."
5. Zaller, *The Nature and Origins of Mass Opinion*.
6. Fiorina, Abrams, and Pope, *Culture War?*
7. Zaller, *The Nature and Origins of Mass Opinion*.
8. Digital screen capture from author's DVR, exact date unknown.
9. <http://pollingreport.com/health4.htm>
10. Blumenthal, "Polling Accuracy Held Steady in 2010."
11. Reeve, "The Whole Romney Ticket Believed in Unskewed Polls?"
12. "National Polls," FiveThirtyEight.
13. "General Election: Trump vs. Clinton," RealClearPolitics.
14. Enten, "Trump Is Just a Normal Polling Error Behind Clinton."
15. Bialik, "The Polls Missed Trump. We Asked Pollsters Why."
16. Silver, "Pollsters Probably Didn't Talk to Enough White Voters Without College Degrees."
17. See the archives at Wang, Princeton Election Consortium.
18. The percentages are taken from Keeter, "Public Opinion Polling and its Problems," 37.

AMERICANS DON'T AGREE; SO WHAT?

BY JAMES F. SHEFFIELD JR.

LEARNING OBJECTIVES

Students should be able to:

1. Explain the causes of social conflict.
2. Assess the degree to which Americans are ideological.
3. Explain the major sources of social conflict today.
4. Explain whether political parties are able to manage divisions in society.

"It were not best that we should all think alike; it is difference of opinion that makes horse races."
—Mark Twain

Veteran journalist Dan Rather recently observed that the United States is a deeply divided nation. (Larson 2017) The rifts between the technologically current and those who are not, between those of means and those of modest circumstances, and between those who are fearful of the future and those who are at ease with it all speak to the reality of clear differences among Americans. Anyone who is aware of events of the 2016 presidential election or who has given any attention to the first months of President Trump's administration might easily draw a similar conclusion.

But this is not a condition unique to the second decade of the twenty-first century; for 25 years or more, observers have been wringing their hands over a "culture war"; for 50 years, Americans have worried about the counter-culture proclivities of the Baby Boomer generation and those that followed; and for 250 years, Americans have found themselves in serious disagreement with each other over one thing or another. Two of our most significant national periods featured profound differences—that of the founding (the years immediately preceding the Revolutionary War, those of the war itself, and the post-War years through the election and inauguration of President Washington) and that of the Civil War and Reconstruction.

What is important is not that such division exists, but rather the root causes of the differences that emerge and the consequences of them. In this chapter, we will consider divisions in a context that helps to explain why they occur, we will explore the nature of some of the contemporary divisions, and we will explore their place in the structures and processes of the American political system. Our purpose will be to better understand the divisions that exist among Americans, the ways they influence the structures and processes of the American political systems, and how the system responds to these situations.

WHY ARE THERE DIVISIONS IN SOCIETY?

Perhaps a good starting point is to recognize that there are differences and there are DIFFERENCES. Divisions in the public may occur for many reasons, and they do so routinely. Some engage so many citizens and create rifts so deep that they become major sources of **social conflict** with which society must cope. Such conflicts involve one or more of our basic social institutions—the family, economic structures, religious entities, the political system, and so on. Oftentimes, the political system is caught up in such a conflict because it reaches across those other institutions or because some of the other institutions themselves become competitors in a particular conflict. An example in the first case might be at what age a person may legally consume alcohol; an example of the second is how medical care is to be made available to those who need it.

Social conflict, which describes the situation in which we are interested, results from (1) two or more entities having some need, preference, or desire; (2) those needs, preferences, or desires being impossible for the various entities to reconcile simultaneously; and (3) the entities nonetheless pursuing maximization of their respective goals. This is the classic "zero sum game," where one entity loses if the other entity gets what it wants. But, the outcome can be less than that; one entity might be able to gain a sufficiently acceptable quantity of its goals and the other accept something less than a completely satisfactory outcome if this **"satisficing"** point for both entities can be found.

There are two problems here. First, in some cases the competing goals may be too fundamental for the people or groups involved to permit either or both to accept a satisficing outcome; for example, those who oppose capital punishment may well not accept its limited use instead of its being employed as a punishment for a wide variety of crimes. The other is that when satisficing might be possible, conditions must exist to encourage pursuit of such an outcome until it is achieved; for example, an encouraging third party might help the contending entities to find a solution. President Lyndon Johnson was noted for urging competing interests to negotiate their differences by invoking the Biblical encouragement, "Come, now, let us reason together" (Presidential Profiles, n.d.).

So, where do conflicts originate? Simply put, they result from the differences in ourselves, our values, our preferences, and the conditions in which we live. That core diversity is magnified in impact by the growing size of our population. Larger populations encourage an even greater expression and pursuit of diverse goals than would otherwise occur. Some Americans are young, others old; we vary by race, ethnicity, religion, economic circumstance, and place of residence. Some are well informed, others not; some are thoughtful, others emotionally reactive. These and many other variations in our citizenry make social conflict a routine fact of life, and the more who share a particular outlook, the greater the tendency to pursue it.

Then, what are some of today's important conflicts? In any political system, there are always basic controversies that arise in various formats. One is who will make the governing decisions? And another is who will have influence over and be involved in the governing decisions that will be made? A third is what are the areas in which government may properly exercise authority, and to what extent? The elections that are held periodically in the United States address the first. The second question has given rise to controversies over voting rights today in the United States that often concern how election processes are arranged can ease or impede certain kinds of voters' participation. Several states have adopted "voter ID" laws of various sorts that require prospective voters to document affirmatively their eligibility to cast ballots. That third question flows from a basic tenet of American politics, limited government; not every controversy is considered fair game for government to consider. Should government, for example, require private businesses to provide paid leave for one or both parents of newborns to ease the addition of a new family member, or is that a decision properly left to individual businesses?

Other issues, of course, flow from somewhat less basic sources. The issues highlighted in the 2016 election cycle are good examples of these. In some ways, these might have been specific to the times and the conditions in which we Americans found ourselves, and some of them may have been persistent over a number of years without stemming from obviously fundamental differences in values. But, do note that in many ways these issues do trace back to some basic and competing values held by Americans and incorporated into our social and political fabric.

To better understand these basic divisions among Americans let us now turn to, first, an effort to organize issues that arise, and second, to integrate management of issues into the structures and processes of the American political system.

Is There an Ideological Divide?—Conservatives, Liberals, and Spineless Jellyfish?

In the 1990s, it became fashionable to describe America's popular culture and its politics in terms of a "culture war." Supposedly, American society was deeply and persistently divided on a variety of fundamental values, to the degree that some observers even suggested the likelihood that contending citizens and groups would resort to violence. These value differences have long been used to categorize people as "conservatives" or "liberals," labels that neatly meshed with the culture war perspective. A partisan element was added to this view when it became conventional to connect the different political parties to one of those labels and to depict electoral outcomes as "red" (conservative or Republican) or "blue" (liberal or Democratic). Consequently, liberal-blue-Democratic became one contender in this culture war, and conservative-red-Republican became the other.

This is a simple reduction of some complex characteristics of Americans and of the American system; simplicity makes it attractive, but there are problems with it. Democrats vary in terms of how liberal they are, and Republicans—to a lesser extent—vary in terms of how conservative they are. In fact, if we were to explore this over a somewhat longer time period, we would see that our two major political parties have traditionally been much less single-minded than is presently the case; conservative and moderate Democrats and liberal and moderate Republicans were commonplace.

Another problem is more subtle. The large number of elective offices in different types of government bodies (notably executive and legislative branches) and at different levels of the American political system (local, state, and national) makes the simplification of electoral outcomes and the issue or public policy meanings they convey very suspect. For example, a congressional district may choose a Democrat to represent it in Congress and in the same election give more votes to the Republican presidential candidate; or a Republican candidate for the state legislature may win a seat in the same district that gives most of its votes to a Democratic candidate for governor. This is starkly illustrated by electoral results from the 32nd congressional district of Texas in 2016; incumbent Republican Pete Sessions was reelected with 71% of the vote, but voters in that same district gave Hillary Clinton 48% of their presidential votes, as opposed to 47% for Donald Trump (Leslie 2016). Election results may say little about party, issue preferences, or **ideology**—the same voters supported a candidate from each party for different offices.

All of this begs a more fundamental question: Are Americans ideological? An ideology is a set of constrained, consistent, fundamental beliefs and values; that means one's beliefs and values should not be in logical conflict with one's other values. The function of an ideology's contents is to prescribe how a citizen should respond to some situation or issue. So, is this true of Americans? Are Americans ideological?

Evidence suggests that the general answer to this question is, "No," although some Americans may appear to satisfy the requirements of ideological thinking. On reflection, the general answer should not be terribly surprising; the opportunity for contradictions in American life is common. One hypothetical example involves a central component of American political culture, personal liberty. That value not only refers to the right to act in some particular fashion, but also to the right to formulate one's own ideas and values. "Personal liberty" does not suggest limits on the contents of those ideas and values, so incompatible ideas and values are neither forbidden nor discouraged. And Americans often do not consider the compatibility of different ideas when forming or employing them. Consider this example of inconsistent values: free speech versus opposition to someone else's advocacy of a socialist political system for the United States. Such inconsistencies are frequently present in Americans' opinions, attitudes, and values and are consequently reflected in their behaviors, which are guided by those beliefs.

A less precise illustration of the limited degree to which ideological thinking is common among Americans can be seen in their collective responses to questions probing the degree to which they are ideological. The informal, but widely used, shorthand terms "liberal" and "conservative" are sometimes presented to citizens in public opinion polls, and they are asked whether those terms apply to them personally. Over the years, there is variation in the overall responses to such questions; today, more respondents indicate that they are conservative than liberal, but the important point is that a large minority, sometimes a plurality (more than any other group), freely identify themselves as being neither conservative nor liberal, but somewhere in between, or moderate.

Data from research by the Gallup organization speaks directly to this point. As you consider this information, take particular note of three of its aspects. First, a significant proportion of the public declines to place itself at either end of the conservative–liberal continuum. Second, even though many of those who consider themselves partisan take ideological positions consistent with what we might expect for members of that party (conservative for Republicans, liberal for Democrats), a significant percentage of each party's respondents choose a different ideological position. Third, it does not matter in general whether the question of ideology is posed in terms of social issues or economic issues (although there are some differences in the pattern between the two issue categories), the overall outcome is fairly similar. Last, and as expected, Democrats and Republicans as a whole respond differently to these questions of ideology.

So what do these data look like? Respondents were asked, "Thinking about social [or economic] issues, would you say that your views on those issues are very conservative, moderate, liberal, or very liberal?" For social issues 34% of respondents answered "conservative," and another 32% answered "liberal," and 31% chose the "moderate" alternative. If we consider Democrats and respondents who said they were leaning toward the Democratic Party in partisan preference, 57% reported being liberal, 28% chose the moderate alternative, and 13% identified themselves as conservative. Among Republicans and those leaning to the Republican Party, 62% said they were conservative, 27% said they were moderate, and 10% said they were liberal (a cynical pundit might say that these latter respondents are RINOs, Republicans In Name Only).

The data for a similar question that referenced economic issues produced slightly different results, but the same general and expected pattern. On economic issues, 41% of all respondents labeled themselves conservative, 35% moderate, and 20% chose the category liberal. For Republican partisan identifiers and those who lean Republican, 73% consider themselves conservative, 23% reported a preference for the moderate label, and 4% termed themselves liberal. Among Democratic identifiers and leaners, 44% reported being liberal, 37% identified as moderate, and 21% selected the conservative category (Jones 2016).

These results are consistent with results from polls in which respondents were simply asked to locate themselves in one of three categories—liberal, moderate, or conservative. Robert Erikson and Kent Tedin (2008) summarize outcomes of some such polls taken at various times in 1976–2008. The proportions of each group were relatively stable throughout the period with conservatives centering around 35%, liberals clustering around 23%, and moderates averaging about 42%. Updating those numbers using 2009–2012 data from the CBS News/*New York Times* polls of that period essentially duplicates the outcome Erikson and Tedin report for the earlier three-decade period.

In summary, many Americans do not consider themselves extreme in views; there are acknowledged inconsistencies in those preferences that lead them to prefer a middle-of-the-road description of themselves. Also, Democrats and Republicans do have predominantly differing ideological leanings, but there is clearly variation within each party as to members' ideological stances. Finally, perhaps the largest group of Americans do not subscribe to extreme ideological positions, but offer more restrained assessments of their value and belief inclinations.

A similar exploration of Americans' ideological preferences might ask a series of questions that dichotomize respondents toward either the liberal or conservative end of the ideological continuum, then summing the series of responses to produce an overall profile not rooted in the answer to a single question. Erikson and Tedin also used this procedure to gain a more specific profile of the American public with regard to its ideological tendencies. In 2008, they asked respondents in a poll 10 specific questions, each of which requested a liberal or conservative response. The cumulative number of liberal answers and conservative answers given by each respondent could then be represented on a continuum ranging from −10 (all liberal answers) to +10 (all conservative answers). A series of bar graphs representing the number of respondents falling at each point along that continuum were then drawn, and a line connecting the peaks of those bars formed a very distinctive shape, one similar to the familiar bell-shaped curve. Most respondents were in the middle, and relatively few were at the extremes. Again, the evidence suggests that Americans are not distributed into a pair of bitterly opposing groups. They tend toward the middle of the ideological spectrum, with successively fewer fellow citizens self-locating to more ideological postures as one moves away from the middle and toward the extremes of the continuum.

In sum, Americans as a whole do not satisfy the requirements of ideological thinking, and their political behaviors are similarly more varied than use of a personal ideology would anticipate. That is not to say Americans do not display general tendencies in either beliefs or behavior; they do, but the degree to which those beliefs and behaviors are constrained and consistent is modest. Still, they do seek out and use simple means to respond to the political world. Sometimes reduction of an event, issue, or situation to conservative or liberal characterization seems helpful or appropriate. And often, probably subconsciously, reliance on partisan cues is an adequate guide. There are, moreover, undoubtedly cases when something else provides guidance; the proverbial assertion that "I vote the candidate, not the party" is an example. When true, party is not relevant, but rather the candidate's personal attributes, usually as distinguished from the traits of an opposing candidate, serve to guide voting behavior, and this situation is not only true of elections, but of issue controversies that pit competing advocates. Citizens observing the issue debate take sides not so much on the merits of either argument as on their assessments of the leaders of the two sides in the debate.

All of this somewhat ignores those who appear to be neither conservative nor liberal. Do they simply have no backbone, unable make up their minds? Should they be considered spineless jellyfish?

Not at all. Some people DO find it harder to choose when presented options, but the presence of many moderates in the American public is more the product of a tendency to be pragmatic, to accept solutions that seem to work for the moment, and to compromise when other solutions cannot be achieved. This character is evident as far back as the Constitutional Convention (the Connecticut Compromise, the Three-Fifths Compromise) and later (the Missouri Compromise). And today, we see this same practice in much of the important legislation passed by Congress. President Obama and his congressional allies found it necessary to accept a variety of provisions they did not want to accomplish enactment of the Affordable Health Care Act several years ago, and President Trump's unsuccessful first effort to repeal that act in 2017 centered on compromises that eventually could not be agreed to by moderate and conservative wings of the Republican Party in the House of Representatives. "All things in moderation," "something beats nothing" is not an overt American philosophy, but there are certainly a lot of examples of its being employed in our history. To be moderate is not the same as being indecisive.

Managing Divisions to Maintain Public Order

If society is to function in an organized fashion, if it is to be a stable entity that survives for a lengthy time, then those elements that would endanger that balance must be regulated. One institution that a society will create to assist in that process is a political system. It is the task of such a system to determine how diverse values and preferences, as well as behaviors consistent with those differences, are, ideally, resolved. Failing that, those conflicts must be managed. To do so, we return to those earlier questions: who rules, who has influence in rule-making, by what processes will these things be determined, and what will be the outcome in the case of any specific conflict?

Elections and Conflict

The political system of the United States is often asserted to be a "democratic" one, meaning that policies made by government are and should be consistent with the preferences of American citizens. Technically, however, democratic systems produce **public policy** (public policy is the official decision by those who have the responsibility for making it, which is intended to resolve or at least regulate a conflict) by having those who make up the system actually make those policy choices. The citizenry makes the decisions. In this fashion, assuming that the principle of majority rule determines the outcome of public decision-making, the resulting policies obviously DO reflect the public's preferences.

But clearly that is not the way we do things in America. Ours is more accurately described as a **representative democracy**, or an **indirect democracy**. Some dispute this view, saying that only citizen policy-making qualifies a system to be democratic, but we will save that debate for some other time. Instead, let us think about how this "indirect" democracy works. Very quickly, and simply, we achieve indirect democracy by having citizens choose a group of official policy-makers and leaving to them the duty of determining which public policies will guide the system and its constituent members.

This is how elections become an essential part of American politics. There are many ways in which someone may gain **political authority**—the responsibility for making choices that are binding on others. Throughout history, force has been a prominent means of asserting one's authority; in other circumstances, actors have insisted that they have been made decision-makers by a supreme being. More informally, societies have sometimes been led by small groups of people—an elite—who have employed family prominence or wealth to gain and exercise political domination. The problem with these devices for determining who will make choices for a society is that they offer little assurance that those who are governed will have any voice or role in the policies that define their lives.

Elections need not suffer that shortcoming. By giving members of society the responsibility to choose those who will make policies in their behalf, voters not only determine who the policy-makers are, but they also can influence the policies those elected officials make by choosing policy-makers who are responsive to their policy preferences. In other words, voters may elect public offices individuals who share their views as to which policies should be adopted, and they may reject candidates who do not share those views.

As our discussion unfolds, it will, of course, become obvious that the process is not quite so simple. For example, the question of who is entitled to vote can easily influence the outcome of the election and the policies adopted by those who are elected. Ancient Athens is sometimes considered an early example of democracy, but only citizens were permitted to participate in Athenian democracy, and the definition of "citizen" was very narrow, causing many people who lived in Athens to be excluded from its political processes.

Today, there is general agreement on who may legitimately participate as voters in the United States; the general principle is "**universal adult suffrage** for citizens." But, note that those who are younger than 18 and those who are not citizens (even if they have legally resided in the United States for their entire lives, paid the taxes for which they were responsible, and abided by the laws that have been adopted) may not vote. It is also common in the United States to exclude those in jail from voting, and some states impose additional voting limits on those who have been convicted of felonies. Perhaps the most common means of excluding Americans from voting is the requirement imposed by most states that a prospective voter register, officially add his or her name to the list of persons eligible to vote in elections. This is a responsibility of individuals in the United States, but in other "democratic" nations it is the government's responsibility to develop and maintain the lists of eligible voters.

The basic point, however, is that indirect democracies give to members of their societies the opportunity to choose who will govern those societies through elections to offices that exercise governing authority, or public policy decision-making responsibility. It is through this mechanism—elections—that the more basic concern of which policies shall guide a society is addressed.

There are a couple of additional considerations which play into this process, however. One is that voters have a choice among candidates; if only one candidate is featured in an election, those voters who disagree with that candidate's policy preferences have no opportunity to insert different messages into the policy process. But, it is also necessary that multiple candidates represent different policy viewpoints; if they all agree on a common policy agenda, again, those voters who prefer a different agenda have no means of advancing other policy ideas. It is at this point that we must consider where candidates come from: political parties.

Can Parties Manage the Divisions?

Political parties began to emerge in the United States soon after the nation was founded, a development that proceeded from a simple fact: not everyone agreed as to which policies the government should adopt. Some leading politicians attempted to increase their influence and the likelihood that their views would become policy by organizing others who agreed with them. That way they could concentrate their influence and elect as many of their number as possible to public office, which continues to be the goal of parties. As they seek electoral success, political parties inevitably simplify the complexities of politics to attract voters to their policy agendas.

Parties as an Ideal

To better understand this, perhaps we should clearly state a formal definition: a **political party** is an organization of people sharing some agreement on how to respond to major issues of the day and seeking to influence the actions of government on those issues by gaining seats in that government for its members in duly constituted elections. The four basic points to this definition are (1) there is an organizational structure of a party—membership, common purpose, leadership, procedural rules, and so on; (2) party members have at least a general, common outlook on policy issues that confront the political system; (3) the intent of a party is to influence government to adopt policies consistent with the policy preferences of the party and its members; and (4) a party seeks to accomplish this by getting its candidates elected so that they will make the kinds of policy decisions that reflect the party's issue positions. In other words, to be successful a party must win elections.

With those basics in mind, the theory of political parties in a representative democracy can be summed up in what has been referred to as the **responsible parties model**. "Responsible" parties seek to reward members by being successful in the competition for government offices and by seeing those successful party representatives in government make public policies that correspond to the preferences of party members. The model assumes that more than one party is competing for seats in government and that the preferences of the public as a whole are reflected in its selection of government officials. The model then says, first, that each party will offer the electorate a unique policy platform upon which to base its votes. Second, voters consider the alternative party offerings and vote in favor of the party whose platform best corresponds to their preferences. The winning party, third, is expected to enact its platform promises. Finally, if the party succeeds in this regard, the public will be inclined to reelect that party and its candidates for office in the next round of elections. However, if it fails to perform as promised, the public may well punish that party by choosing some other party's candidates in the next election.

Parties in Reality

There is, obviously, a coercive element to this model—a party must do what it promised when elected to office or face being cast aside in the next election; that is how party integrity is supposed to be encouraged. But, some other things are also apparent. First, even within a party there is likely to be such diversity of views that the party platform will be a fairly general statement that is capable of including specific differences. To use an elementary example, a party that emphasizes a strong national defense might include people who wish to see a major new weapons system developed and employed, others who wish to see compulsory national military service instituted, some who prefer that the Defense Department budget be increased by 50%, and some may want a major change made in the way that basic training is accomplished for new members of each military branch.

Second, voters must be active and informed; they must seek out the differences in party platforms, then make judgments as to which party's platform best reflects their personal preferences, and then act (vote) in a manner consistent with that analysis. They must then monitor the behavior of the elected party and either reward or punish that party in a subsequent election by determining whether the party behaved as they wished after the previous election. This puts significant responsibility on the shoulders of voters.

Third, the possibility for effective party governance is limited by two characteristics of the American political system: separation of powers and federalism. There is not one agency that governs; there are many. At the national level, three branches with separate selection procedures exist: the presidency, the Congress, and the national courts. Then, this is substantially duplicated in each of the 50 states and significantly so in the thousands of local governments, which also exist in the United States (there are some 90,000 governments and perhaps as many as 500,000 elected officials in the nation). The policy issues of concern may not be the same in a state's political system as compared with the national system, and getting thousands of local, state, and national elected officials who are members of the same political party to agree on a major controversial issue is highly unlikely. On the latter point, consider, for example, the diverse views on immigration that are held by various Republican officeholders from across the nation.

We will return to this matter of variation in party members' political opinions and preferences below, for it is a significant reality in American politics, AND it is an important dimension of the opinion and values divide that can be seen in the United States.

Meanwhile, what do parties contribute to the system as they attempt to satisfy the kinds of expectations expressed and implied by the responsible parties model? First, they help inform the electorate, especially their members. Studies of the American electorate have repeatedly found that Americans are not terribly well informed on public affairs and that they do not go to great lengths, typically, to become better informed. Americans are, however, very social creatures, and they can be influenced as to what is important and what should be done by the social institutions to which they are attached. Parties attempt to take advantage of this, reinforcing the commonalities their members have, alerting members to new information or new issues, and reminding them of what to do to satisfy their preferences on public issues. This includes overt cues as to how to vote in upcoming elections.

Second, parties recruit and train candidates it may wish to sponsor in quests for public office. It is essential to have candidates with traits voters find attractive to give those voters even more reason for supporting the party candidates in an election. Third, parties mobilize their members to vote; turnout in presidential elections these days is less than 60% of the potential electorate and only about 40% in off-year congressional elections. Contests for state and local offices typically draw even fewer voters. Overcoming that pattern is important for a party to be successful, so they invest a great deal of effort into "getting out the vote."

Finally, parties provide a basis for those who win office as members of the same party to act in concert. Presidents may approach members of their own party serving in the Congress with some expectation that those legislators share a common general perspective with them, allowing them a better chance of accomplishing common party policy goals.

Do Parties Influence Individual Voting?

Parties have influence over voters to a degree that should not be underestimated. The single best predictor of which candidate a voter will support is the voter's party membership. Democrats tend to vote for Democratic candidates, and Republicans tend to vote for Republican candidates. Various reports of exit poll results across the nation in 2016 indicate that approximately 90% of voters who consider themselves Republicans voted for Republican presidential nominee Donald Trump, and approximately 89% of voters who identify as Democrats voted for the Democratic presidential nominee Hillary Clinton. The relationship between voter and party is a psychological attachment that voter has to a particular political party. We refer to this as party identification. The stronger that attachment, the more attuned the voter is likely to be to party pleas to go to the polls on Election Day and to ballot for the party's candidates when voting.

Political parties are a characteristic element of the American political system. Interestingly, not only do many Americans insist that they have little regard for politics, they also have little regard for political parties. The irony in this is that most Americans profess this psychological attachment to one party or another.

There are various sources of information on the partisan leanings of the American public; two of the more accessible sources are the Gallup polling organization (www.gallup.com)

and the Pew Research Center (pewresearch.org). The technique is to ask opinion poll respondents their partisan preferences, if any. The question is usually framed something like this: "Generally speaking, do you consider yourself to be a Republican, a Democrat, or an independent?" If the respondent gives the answer "independent," there is usually a follow-up question such as: "Do you lean more to the Republican Party, the Democratic Party, or neither?"

There has long been some debate as to whether a discussion of partisanship should present "leaners" as identifiers of a party or whether they should be understood simply as independents. The data suggests the importance of this distinction, and my understanding of the research would seem to suggest that most leaners are clearly partisans, regardless of their initial response to the partisanship question.

Gallup poll (Gallup) findings indicated that in 2016, 31% of respondents considered themselves to be Democrats, 28% Republicans, and 39% independents. The Pew Center (Pew) found 33% Democrats, 29% Republicans, and 34% independents. While the results of these two sources are slightly different, the overall findings are consistent. Additionally, the data for 2016 is consistent with that from previous years.

If, however, the follow-up data on independents that breaks out leaners are considered, in the Gallup survey 47% of respondents fall into the Democratic/Democratic leaner category, 42% into the Republican/Republican leaner group, and the set of independents is reduced to 11% of the sample that asserts it has no partisan inclinations at all. Again, the Pew Center's numbers are similar: 48% are Democrats/Democratic leaners, 44% are Republicans/Republican leaners, and pure independents are 8%. (Totals in both cases do not equal 100 exactly due to rounding and to respondents who did not answer the questions.) Regardless of the approach employed, partisanship is a common trait of Americans.

An obvious question at this point concerns whether all members of one particular party have identical views on issues of the day. Even a casual examination of contemporary party members or party leaders makes it clear that they do not, although there may well be a lot of agreement on some matters. We usually think instead that parties are coalitions of people who have similar views (usually basic, general views) on various issues. This is because parties must win elections in order to be successful, and to win elections the party must attract large numbers of voters. The greater the number of voters in the electorate, the greater the issue stance variation that electorate is likely to display. Since voters do vary in their issue stances, parties tend to downplay the differences that are possible in an issue position and emphasize the common general stance they advocate.

Is Party the Same as Ideology?

In recent years, however, many have asserted that a basic divide exists in the American public in terms of the values Americans hold. This divide is often said to parallel the partisan divide; in other words, Democrats tend to have one set of values on some fundamental issues and Republicans have opposite values on those same issues. For several decades, the Democratic Party has generally supported political and social equality, assistance for those lacking in resources to participate in contemporary life, and government action where necessary to insure those things. The Republican Party has generally advocated personal responsibility for one's political and social circumstances, a society that leaves opportunity's doors open, and an economic system largely independent of government regulation.

These have loosely been referred to as "liberal" and "conservative" approaches to governance. But historically there have been "liberal" and "moderate" Republicans, just as there have been "conservative" and "moderate" Democrats.

Over the past 50 years or so, however, there has been a quiet, gradual shift in party adherents. The Democratic Party has become a party of, predominantly, liberal views, although it still reflects at least some diversity in its ranks. In contrast, the Republican Party has clearly become a conservative party, having little patience with those who deviate from a conservative posture on any issue.

If these general party descriptions are valid, then partisanship is little more than ideological difference, right? No, not really. Democrats are generally liberal, and to an even greater extent Republicans are generally conservative, but in both parties there are some members who differ from their parties' general posture. Such groups were obvious in the 2016 elections and show evidence of continuing their visibility (and importance?) in the years that follow.

In the case of Democrats, these voters coalesced around the presidential candidacy of Senator Bernie Sanders and his advocacy of government's actions to enable citizens; although the election outcome quieted this group, is it merely latent—hibernating until its next opportunity to gain success? Republicans are somewhat more interesting for their diversity and their continued visibility. "Mainstream" Republicans continue to dominate elective office; they are generally conservative, but in comparison to some Republicans, they are "moderate." The House Freedom Caucus and its adherents are more assertively conservative, uncompromising, and vocal. During the 2016 presidential election campaign, they often allied with a third group, which for lack of a better label, we will term Trumpsters.

Like the Sanders Democrats, the Trumpsters have ardently protested their lack of influence in government and their perceived lack of government responsiveness to their needs (the two do differ in the needs they want met); Trump supporters have tended to be conservative and appear to be less limited by traditional American values (e.g., willing to silence or marginalize those who disagree with them without regard to the value of free speech). Trumpsters also (apparently in contrast to the Freedom Caucus) depend on cues from their adopted leader, President Trump, endorsing almost without question anything he says or does. In turn President Trump plays to them, often in a manner that produces emotional, rather than thoughtful, response.

Jonathan Martin (2017), reporter for the *New York Times*, captured this dynamic in an April 9, 2017 article describing the Georgia sixth congressional district special election. He describes a condition wherein personal loyalty and a desire to "win" have diminished political philosophy; the rift between the Tea Party and "establishment" factions has been upset.

So What Have We Learned?

Political parties cannot corral significantly the diverse perspectives in the citizenry as a whole or even those within their individual party ranks. The consequence is that advocates of diverse viewpoints continue to compete in the political arena, none large or strong enough to dominate policy-making for any prolonged period. The policies that do get made are compromises, mixtures, hybrids of the perspectives contending in a particular issue arena, instead of reflecting a pure value strain.

Americans are not cut out of a single bolt of cloth. We differ, and we bicker because of it. We compete to gain what we prefer, even as we say that we do not like conflict. But, this variety of perspectives, preferences, and needs distributed over a large population, a multiplicity of governing agencies and authorities, and the limitations of general values that govern who rules and how all cause satisficing, compromising governance to occur. Or, as one observer has termed the process, it is one of "muddling through." Only when, or if, some difference becomes so basic that compromise becomes impossible and reason becomes unyielding that the fact of disagreement be a genuine threat to the nation. Meanwhile, if we are sufficiently concerned about something, we engage in efforts to gain an outcome that is rewarding, and if we are not concerned, we simply proceed until something else does mobilize us.

Key Terms

Ideology—a set of ideas a person holds about politics and the role of government; usually discussed in terms of conservative or liberal.

Indirect democracy—a political system in which elected representatives govern on behalf of the citizenry; also called representative democracy.

Political authority—the responsibility for making political and policy choices for others.

Political party—an organization of people sharing some agreement on how to respond to major issues of the day and seeking to influence the actions of government on those issues by gaining seats in government through elections.

Public policy—any law, rule, or official governmental decision made by those who have the political authority and responsibility for making it, which is intended to resolve or at least regulate a societal issue.

Responsible parties model—foundational idea behind parties in a representative government. The model assumes that in a system with multiple political parties, each party will represent substantially different ideological view points, voters will make electoral decisions based on these positions and once elected parties will govern in a manner consistent with these views and the will of the people.

Satisficing—a process of compromise in which each of the participants agrees to accept a decision that meets some but not all of their objectives.

Social conflict—the struggle between groups or individuals for power or influence in society.

Universal adult suffrage—the provision of the right to vote to all adults in a society.

Multiple Choice Questions

1. The contents of this chapter suggest that
   a. serious issues rarely arise in American society.
   b. the only issues in American history that have caused significant problems have been associated with armed conflict.
   c. eliminating political parties would significantly reduce the number of conflicts Americans face.
   d. issues are inevitable in society.

   Answer: D

2. Which of the following is an aspect of social conflict?
   a. At least two persons or groups have some goal.
   b. Goals of differing persons or groups cannot be simultaneously satisfied.
   c. Those persons or groups actively pursue their conflicting goals.
   d. All of the above are aspects of social conflict.

   Answer: D

3. What is a potential source of social conflict in American society?
   a. Residents of geographically small states versus those who live in large states.
   b. People who travel to work by private automobile in some large city versus those who use mass transit.
   c. Members of the U.S. Chamber of Commerce versus members of the Brotherhood of Electrical Workers.
   d. All of the above are potential sources of conflict in American society.

   Answer: D

4. Which of the following statements is consistent with the contents of this chapter?
   a. More Americans report being moderate than report being either conservative or liberal.
   b. Most Americans consider themselves conservatives.
   c. Most Democrats label themselves moderate.
   d. Equal proportions of Americans divide themselves into the liberal, moderate, and conservative categories.

   Answer: A

5. Why do election outcomes so often fail to resolve issues before the American public?
   a. Winning candidates for one set of offices often disagree with winning candidates who gain a different set of offices as to what should be done.
   b. Competing candidates for public office do not address the same issues during the election campaign.
   c. Different candidates for public office agree on the issue but disagree as to the best way to achieve the goal that they agree upon.
   d. All of the above limit the ability of elections to resolve issues.

   Answer: A

Discussion Question

Select one issue that was a significant element of the 2016 U.S. presidential general election campaign. Describe the basic differences in the major party candidates' responses to that issue. Identify at least two types of Americans who might have taken a side on this issue; explain which side would each have taken and why. Did the election outcome determine how this particular issue will be resolved? Why or why not? Discuss.

References

Erikson, Robert, and Kent Tedin. 2008. *American Public Opinion,* 8th ed. Boston: Allyn and Bacon.

Gallup. 2016. Accessed December 14, 2016 from www.gallup.copm/poll/201638/independent-political-lowest-six-years.aspx?g_Source=party+identification+2016&g_medium=search&g-campaign+tiles.

Jones, Jeffrey M. 2016. "Democrats More Liberal on Social Issues than Economic Ones." Accessed July 1, 2017 from www.gallup.com/poll/191741/democrats-liberal-social-issues-economic-ones.aspx?g_Source=ideology+and+social+isues&g_medim=search&g_campaign+tiles.

Larson, Serena. 2017. "Dan Rather: We Are a Deeply Divided Country." www.money.cnn.com, March 11, 2017.

Leslie, Katie. 2016. "Is Dallas Rep. Pete Sessions Vulnerable after Clinton Won His District?" *Dallas Morning News.* Accessed July 1, 2017 from www.dallasnews.com/news/local-politics/2016/12/12/sessions-culberson-see-districts-turn-blue-presidential-race-age-trump-signal-long-term-trouble.

Martin, Jonathan. 2017. "For the GOP, A House Race Blurs Identity." *New York Times,* April 10, 2017, p. 1A.

Huang, John, Jacoby, Samuel, Strickland, Samuel, and Lai, Rebecca. 2016. "Election 2016: Exit Polls," *New York Times.* Accessed December 14, 2016 from https://www.nytimes.com/interactive/2016/11/08/us/politics/election-exit-polls.html?_r=0.

"The Parties on the Eve of the 2016 Election: Two Coalitions, Moving Further Apart." 2016. Pew. Accessed July 1, 2017 from www.people-press.org/2016/09/13/the-parties-on-the-eve-of-the-2016-election-two-coalitions-moving-further-apart/.

"Presidential Profiles." n.d. Accessed July 1, 2017 from http://www.presidentprofiles.com/Kennedy-Bush/Lyndon-B-Johnson-Consensus-politics.html.

NOT EVEN A GOOD SCANDAL? THE POWER OF INCUMBENCY IN CONGRESSIONAL ELECTIONS

BY JEFF FINE
Clemson University

LEARNING OBJECTIVES

Students should be able to:

1. Identify recent trends with respect to the rate at which incumbents are reelected to Congress.
2. Explain why incumbents are advantaged over challengers in races for the U.S. House and Senate.
3. Describe how being members of the House or Senate provides institutional advantages that help legislators keep their jobs in Congress.

"In the vast majority of races around the country, there is no question who is going to win. Absent an indictment or scandal or $1 million in the bank, it's awfully difficult to unseat an incumbent."
—Larry Makinson, Former Executive Director of the Center for Responsive Politics[1]

INTRODUCTION

During the 2016 presidential election, Donald Trump vowed to "drain the swamp" in Washington if he were elected. This rhetoric was aimed largely at Congress, which Trump characterized as being corrupt and beholden to special interests over the well-being of constituents (Hulse 2016). Trump regularly bragged about how he had been able to gain access to and influence with legislators as a result of his own contributions to their campaigns in the past. During the 2016 campaign and shortly after his victory, Trump advocated for term limits in Congress to solve this problem as he saw it. This type of campaign language is not surprising, as politicians often run for national office by criticizing Washington. That is one of many reasons why Congress's approval ratings have been abysmal in recent years, and why many Americans report "dissatisfaction with politicians" as the most important problem facing the nation.

Contributed by Jeff Fine. Copyright © Kendall Hunt Publishing Company.

Calls for term limits in Congress are the direct result of the high reelection rates of its members, both in the House and in the Senate. The overwhelming advantage held by **incumbents**—those who currently hold that political office—is underscored in the quotation above from Larry Makinson. We have seen numerous examples in recent years of sitting members of Congress winning reelection despite scandals, indictments, and/or wealthy challengers.

To be clear, the vast majority of elected officials are honorable and trustworthy leaders working to better the lives of their constituents and the country. However, the high reelection rate for even those members who have been embroiled in scandal underscores that all incumbents hold significant advantages in elections over those who seek to unseat them. This chapter explores the many advantages afforded to congressional incumbents, and discusses how even an indictment, a scandal, or even an opponent with a million dollars in the bank is often not enough to defeat an incumbent.

Indictments, Scandals, and Millions in the Bank

Indictments

Democratic Congressman Mel Reynolds was elected to Congress from his Illinois district in 1992. Reynolds is one of only a few politicians to have been selected as a Rhodes Scholar, and he earned a law degree from Oxford as part of this prestigious scholarship. His familiarity with the law failed him, however, as Reynolds found himself on the receiving end of the federal judicial system. In August of 1994, Reynolds was indicted on charges of sexual assault and child pornography for having sex with and taking nude pictures of a 16-year old worker on his congressional campaign ("Mel Reynolds" 2008). While an indictment is simply the formal charge of a crime, in politics these accusations are often painted by an opponent as equivalent to being convicted, and this characterization can lead voters to presume the guilt of the person charged with the crime. Even though he had been indicted, Reynolds continued his bid for a second term in Congress. Despite the criminal proceedings against him and the sensitive nature of his sexual abuse charges, the Republican party did not even field a challenger to run against Congressman Reynolds. Without major party opposition in the race, Reynolds was safely reelected. In 1995, Reynolds was convicted and sent to prison, forcing him to resign from Congress. However, the fact that Reynolds was reelected in the first place in the wake of being indicted on sexual assault charges, and his lack of a Republican challenger in the race, suggests that sometimes not even an indictment can unseat an incumbent.

Perhaps more troubling than the Reynolds case is that of Democratic Representative Jim Traficant of Ohio. Traficant was first elected to Congress in 1984, and was reelected eight times by the people from his district. However, Traficant's political career was derailed in 2002 when he was indicted on 10 felony counts including tax evasion, racketeering, bribery, and obstruction of justice. After a lengthy trial, Traficant was convicted and sentenced to eight years in prison. He was sent to jail by a federal court. However, he could have been punished by his colleagues since the Constitution affords Congress the power to punish its own members. Following his conviction, the House of Representatives therefore held a vote to expel Traficant from membership in the chamber, which passed by a 420-1 vote. Traficant's expulsion marked only the fifth time in history that a sitting member of Congress was removed from office by their colleagues (Mitchell 2002). Amazingly, Traficant vowed to run for reelection from his prison cell. Despite being limited to campaigning from the inside of a federal penitentiary, Traficant still received 15% of the vote in the November 2002 election. While he lost the race, Traficant's ability to receive 15% of the vote after not only being indicted but also convicted and expelled from office is a testament to the strength of incumbency.

Scandals

There have been many high-profile scandals involving a member of Congress, and some of the biggest offenders are still in Congress today. In 1994, freshman Republican member Kenneth Calvert of California was found in his car by police officers in his congressional district after 2 a.m. Calvert was caught in a compromising position, and the woman with him told police officers that she had previously been arrested for prostitution and possession of heroin (Merida 1994). After initially trying to flee the scene in his car, Calvert eventually stopped and told the officers who he was. While he was not arrested at the time, the police report (filled with a detailed account of the incident) was printed in the local newspaper in Calvert's congressional district. Calvert eventually apologized for the incident and defended his actions by saying he was "intensely lonely." Despite this scandal, Calvert ran for reelection and easily won with over 55% of the vote, and remains in Congress today.

Senator David Vitter also was caught in a sex scandal while in office. Though he was not arrested, Vitter's phone number surfaced on the records of a prostitution service known as "D.C. Madam." Vitter acknowledged that he had committed a "serious sin" and asked for forgiveness. His wife appeared with him at a press conference during which he apologized publically. The scandal made national headlines, including a featured story on ABC's "20/20." The intense media spotlight was driven by reports of several prominent figures being involved, including Vice President Cheney, a U.S. Attorney, and a top official at the State Department. Following the D.C. Madam scandal, a Louisiana brothel also claimed that Vitter had previously been a customer. The use of brothels and prostitutes has not seemed to faze Vitter's political career. The scandals surfaced in 2007, and they were the subject of several campaign commercials made by Charlie Melancon during his 2010 campaign against Vitter. However, Vitter cruised to reelection, defeating Melancon 57% to 38%. Vitter remained in the Senate until he retired to run for governor of Louisiana in 2016.

In both the Vitter and Reynolds instances, a sitting member of Congress was embroiled in a sex scandal that made local and national news. However, even these tawdry scandals were not enough to unseat an incumbent.

Millions

An independently wealthy opponent represents a formidable challenge for a sitting member of Congress. The perceived threat posed by such an individual was sufficiently large for legislators to modify the campaign finance laws as part of the Bipartisan Campaign Reform Act of 2002 to allow an incumbent to accept larger donations when facing a wealthy, self-financed opponent. While this so-called "millionaire's amendment" was struck down by the U.S. Supreme Court in 2008 (*Davis v. Federal Election Commission*), the original inclusion of this provision is an indication of the perception that the uber-wealthy might be formidable opponents for incumbents. However, despite this fear on the part of incumbents, being independently wealthy may not be enough to help a challenger overcome the massive advantages of incumbents.

In 2010, former Hewlett-Packard CEO Carly Fiorina mounted a challenge to incumbent Senator Barbara Boxer of California. Boxer was seen as a vulnerable incumbent, and experts rated the election as a "toss-up" (Cook 2010). Fiorina was a rising star in the Republican Party and at one point was considered as a possible running mate for John McCain during the 2008 presidential election. Fiorina's business experience made her an attractive candidate. Her personal wealth—she has a net worth of over $20 million—coupled with her willingness to use it made her a viable challenger. However, despite contributing over $5.5 million to her own campaign (OpenSecrets 2010) and Boxer's seeming vulnerability, the three-term incumbent defeated Fiorina by a 52–42% margin.

In fact, examples of challengers using vast personal wealth to defeat an incumbent are relatively uncommon. One such example was heart surgeon Bill Frist of Tennessee (R-TN), who later went on to serve as Senate Majority Leader. During his 1994 campaign against incumbent Democrat Jim Sasser, Frist lent his campaign $2.2 million to win the race ("FEC Fines Frist's 2000 Senate Campaign" 2006). Although Frist's victory was an exception, it is not because wealthy challengers do not win congressional elections. Rather, it is because affluent would-be candidates are strategic and tend to wait for an open seat before mounting a run for Congress.

Incumbency Advantage

One of the most persistent phenomena observed by political scientists is **incumbency advantage**, whereby the individual who currently serves in office is overwhelmingly likely to win reelection. Over the past 60 years, over 90% of incumbents seeking reelection have won. While this pattern is strongest in the House of Representatives with roughly 93% of incumbents winning reelection since 1950, senators also benefit from incumbency as roughly 80% of senators have been reelected over the same time period (OpenSecrets 2010). In 2016, 97% of House incumbents seeking reelection were victorious, as were 87% of incumbent Senators.

The 2010 midterm congressional elections received widespread media attention, partly due to the unprecedented amount of anti-incumbent sentiment. In public opinion polls, voters reported high levels of disapproval of both parties in Congress and with incumbents overall. These anti-incumbent attitudes helped fuel the rise of Tea Party candidates who ran against the system and incumbent politicians alike. In the election, the Republican Party (including the Tea Party candidates running as Republicans) regained control of the House of Representatives by gaining 63 seats and picked up 6 seats in the Senate. This was called a "wave" election, as a flood of challengers washed out existing legislators. However, even in an election where such massive turnover occurred, 85% of House incumbents who sought reelection won their race, as did 84% of Senate incumbents. This pattern is consistent with other similarly tumultuous congressional elections in 1994 (where Republicans regained control of the House of Representatives for the first time in 40 years) and 2006 (when the Democrats finally recaptured the House majority). In both of these elections, over 90% of incumbents seeking reelection in the House were victorious (OpenSecrets 2010).

Causes of Incumbency Advantage

Money

When seeking factors that cause incumbency advantage, the media often points to the role that money plays in elections. The argument is that money affects electoral outcomes whereby the candidate with the most money wins. The candidate with the most money does win more often than not, but this obscures the true relationship between money and electoral outcomes.

There have been instances where individuals were able to use their enormous personal wealth to win a seat in Congress. In 2000, former Goldman Sachs CEO Jon Corzine spent $62 million—a record at the time—to win a Senate race in New Jersey in 2000. Those who argue that money has undue influence on American elections often point to the Corzine race as a prime example. When we think about the role of money, we are prone to remember those instances where wealthy candidates won their race. But for every Jon Corzine there are other wealthy candidates who lost their elections. For example, beer-maker Pete Coors, Chairman of Coors Brewing Company (now MillerCoors), failed to win his 2004 Senate race in Colorado despite contributing over $1 million of his own money to his campaign (OpenSecrets 2010). This amount, however, pales in comparison to the amount of self-financing in the 2010 Connecticut Senate race. Former World Wrestling Entertainment CEO Linda McMahon, whose husband Vince is the founder and current CEO of the professional wrestling league, spent over $50 million of her own money in a losing effort to Richard Blumenthal (OpenSecrets 2010).

The argument that money causes electoral outcomes goes beyond those few races where one candidate funds all or part of their campaign with their own personal wealth. It also centers on the disproportionate financial advantage held by incumbents over challengers. In recent House elections, the typical incumbents held a four-to-one money advantage over the average challenger. In Senate elections, the ratio is even higher, with Senate incumbents outraising their opponents by a seven-to-one margin. Since incumbents have more money and they win at such high rates, many casual observers of congressional elections suggest that the money gap drives incumbency advantage. However, political science research has shown that candidates do not win elections because they have more money than their opponents. Rather, candidates have more money than their opponents because we already know they are going to win the race (Jacobson 1983). Many contributions are motivated by the desire to have some influence on the political process, or at least to buy access to an elected official to voice concerns on a variety of issues. Therefore, it makes the most sense to contribute money to the candidate who is most likely going to win the race. Since incumbents win the vast majority of races, rational contributors funnel their money to them. Some donors attempt to cover their bases by contributing money to both major party candidates in a race, in an attempt to secure influence and access as described above.

Overall, it is clear that challengers are significantly disadvantaged on this front. Incumbents typically raise much more than do challengers, and even those challengers with large financial assets still tend to lose when facing an incumbent. So, if money is not the culprit, what factors drive the high rate at which incumbents are reelected?

Experience

Incumbents possess a variety of resources at their disposal that allow them to win reelection at such high rates. Perhaps the most obvious advantage for incumbents is their experience. These individuals have worked for years (and in many cases, decades) serving the public, navigating political waters, developing expertise on issues that are important to them and their constituents, and crafting messages that resonate with voters. These politicians often have staff members who have worked with them for years who also have developed their own experience in their issue areas or in helping constituents with concerns. This type of advantage for incumbents is exactly what we *should* want in a representative democracy; voters are rewarding politicians who are performing good public service with another term in office.

Beyond their experience governing, incumbents also have experience running (and winning) elections. Having successfully run a campaign in the past can be a strong advantage, as these politicians have honed their campaign techniques and strategies. Their experience winning in that district or state also gives them insight that a challenger might not possess. They know which neighborhoods are good and bad for them, they know what messages resonate with the voters, and they have extensive networks of contacts within their constituencies that can be used to staff their campaigns, help raise money, and canvas for votes.

Members also have legislative records that aid their chances at reelection. This can come in a variety of forms. They can introduce bills or amendments, or hold hearings on issues of importance to their constituents. They also can work to defeat legislation or amendments that they oppose. Further, until recently, members of Congress could try to secure **earmarks** (also called **"pork-barrel spending"**), which brings money back to their district or state for local projects. These projects helped members of Congress demonstrate tangible benefits that they provide to their constituencies. Robert Byrd (D-WV) earned the nickname "The King of Pork" for securing hundreds of millions of dollars for pet projects in West Virginia. Byrd was even quoted as saying that he wanted "to be West Virginia's billion-dollar industry" (Clines 2002). A notable pork-barrel project is the John Murtha Airport in Johnstown, Pennsylvania, named for the former member of Congress who secured over $150 million in federal funding for the airport. The Murtha airport only services three total arriving flights a day, two of which arrive from Washington, D.C. (Kady 2009). Citizens roundly disliked earmarks designated for other districts or states, but favored the funding that was brought home to their own area. So, although Byrd and Murtha may be scorned elsewhere for their pork-barrel projects, such activities only strengthened public opinion toward them locally and increase their chances of being reelected.

This type of spending was criticized as a source of waste and bloat in the federal budget, as well as giving the appearance of impropriety and special-interest influence. In 2010, Congress banned the use of earmarks. There are some members who lament the removal of this tool, as it makes it more difficult to build coalitions to get legislations passed. Further, even with the ban there are ways that legislators have tried to sidestep these reforms in an effort to channel more resources to their districts and states.

Challengers often criticize the incumbents' experience by trying to paint them as "Washington insiders" who are out of touch with their constituents. When the incumbent has secured pork-barrel projects, challengers can criticize the member for contributing to large budgets and deficits. However, the other resources afforded to incumbents help combat these strategies and contribute to their continued success at the polls.

Name Recognition

Name recognition is another factor that reinforces incumbency. Voters are reluctant to cast a ballot for someone they do not know, and they are overwhelmingly more likely to know the name of the incumbent representative or senator. The incumbent has met countless constituents during previous elections, when visiting the congressional district, and in the district or Washington, D.C. offices. The incumbent also benefits from news coverage of visits back to the district or state as well as legislative achievements. These face-to-face interactions with constituents as well as print, TV, radio, and internet coverage of them, increases the number of voters who recognize the name of incumbents and boosts their chances of reelection.

Institutional Advantages

In addition to the informal resource of experience, members of Congress are also afforded several institutional advantages that aid in their reelection efforts. One perquisite of the job is the **franking privilege** whereby members of Congress are able to send mail to their constituents free of charge by using their signature in place of a stamp. Legislators use the franking privilege to send various types of mail to their constituents. For example, most congressmen send periodic flyers that tout their legislative accomplishments and work on behalf of the people back home. These flyers are a tangible reminder of the work the member is doing on behalf of the district or state. These flyers help boost name recognition of incumbents, and recent advancements in this type of communication allow incumbents to target specific messages to particular constituents. For example, an incumbent can send a pro-choice message to one household who cares a great deal about that issue, and send a message about gun control to a different family for whom that issue is more of a priority. This allows incumbents to pump up their favorability rating with many different would-be voters.

While there are restrictions preventing legislators from sending franked mail in close proximity to an election, members still use this resource with such frequency that it helps increase name recognition and promote their record. Recent studies have shown that the value of the franked mail that the typical member of Congress sends every 2 years is more than the typical challenger spends on his or her entire campaign altogether. Since this privilege is not extended to challengers, it represents a sizable advantage to incumbents.

Members of Congress also have travel allowances that allow them to visit their home districts or states frequently. The typical member of Congress returns home at least every other week while in office (even the ones from far-flung states like Alaska or Hawaii), and many return home every weekend. The schedule of business in Washington, D.C. is such that it allows legislators to visit home every weekend, and spend perhaps as few as three days a week in Washington. Many members of Congress retain their residencies back home, and keep more temporary housing in D.C. Some members of Congress have even resorted to sleeping in their offices while in Washington, and then flying home every weekend. Joe Biden famously commuted nightly to and from work in D.C. from his home in Delaware via the Amtrak train home during his time in the U.S. Senate. These travel allowances give members a greater ability to have a tangible and visible presence in their districts and states. So, even though they are "in D.C.," they are not gone from the district. While they are back home, legislators can be seen interacting with constituents in a variety of settings. For example, they might deliver a speech at a high school or university graduation, give remarks at the opening of a new public transit project, stop by to see wounded soldiers in a hospital, visit students in a local school, or frequent a business or factory in the state or district. Some members of Congress also hold weekly meetings, call-in shows, "office hours," and/or participate in town halls while they are home visiting their constituencies. Others use social media to interact with constituents regularly online. For example, Senator Grassley (R-IA) answers questions from constituents weekly via YouTube, and Senator Booker (D-NJ) is a frequent Twitter user who even replies when people respond to his tweets. These activities enhance the connection that voters feel to their legislator, and it gives incumbents a decided advantage when seeking reelection.

Congress also contains its own media production facilities for members to use. Both the House of Representatives and the Senate have their own media studios in their respective sides of the Capitol Visitor Center complex. With a short walk or subway ride in the tunnels connecting their Washington, D.C. office buildings to the U.S. Capitol, members can use these facilities to quickly leverage the media to communicate with constituents and the broader public. Members of both chambers often hold press conferences in these studios, or use them to record video packages that might be used to convey their messages back home. Occasionally, clips from these press conferences or packages may be aired on local news, posted to a member's YouTube page, or disseminated to constituents more directly. As with the franked mail, this resource raises the incumbent's name recognition and can increase voters' perceptions of the accomplishments of their legislator. Together, these institutional perquisites are advantages that bolster the incumbent's chances of winning reelection.

Casework

Congressmen and senators also build a rapport with their constituents through **casework**. Casework is the term used to describe legislators work to help constituents navigate the cumbersome political process and federal bureaucracy. When citizens have difficulty obtaining a visa, getting a passport, or securing their Social Security checks, they often call their representatives or senators for assistance. Members of Congress have fulltime staff, both in Washington, D.C. and in the district or state, that help constituents with these requests. Many members and senators have multiple offices in their congressional districts and states, each with caseworkers devoted to providing this type of aid to constituents. Some legislators, often those who represent larger rural districts or states, even have mobile "offices" that allow staffers to drive to constituents to help provide casework. This assistance is nonpartisan, as legislators aid any constituent that calls regardless of their party affiliation or vote support.

By providing this crucial service, members of Congress form a bond with the individuals who benefit from the casework. Even though a particular constituent may not have received such help from their legislator, they are more likely to know other citizens who have. Further, this type of "casework" allows the incumbent to build a dataset of the concerns of their constituent, as well as potential voters who might be mobilized by particular messages. This is a powerful advantage over challengers who lack this information.

Casework reinforces incumbency advantage because this work, usually done by the members' staff, give voters tangible evidence that the current member is working for people back home. It also provides them critical information on the interests or concerns of their constituents.

Configuration of the District

Redistricting, the redrawing of congressional districts that occurs every 10 years following the census, also contributes to incumbency advantage. In the vast majority of states, the boundary lines for congressional districts are determined by members of the state legislature. This gives the state legislature the ability to draw a district map in a way that is favorable to their political party. For example, the Democratic-controlled state legislature in Maryland has drawn district boundaries that help maximize the number of congressional seats that will be won by Democratic candidates, while in North Carolina and Texas, Republican-controlled state legislatures have drawn districting maps that help the GOP gain additional seats in Congress.

In addition to districting plans that advantage a political party, district boundaries are sometimes reconfigured in such a way that it makes incumbents even safer. Under these plans, districts are created so that they are composed of a sizable (and sometimes overwhelming) number of Democrats or Republicans. This provides a substantial advantage to the incumbent, all but assuring victory for one political party in that district. California is a notable example. We often think of California as a Democratic state, but 14 of the 53 congressional seats from California were won by Republicans in the 2016 elections. You might assume that in such a liberal state, that these 14 Republican congressmen would be vulnerable, and thus they might be incumbents who might be beatable by Democratic challengers. However, the configuration of California's 53 districts through redistricting makes that unlikely.

In California, district boundaries are drawn by the nonpartisan California Citizens Redistricting Commission. The commission has drawn the boundaries so that both Democratic and Republican legislators are politically safe and insulated from a meaningful challenge. The district boundaries in California are drawn so that districts are either overwhelmingly Democratic or Republican, with very few districts closely split between the parties. That means that incumbent congressmen from both parties are relatively safe. In 2016, only 4 out of 53 congressional races had the 2 candidates finish within 6 percentage points of each other, and only 11 races were within 15 percentage points ("CNN Election Center—The States: California" 2010). The remaining 42 races were not competitive. Thus, the configuration of the districts reinforces incumbency because many districts nationwide are either solidly Republican or Democratic, making defeat that much tougher.

Discouraging Quality Challengers

One of the biggest advantages held by incumbents is that would-be challengers know all of the above information. They know the statistics about the percentages of incumbents that win reelection. They know the benefits that incumbents enjoy in terms of name recognition and institutional advantages. Any individual considering a run for Congress realizes that taking on an incumbent would be a steep, uphill battle. Since challengers know all of this, most of the quality challengers (e.g., those with previous political experience, strong personal backgrounds, and those with name recognition or access to wealth) choose not to run against an incumbent. Instead, these aspiring congressmen will wait for an open seat race, when the incumbent has either resigned, chosen to run for a higher political office, or when a new congressional district is created. By waiting for an open seat, challengers avoid tarnishing their political careers by losing to an incumbent.

Thus, the ability to scare off quality challengers is an important cause of incumbency advantage. Members of Congress raise large sums of money for their next political battle, and use this "war chest" to signal that they have the resources to run a strong campaign. Using their institutional advantages to visit their district or state regularly, building strong policy records that benefit the people back home, and performing casework to help constituents navigate the political system and cut through red tape, all send signals to potential challengers that they should wait for a later opportunity to run for Congress.

CONCLUSION

The power of incumbency is one of the most persistent features of the modern Congress. Over 90% of incumbents seeking reelection have won their races over the last 50 years, and even "wave" elections like those of 2010 or 1994 see reelection rates over 80%. In 2016, 97% of House members seeking reelection won their races, as did 87% of senators seeking reelection (OpenSecrets 2010). The advantages that members of Congress possess make it extremely difficult to unseat them. Former Senator Chris Dodd (D-CT) summarized these advantages well:

> "[W]e . . . have treasuries of significant amounts and the power of the office which allows us to be in the press every day, if we want. We can send franked mail to our constituents at no cost to us. . . . We do radio and television shows. We can go back to our States with subsidized airfares" (Steen 2006).

Incumbents exploit these factors and others to their benefit, both in scaring off quality challengers and in defeating those candidates that do emerge to run against them. As this chapter has shown, even the most unscrupulous elected officials are able to ward off these challenges in the face of indictments, scandals, or millions in the bank.

To be sure, there are examples where an indictment or a scandal was enough to unseat an incumbent. However, most recent scandals have resulted in resignations. Often members of their own political party call on these beleaguered politicians to resign to prevent negative press from tarnishing their party's image or the scandal to distract from the party's political agenda. This trend has been more common in recent years, likely due to the rise of 24-hour news networks, the internet, and technological advancements like camera phones, Twitter, and YouTube.

Chapter 6: Not Even a Good Scandal? The Power of Incumbency in Congressional Elections

Former House members Bob Ney (R-OH) and William Jefferson (D-LA) both resigned and went to prison due to illegal financial activities while in Congress. Rep. Mark Foley (R-FL) resigned due to a scandal involving inappropriate text messages he sent to male pages. Senator John Ensign (R-NV) resigned after reportedly funneling money to the family of a former staffer to cover up an affair that Ensign had with the staffer's wife. Each of these members of Congress could have faced an expulsion vote had they remained in the chamber. Senator Larry Craig (R-WY) resigned after being arrested and pleading no contest to charges that he solicited prostitution from an undercover police officer in the Minneapolis airport. Craig initially stated that he would seek reelection, but immense pressure from his own party helped convince him to resign.

These scandals were covered at length in the 24-hour news cycle. Audio clips of Craig's interview with the police were released and went viral on YouTube. Former Congressman Anthony Weiner (N-NY) became infamous for sending explicit pictures to various women, resulting in one of the first scandals involving a politician to arise due to Twitter. Although initial public opinion suggested that Congressman Weiner could maintain his seat even amid the scandal, he ultimately resigned from office. As social media websites and technology becomes even more widespread, it will likely become increasingly difficult for scandal-plagued legislators to sustain the political fallout once news becomes public. However, Vitter's smooth reelection and Weiner's sustained approval in the wake of his scandal suggest that legislators who refuse to resign despite allegations are still formidable candidates who have massive advantages as incumbents.

These advantages held by incumbents have important consequences for elections and for the political system more broadly. On the positive side, high incumbent reelection rates help the best and most experienced elected officials remain in office, providing a wealth of good institutional knowledge to Congress and helping improve the quality of representation. However, as noted above, incumbency advantage can have negative impacts on the system. It can reinforce itself by deterring quality challengers who are afraid to run against someone who has such an overwhelming chance of winning. The voters therefore are denied the most qualified pool of candidates, which hampers the quality of governance. Some argue that the power of incumbency might lead to more corruption, or at the very least a decreased incentive to respond to the preferences of the constituency, though the evidence is mixed at best on this. More broadly, the high rate of reelection for incumbents can weaken the sense of political efficacy among citizens, who may be less likely to think that their vote matters when the outcome is decided before more races begin and certainly well before Election Day.

Key Terms

Incumbent—the individual who currently holds a political office.

Incumbency advantage—the phenomenon whereby an overwhelming number of congressmen and senators win reelection if they choose to run for another term.

Earmarks/Pork-barrel projects—pet projects created by members of Congress to bring money, jobs, and resources back to their district or state.

Franking privilege—a perquisite of the job of a member of Congress; members of Congress are allowed to send mail to their constituents by signing their name instead of using a stamp.

Casework—work done by members of Congress and their staffs to help solve a problem for their constituents or to help constituents navigate red tape in the bureaucracy.

Multiple Choice Questions

1. Through the franking privilege, members of Congress are:
   a. allowed to send free mail to their constituents by including their signature instead of a stamp.
   b. protected from being arrested on the way to or from the U.S. Capital.
   c. allowed to introduce legislation on any topic.
   d. allowed to speak "frankly" on the record about an issue of concern.

   Answer: A

2. Which of the following is most correct with respect to the percentage of incumbents who seek reelection that win?
   a. Less than 10%
   b. Approximately 25%
   c. Approximately 50%
   d. Over 85%

   Answer: D

3. Which of the following is correct with respect to advantages *typically* held by incumbents seeking reelection to Congress?
   a. The opponent has more money than the incumbent.
   b. The incumbent has less political experience than the opponent.
   c. The opponent has less name recognition than the incumbent.
   d. The incumbent has less access to franking than the opponent.

   Answer: C

4. If a constituent is having trouble getting her Social Security check or obtaining a work visa, she might call her member of Congress or senator to help with this process. The work conducted by the office of the legislator on behalf of the constituent is called:
   a. earmarks.
   b. casework.
   c. franking.
   d. filibustering.

   Answer: B

5. Which of the following is an example of a member of Congress using an earmark (also called a pork-barrel project)?
   a. Adding an amendment to a bill bringing money to the district to build a bridge
   b. Helping a constituent obtain a Social Security check that has been delayed
   c. Voting against a bill that requires every American to have health insurance
   d. Giving a speech on the floor of the chamber to persuade other members

   Answer: A

6. Which of the following best captures why incumbents typically have more money than challengers in congressional elections?
   a. Challengers prefer social media outlets so they need less money to be competitive.
   b. Incumbents have written laws restricting how much money opponents can raise.
   c. Members of Congress can use taxpayer money to fund their entire campaign.
   d. Donors contribute to the candidate who seems the most likely to win.

   Answer: D

Discussion Questions

1. Incumbents are advantaged in congressional elections, allowing them to win at high rates. Explain why incumbents have such a strong advantage over their opponents and then make an argument about whether steps should be taken to prevent incumbents from winning elections repeatedly.
2. Make an argument that incumbents winning elections at high rates is good for American democracy, as well as an argument that this phenomenon is bad for the political system.

References

Clines, Francis X. 2002. "How Do West Virginians Spell Pork? It's B-Y-R-D." *The New York Times*. May 4.

CNN Election Center—The States: California. 2010. http://www.cnn.com/ELECTION/2010/results/state/#CA.

Cook, Charlie. 2010. "2010 California Senate Race." *The Cook Political Report*. Retrieved from http://www.cookpolitical.com/node/3341.

FEC Fines Frist's 2000 Senate Campaign. 2006. *USA Today*. Retrieved from *USA Today* website: http://www.usatoday.com/news/washington/2006-06-01-frist-fine_x.htm.

Hulse, Carl. 2016. "As Trump Embraces Term Limits, Allies in Congress Pull Away." *The New York Times*, November 16.

Jacobson, Gary C. 1983. *The Politics of Congressional Elections*. New York: Longman.

Kady, Martin II. 2009. "GOP's Next Target: John Murtha's Airport." *Politico.* Retrieved from Politico.com website: http://www.politico.com/news/stories/0909/27261.html.

Mel Reynolds. 2008. In Office of the Clerk Office of History and Preservation (Ed.), *Black Americans in Congress, 1870-2007.* Washington, D.C.: U.S. Government Printing Office.

Merida, Kevin. 1994. "America's Latest Soap: As Congress Turns; Alleged Indiscretions Feed Public Mistrust, Jeopardizes Careers." *The Washington Post*, June 5, p. A1.

Mitchell, Alison. 2002. "House Votes to Expel Traficant From Ranks." *The New York Times.* Retrieved from *The New York Times* website:

OpenSecrets. 2010. Congressional Elections. *Center for Responsive Politics.* http://www.opensecrets.org/races/index.php

Steen, Jennifer A. 2006. Self-Financed Candidates and the "Millionaires' Amendment." In Michael J. Malbin (Ed.), *The Election After Reform: Money, Politics, and the Bipartisan Campaign Reform Act.* Lanham, MD: Rowman & Littlefield, Inc.

Note

1 The Center for Responsive Politics is a nonpartisan, nonprofit organization that runs the website Open Secrets (www.opensecrets.org). This site helps provide transparency in elections by disclosing campaign donor and spending information in an easily searchable format.

HOW DO YOU KNOW UGLY WHEN YOU SEE IT? STANDARDS AND STRATEGIES FOR REDISTRICTING

BY RICHARD N. ENGSTROM
University of Maryland, College Park

LEARNING OBJECTIVES

Students should be able to:

1. Identify and demonstrate understanding of key details in the redistricting process.
2. Describe the connections between various political actors and the redistricting process.
3. Explain the benefits and limitations of the current redistricting process, and will be able to discuss alternatives to the current approach to redistricting.

In the spring of 2010, households and individuals all over the United States filled out a census form identifying how many people lived at their address as of April 1, 2010. Governments, businesses, interest groups, and other institutions use this information for many things: resource allocation, local government planning, and marketing, to name a few. But the main purpose of the census is to determine how the 435 seats in the U.S. House of Representatives will be apportioned among the states.

In the reapportionment process, census data are used to calculate how many House seats each state will have for the next 10 years.[1] The new census numbers mean that many states with large gains in population will gain additional House seats (Texas gained four House seats as a result of the 2010 census), and other states will lose seats (New York and Ohio each lost two seats). Once the reapportionment of seats has been determined, and every state knows how many House seats they have in the new decade, the process of redistricting begins. Representation in the United States is based on a single-member district system; that is, states divide themselves into as many geographic areas as they are assigned seats in the U.S. House, and each area's voters select a representative who will serve their congressional district in Congress. Whenever a state gains or loses seats, or when the population shifts from some areas of a state to other areas, a state's congressional districts have to be redrawn to accommodate the changes. Those new congressional districts are then used in the state's next set of congressional elections.

Contributed by Richard N. Engstrom. Copyright © Kendall Hunt Publishing Company

Redistricting may sound straightforward, but it has become a very controversial and contentious part of elections in the United States. Americans often think that the battle over the congressional district map is both unreasonably contentious and messy; and that the end result is an ugly set of bizarre districts that exist to serve politics in a process that seems to confuse "John Q. Public," the average person. This chapter summarizes the redistricting process, discusses the issues surrounding redistricting, and outlines a few solutions to the problems that are raised in debates on the issue. If geographically odd, difficult to understand congressional districts are a problem, solutions to that problem are available. Americans simply have to accept changes to some assumptions we have about who makes decisions, what rules must be followed, or what representatives in Congress are thought to represent.

WHY REDISTRICT?

Drawing new districts every 10 years lessens the problem of malrepresentation—a situation where some representatives are elected by many people, while other representatives are elected by relatively few people. When people from different congressional districts in a state send representatives to the U.S. House of Representatives, those representatives should, ideally, be serving roughly the same number of people. Balancing the number of people in a state's congressional districts not only means that representatives will have to serve roughly the same number of people, but also that people who cast a vote for a congressional candidate are having close to an equal influence on the outcome of the election. If a state, for example, had one million residents and five congressional districts, the redistricting process would require that the new district boundaries each contain 200,000 people, giving each resident of the state an equal influence in the outcome of the congressional election. Over the next 10 years, the population in the state might increase or decrease, and the population within the state might move around, requiring the redistricting process to readjust the districts during the next redistricting cycle.

If a state does not redistrict periodically, malrepresentation can become more and more of a problem. In fact, the Supreme Court, in *Wesberry v. Sanders* (1964), ruled that U.S. House districts must be drawn in a manner that divides a state's population as equally as possible. Before *Wesberry*, many states did not regularly redraw their congressional district boundaries, causing the populations of congressional districts in many states to vary a great deal. Alabama, for example, did not redistrict between 1900 and 1964, and by that time the populations of districts in rural Alabama were much lower than in a district in cities such as Birmingham or Montgomery. This basically meant that a person in a rural section of Alabama cast a vote that counted more toward the election of a congressional representative than a person casting a vote in an urban area.

The court required states to follow the principle of "one person, one vote." This means that the value of a vote that an individual casts for a representative in Congress should have the same value as a vote cast by other individuals in other parts of the state. Since the "one person, one vote" principle was established by *Wesberry* (and applied to state legislative redistricting in *Reynolds v. Sims* (1964)), states have had to take the data provided by the census every 10 years, and use it not only to learn how many representatives they will elect, but also to balance the populations in the state's newly drawn congressional district plans.[2]

Notice that redistricting only applies to one chamber in Congress: the House of Representatives. The U.S. Constitution does not allocate Senators based on population, but simply provides for each state to have two Senators. Even though states have dramatically different populations (in 2010, California had over 37 million residents, while Wyoming had fewer than 600,000), each state is represented equally in the Senate. In other words, the Senate has a high degree of malrepresentation. This is by design, as the framers of the Constitution crafted the Senate to protect the interests of smaller states from legislation that might benefit states with large numbers of representatives in Congress. The House of Representatives, on the other hand, is designed to represent the residents of the state, and the Supreme Court has decided that redistricting is an important component of that process.

WHO DRAWS THE LINES?

The nature of the congressional district plans that result from the redistricting process has a great deal to do with who draws the congressional district lines. In most states, a redistricting plan is handled the same way any other change is a state's laws is managed: by passing a bill in the legislature. Bills outlining proposed changes are filed by members of the state legislature, those bills are assigned to a committee (often a committee dedicated to handling redistricting issues) that hears testimony about the plans and makes changes before recommending a plan to the legislative chamber as a whole, which then votes to accept or reject the new districting arrangement.

Like bills that move through the U.S. Congress at the national level, bills being considered by state legislatures are usually required to pass in both chambers of the state legislature.[3] Therefore, bills are proposed in both the State House and State Senate. When the process produces different congressional district plans, the bills have to be reconciled in a conference committee. Most states also give governors the power to veto legislation, so a redistricting plan often has to account for the preferences of a state's governor. Legislatures can then either override the veto, or revisit the process by considering an alternative plan.

Since legislators must approve the new congressional district plan, the preferences of legislators matter a great deal. Legislators are members of political parties, for example, and they typically want to make sure that the new district plan does no harm to their party's chances in future elections; and they may even want to make sure that the new plan gives his or her party an advantage. State legislatovrs are also often "progressively ambitious," meaning that they intend to seek higher elected office—often congressional office. Plans that harm a politician's chances of winning a congressional seat in the future (one that, for example, splits an area where he or she could expect a great deal of support such as a hometown or current state legislative district), are plans that legislators, particularly those legislators in leadership positions, might make sure are altered to provide the best chance that he or she can win an election in the congressional district in the future.

WHAT FACTORS DETERMINE THE LINES?

In addition to the many interests who provide input into the process of redrawing the lines, there are several factors that policy makers must and do account for in the redistricting process. The first is the population data provided by the U.S. census. In order to conform to the "one person, one vote" standard, the Supreme Court actually requires that congressional districts in a state have as close to equal populations as possible. This means that district plans should divide the state's population equally among its districts. Deviations should be no more than one person (which may be necessary depending on whether or not a state's population is divisible by the number of districts apportioned to the state).

A second factor is not an official factor that is required to be accounted for when redistricting, but is a common consideration that state legislators take into account: incumbent protection. Since members of Congress are expected to live in their districts, it is possible that a redrawing of the lines could place an incumbent's residence outside of the bulk of his or her district. Legislators often take the location of the homes of incumbents into account when redistricting, though it must be noted that a party that controls the redistricting process in a state can intentionally move district lines so that an incumbent's house is in a district that it would be difficult for that person to win (by placing a Republican's home address in a district with a large Democratic majority, for example). Most often, however, the homes of incumbents of both parties are accommodated early in the process of redistricting.

Another factor that policy makers take into account when redistricting is the location of geographically concentrated interests in the state. Districts are easier to represent when the residents of the district share interests. Urban and rural populations are perhaps the most obvious examples of geographically concentrated groups with particular interests. Urban constituents might be better served by a member of Congress who focuses on transportation and housing issues, while rural constituents would prefer a member who focuses on agriculture and land management policies. Legislators can then draw districts that contain similar populations to ensure that representatives are responsive to those interests.

Race and ethnicity play important roles in redistricting, and populations with shared racial or ethnic characteristics can be thought of as groups with shared political interests. In fact, many important Supreme Court cases related to redistricting concern how the ability of racial and ethnic groups to elect the candidates of their choice has been affected by the redistricting process. The process of drawing lines that advantage one group and disadvantage another is called "gerrymandering," and plans that seem to be drawn with the intent to minimize the chances of racial and ethnic groups to elect candidates to public office are often called "racial gerrymanders," and are illegal under the Voting Rights Act of 1965.[4] Various interest groups, the U.S. Justice Department and the Federal Courts, pay close attention to how racial and ethnic minorities are grouped together or split apart, and courts will require a state to redraw a redistricting plan (or will even impose a court-ordered plan) if a state does not produce an arrangement that protects the representation of racial and ethnic minorities.

Politics is another factor that guides the redistricting process. Just as a redistricting process can produce a racial gerrymander, policy makers can produce a "partisan gerrymander." Just as other groups can be geographically concentrated, supporters of political parties can be found to live in particular parts of a state. Rural areas, urban areas, areas with populations that have similar incomes, suburbs, and other places in a state can be strongholds of supporters for one party or the other. By carefully drawing the lines to create as many districts filled with a majority of voters who can be counted on to support their party, those who control the redistricting process can give their party an advantage when it comes to electing their fellow partisans to Congress.

An important factor in the redistricting process that is not discussed as often as the factors mentioned above is time. The census takes place in the spring of every year with a zero as its last digit (the last census took place in 2010), and the data are not processed and available to states until the spring of the next year. States are required to have their new district plans in place for the congressional elections that take place the year after the data are available, so states really have one legislative session to hammer out the details of the following year's congressional elections. This is a very short period of time to address all of the concerns and legal issues related to a new congressional district plan. Add to this short timeline the fact that many states limit the amount of time their legislatures are in session, and redistricting may have to take place rather quickly, which makes it difficult to produce a plan that satisfies all of the individuals and groups with a stake in future elections.

Given all of these factors that affect congressional district boundaries, it is perhaps not surprising that congressional district lines are often criticized as being "bizarre" or "ugly." Rather than nice, regular shapes, serving as boundaries around cities and recognizable regions, we often find congressional district plans that consist of unrecognizable, jagged shapes. Famously irregular, or ugly, districts are often given nicknames pointing out the district's strange structure. A Z-shaped district that cut through Louisiana was called the "Zorro district," a district in North Carolina was called the "Squashed Bug district," and a Chicago district that connected two parts of the city with a thin connecting band was termed "The Earmuffs." Indeed, congressional districts can wander through a state in ways that do not seem to make geographic sense, and this has generated a great deal of criticism for the redistricting process.

WHAT'S THE PROBLEM?

Are irregularly shaped electoral districts really a problem? They certainly have drawn a great deal of criticism. Critics contend that redistricting provides interested groups the opportunity to give themselves an unfair advantage in elections. The voters, rather than those who have control over the conditions under which the elections take place, should determine the outcomes of elections. Gerrymandering tilts the electoral playing field in favor of the interests of those who get to control the redistricting process. What is supposed to be fundamental to a democracy, the voice of the people expressed at the ballot box, becomes less influential when those results have been subject to a process designed beforehand to produce particular outcomes.

In addition to the manipulation that some say gerrymandering involves, electoral lines that are drawn to produce particular electoral outcomes can also be said to discourage people from supporting or participating in the democratic process. When members of particular groups (say, members of the Democratic party, or rural voters) find themselves in a district that was carefully drawn to facilitate a certain outcome (a district that elects a Republican, or a district that was designed to represent the majority of urban voters included within the district), it is easy to see how one might conclude that the value of voting is diminished.

Even if constituents do not find their role in the democratic process to be compromised by gerrymandering, it is possible that the practice undermines the representative relationship. Ugly districts can be seen to make it difficult for constituents to understand what their member of Congress represents, who is in the district and who is not, and even who a constituent's representative actually is. If the southwest part of a state is represented by a single member of Congress, it is easier for people to determine who their representative is, as well as who else is represented by that person. If three or four different districts wind through the southwest part of the state, residents of that area have to pay closer attention to where the districts begin and end, and which streets, property lines, or other boundaries separate one district from another. It is possible that constituents think that their member of Congress is the same as the member of Congress who represents their friends who live a few streets away, or who is discussed most often on their local news, when in fact they are following the actions of the wrong representative, building support for or opposition to (and perhaps even writing letters to and campaigning on behalf of) a member of Congress who they cannot vote for or against on election day.

SO WHAT IF THE LINES ARE UGLY?

It is possible, even if there is much to dislike about districts that appear jagged, irregular, and "ugly," that there are also benefits to districts that are drawn with priorities other than the creation of relatively smooth, regularly shaped, districts that have outlines that appeal to the eye. Though electoral districts are geographic, they are meant to represent people, not geography. People, it turns out, can share interests without living together in regions with smooth outlines. If a group of significant size with common interests lives across three communities in a state, why shouldn't they be able to constitute a community that selects a member of Congress to express their shared interests? Providing that group with a district may involve drawing district lines that are irregular, as the district extends across the state to gather those community members together for the purposes of representation.

This is particularly true of groups that have historically been discriminated against when trying to participate in democratic elections in the United States. The Voting Rights Act identifies groups that have had trouble participating in American elections in the past, and requires that states take special care to ensure that those groups are not disadvantaged by any implementation of, or change to, election procedures. Redistricting is one change to elections to which government officials charged with conforming to the Voting Rights Act pay close attention, ensuring that districts are not drawn in a way that minimizes or decreases the opportunities for these groups to elect a representative of their choice.

It is also true that other political boundaries have the "ugly" characteristics that receive so much criticism when they appear on congressional districts, but those boundaries do not seem to be of much concern to critics. U.S. States, for example, are often irregular. The panhandles of Oklahoma and Florida extend away from the core of the state in a manner that would qualify as reducing the shape of the state's regularity. The Upper Peninsula of Michigan is another example of a geographic feature of a state that would draw the attention of critics if it were an area that was not connected to the bulk of the rest of its House district. Though it's true that none of these features of state geography can be accused of existing to manipulate the outcomes of contemporary elections, they may have electoral consequences, the arguments about the difficulties for the representation process should hold, and nobody seems too concerned about the varying shapes of what are essentially the electoral districts used for the U. S. Senate.

It is also possible that some districts drawn to be smooth and regularly shaped can serve the function of a gerrymander. A straight line can divide populations in two that could otherwise elect representatives of their choice, as easily as an irregular line can. So, it is not clear that regular shapes, as opposed to irregular ones, better serve the goals of representation. The southwest portion of the state may be easy to identify, but if three separate communities of interests, who could receive representatives separately, are grouped together, then the district serves the same function as the situation where three districts cut through a region with a shared interest: the groups are divided from the rest of their communities, and some other group benefits from their reduced ability to select representatives of their choice.

WHAT CAN BE DONE?

For those concerned about what results from the current congressional redistricting process, the essential question is: Is there a way to draw electoral districts that cannot be manipulated? Or, at least, is there a procedure that can allocate representatives to states, and makes it difficult to manipulate the outcomes of elections? Several possibilities exist, though none seem to satisfy everyone.

One solution would be to draw districts randomly. It would certainly be possible to create a computer program that would, for example, take a map of a state and systematically build a district from a random point while accounting for the district's population as the boundaries expanded. Once the district reached the population size for a district in that state, the computer program would begin the process of creating a second district, adjacent to the first, and continue this procedure until the new districts were completed. Though this procedure would eliminate the manipulation of outcomes that concerns many critics, there are not many fans of the idea of drawing congressional districts with no concern for the shared or different characteristics of the underlying population. And, it should be noted, the process would not ensure that some groups were electorally better or worse off than other groups, rather that the advantages that emerge from the plan would occur randomly. Though this approach aggressively addresses the problem of interested policy makers drawing lines to suit one group and disadvantage another, it does not seek to create districts that achieve any goal other than addressing that problem, and it may be better to settle on a process that is at least somewhat concerned with creating districts that serve constituents well.[5]

A common response to the question of what can be done to address concerns about redistricting is to require policy makers to apply what are often referred to as "traditional districting principles." Traditional districting principles, in short, require that electoral districts be drawn so that they are compact, contiguous, and conform to the boundaries of existing communities. Compact districts do not have irregular boundaries, and the districts edges are relatively close to its center. Contiguity simply means that all parts of the district should be geographically connected. Conforming to the boundaries of existing communities (such as cities and counties) makes sense in general, but there are questions as to what counts as a preexisting community. It is possible that some feel that their community is their neighborhood, while others feel that a metropolitan area is a proper understanding of a community. Even if that is not an issue, it's possible that preexisting communities exist, but that they are not distributed in a geographically compact way. It is also the case that some communities, such as towns and cities, are cut into sections by other things such as county lines, highways, and rivers. So, traditional districting principles seem to make sense in general, but their application is more complicated than the simple statement of principles makes it appear.

A solution that might help minimize the creation of districts with geographically "ugly" characteristics would be to lessen the equal population requirement. Indeed, a lot of the irregularity can be attributed to policy makers trying to achieve their general goals while still meeting the very specific and exact requirement that the district population be within one individual of a predetermined number. This would allow those who draw the lines more freedom to meet their goals, without requiring them to include and exclude particular pieces of geography because of the need to end up with a specific number of residents in the district. Redistricting plans for state legislatures (which also usually have single-member districts) are not held to as stringent a standard as are congressional district plans. Rather than the one-resident rule, state legislative districts can deviate by as much as 5% above or below the average population of state legislative districts overall. This gives policy makers more flexibility in fixing district boundaries.[6]

A solution being tried in several states is the use of redistricting commissions. Redistricting commissions are groups of experts who are given the responsibility of drawing new congressional district plans; taking that responsibility away from state legislators and their presumably more political process. Alaska, Arizona, California, Colorado, Hawaii, Idaho, Iowa, Missouri, Montana, New Jersey, and Washington all have implemented some form of redistricting commission, though who serves on the commission and what its responsibilities vary by state. Redistricting commissions are usually balanced by party, with an equal number of Democrats and Republicans appointed to serve. Sometimes a tie-breaking member is appointed, who is not a member of either party. Some commissions introduce redistricting plans at the beginning of the process, while others only step in if the legislature cannot agree on a new district plan. All commissions rely on the assumption that independent groups may navigate the redistricting process more effectively than is possible in the regular legislative process, and that party balance and/or independence can lead to fairer plans. Interestingly, single-member districts, when used in the legislatures of other countries, are frequently drawn by independent commissions and are not usually redrawn as part of the legislative process.

Finally, it is possible to select representatives without drawing districts. A state could decide to elect its representatives at-large, or could use a number of nongeographic systems of representation in its elections. Party-list systems, for example, would allow political parties to put a slate of candidates forward to be voted on by the entire state. Voters would then vote on the entire slate of candidates, and the parties would win the number of seats in Congress that was closest to the percentage of the vote the party's slate of candidates won in the election. This system, and several others like it, would allow the House of Representatives to allocate representation by population, without having to draw election districts. It does, of course, come with disadvantages, such as the lack of a direct connection between a state's resident and a particular representative. However, nongeographic representation is a feasible solution for the perceived problems associated with redistricting.[7]

CONCLUSION

Redrawing the lines of electoral districts is a normal process in a system that uses single-member districts to select representatives. The fact that the United States gives the task to states, and that the U.S. courts have determined that districts must, at least every 10 years, contain basically equal numbers of constituents, has brought the politics of the redistricting process to the forefront in American politics. Every 10 years, legislators, governors, specially appointed commissions, interest groups, parties, and eventually courts get involved in the process of determining what parts of the states will be sectioned off to elect their own members of the U.S. House of Representatives. The process is often contentious, and the districts often drawn in such a way that many interested parties feel that the process produced advantages to some groups, and disadvantages to others.

Several solutions exist to address the problems that are raised by critics of redistricting plans in particular, and the redistricting process, in general. But, with the exception of several states experimenting with nonpartisan redistricting commissions (or redistricting commissions balanced between the major parties), critics seem unwilling to alter too much about the current system in the interest of eliminating bizarre congressional district boundaries. If the problem is important enough to generate cases in the Supreme Court, op-ed columns in newspapers across the country, and tense debates on the floors of legislatures from coast to coast, why are solutions to the problem so rarely considered?

It is possible that redistricting is not uniquely partisan, that the stakes are not abnormally high, and that the process is not unusually likely to produce outcomes that are unfair or particularly determined by the process put in place legally. Any issue taken up by a state legislature has to go through the legislative process, accommodate the interests of governors, are subject to lobbying by interest groups, and lead to outcomes that advantage some groups and disadvantage others. So, why does redistricting serve as a prime example of legislatures' inability to produce sensible, rather than manipulated, public policy? In the redistricting process, we see political actors battling to control how the redistricting map will be drawn, and the "battle lines" can look messy, ugly, and partisan. The result of that battle is a map of ugly shapes representing outcomes that serve groups. Redistricting is a battle over a map, and the outcomes, as a result can be explicitly . . . mapped. Because the outcome is visible and easy to display, winners and losers can be identified, and the intent of those who draw the lines can be seen in the twists and turns on the map. But, other legislation also allocates resources to some but not others (special programs for particular agricultural products, for example), and gives one party's constituents advantages (urban housing programs that apply to predominantly Democratic districts), and may even help members of a Congress win subsequent elections (a new tax exemption in part of a member's district that adds economic value to a community).

Though there are many examples of legislation that may have broad policy and electoral implications, they cannot be mapped as easily as electoral districts. No graphics can readily show how the benefits extend to some individuals or groups in a state, but twist around other constituents that do not receive them. A change in how sales taxes are collected will have many winners and losers, but it would be hard to put them on a single map that would clearly identify how the change led to the winning and losing. The fact that a single visual image can reveal that a legislative process created a policy that reflects the interests of policy makers is probably a more important component of redistricting's bad reputation than it being any kind of particularly strong example of dirty or unfair politics.

This is not to say that we should ignore the implications of the redistricting process, or that we should give up on creating a system that produces election districts that are drawn in a way that serve the election system better. Redistricting is an excellent example of the importance of rules and institutions for political outcomes. It is also an excellent tool to consider how our system of representation in the United States works, what assumptions we have about who or what a member of Congress represents, and to consider how the legislative process creates policies that cater to the interests of the many actors who are involved in political decision-making at the state and national levels.

Key Terms

Gerrymandering—the process of drawing district lines to give an electoral advantage or disadvantage to certain groups.

Incumbent protection—a factor taken into consideration in redrawing of district lines in which lines are drawn in such a way as to electorally protect the incumbent for that district.

Malrepresentation—the situation where some elected representatives are elected by many people while others are elected by a very few.

Reapportionment—the process of redrawing electoral district lines to reflect population changes.

Redistricting commission—a group of experts given responsibility for redrawing congressional district lines, in an effort to reduce the partisan and political influence on the process.

Single-member district—an electoral district with a single representative in a legislative body such as Congress.

Traditional districting principles—the idea that legislative districts should be compact and contiguous, and conform to the boundaries of existing communities.

Voting Rights Act—a law passed by Congress that requires states to take special care in redistricting such that groups that have been historically hindered in voting are not disadvantaged by any change to the electoral procedures.

Multiple Choice Questions

1. Congressional redistricting is
   a. the process of assigning returning members of Congress to new congressional committees.
   b. the process of allocating committee hearings to different buildings in the District of Columbia.
   c. the process of appointing federal judges to new Federal District Courts.
   d. the process of drawing new election districts for members of the House of Representatives.
   e. A and B.
   Answer: D

2. Congressional redistricting occurs every 10 years because
   a. the average member of Congress serves in office for 10 years.
   b. the census takes place every 10 years.
   c. District Court Judges serve 10-year terms.
   d. Directors of Administrative Agencies serve 10-year terms.
   e. None of the above.
   Answer: B

3. Congressional redistricting is usually handled by
   a. the Joint Congressional Committee on Redistricting.
   b. the Supreme Court.
   c. state legislatures.
   d. political party committees.
   e. a presidential commission.
   Answer: C

4. In a congressional redistricting plan, population deviations between districts in a state can deviate by only
   a. plus or minus 1%.
   b. plus or minus one person.
   c. plus or minus 5%.
   d. plus or minus five votes.
   e. None of the above.
   Answer: B

5. In a state legislative redistricting plan, population deviations between districts in different states can deviate by only
   a. plus or minus 1%.
   b. plus or minus one vote.
   c. plus or minus 5%.
   d. plus or minus five votes.
   e. None of the above.
   Answer: C

Discussion Question

Every 10 years, the U.S. Government conducts a census of the population. The census numbers are used in the redistricting process to draw new congressional districts.

a. Identify two political actors who are formally involved in the congressional redistricting process.
b. Describe two constraints that exist that can prevent a policy maker from drawing the congressional district lines that he or she prefers.
c. Explain how a redistricting commission can address a criticism of the current congressional redistricting process.

References

Amy, Douglas. 2000. *Behind the Ballot Box: A Citizen's Guide to Voting Systems.* New York: Praeger.

Balinski, Michel L. and H. Peyton Young. 2001. *Fair Representation: Meeting the Ideal of One Man, One Vote.* Washington, D.C.: Brookings.

Bullock, Charles S. 2010. *Redistricting: The Most Political Activity in America.* Lanham, MD: Rowman & Littlefield.

Grofman, Bernard and Lisa Handley. 2008. *Redistricting in Comparative Perspective.* Oxford: Oxford University Press.

Mann, Thomas E. and Bruce Cain. 2005. *Party Lines: Competition, Partisanship, and Congressional Redistricting.* Washington, D.C.: Brookings.

Miller, William J. and Jeremy D. Walling, eds.. 2015. *The Political Battle over Congressional Redistricting.* Lanham, MD: Lexington.

Shelby County v. Holder, 570 U.S. 2 (2013).

Notes

1 The mathematics of how a state's population determines how many seats in the House of Representatives it receives was originally based on a formula created by Thomas Jefferson, but by 1900 it was replaced by a formula originally proposed by Daniel Webster. Today, the House uses a formula proposed by Census Bureau statistician Joseph Hill in 1911. See Balinski and Young (2001).

2 Of course, several states do not have to redistrict congressional districts because their population only requires that one House member be elected from the state. Alaska, Delaware, Montana, North Dakota, South Dakota, Vermont, and Wyoming sent only one U.S. Representative to Washington, each of whom was elected to his or her seat in a statewide election.

3 This is only a general description of the redistricting process in the states. Some states have adopted unique rules as part of their redistricting processes, including early involvement by the governor (Maryland) and input from special advisory bodies (Iowa).

4 The standard of district lines being drawn "with the intent" of discriminating on account of race or ethnicity is a relatively new development in legal cases on racial gerrymandering. A previous, easier to meet, standard of showing that a district plan "resulted" in discriminatory outcomes was replaced in the U.S. Supreme Court's ruling in *Shelby v. Holder* (2013).

5 Using "computer-generated" district lines is a popular suggestion for addressing problems associated with gerrymandering. Though districts drawn by computers may seem appealing because they remove people, and their political interests, from the redistricting process, no algorithm has yet been able to attract a consensus as the most appropriate computer process determining the details for how the lines are drawn. This solution, therefore, is probably not practical in the near term.

6 Other democratic countries using single-member district election systems, interestingly, do not have the strict population equality standards required by the "one person, one vote" principle in the United States. And the redistricting process in other countries is typically less contentious in those democracies. For details, see Grofman and Handley (2008).

7 See Amy (2000) for a discussion of the various alternatives to single-member district elections.

THE SPEECH OF A LIFETIME

BY RICHARD W. WATERMAN
University of Kentucky

LEARNING OBJECTIVES

Students should be able to:

1. Explain the role of presidential speeches in the public perception, understanding of national conditions, and for setting the public agenda.
2. Explain the development of presidential speech format and frequency over time.
3. Explain how popular support for the president can affect the success of presidential speeches.

"'True words, words in conformity with law and justice, are images of a good and trustworthy soul,' and would create a still wider community. Western culture, the education of that civilized West, would be based on this faith in the immortal word."

—Boorstin (1992, 226)

INTRODUCTION

"Have you ever considered what speech you would give if you only had a limited amount of time left to live?" Dr. Randy Pausch of Carnegie Mellon University asked this question. He cites the experience of former basketball coach Jimmy Valvano who gave his last speech at the ESPY Awards. Valvano's address was remarkably emotional and it begs the question, if you were speaking to your peers, your friends, your family members, everyone that matters to you, and this was in essence your last speech, what would you say? It also suggests that you better have something really important to say because you are not going to get another chance.

Well, Jimmy Valvano was literally facing death. He had cancer and was not expected to live much longer. Politicians, on the other hand, often face an equivalent state, a critical or crisis point in their careers, what we might call the possibility of imminent political death. For instance, when Barack Obama's pastor, the Reverend Jeremiah Wright, brought the issue of race to the forefront in the 2008 campaign, the then Democratic presidential candidate faced a moment of crisis. How should he handle the thorny issue of race? This was an issue that the candidate had tried to avoid but with the news media now focusing on the Reverend Wright's daily rants, Obama was forced to directly confront the issue. One misstep at this critical point in his political career could have been devastating, especially with his main competitor Hillary Clinton's resurgent momentum on the Democratic nomination campaign trail.

As a result of all these factors, the whole world literally was watching when candidate Obama stepped onto a stage in Philadelphia. If his message struck the wrong political note there would be no turning back. Writing later, on Obama's inauguration day about the Philadelphia speech, Columnist Derrick Jackson of the *Boston Globe* noted, "No matter how memorable the speech Barack Obama gives today for his inauguration as the 44th president of the United States, he might not have become the nation's first African-American president had he fumbled a single word 10 months ago in his speech on race in Philadelphia." Jackson continued,

> "The speech, an unprecedented combination of nuanced history lesson and an urging of everyone to understand each other's feelings, was all but acclaimed by most newspaper editorials. In an interview in Philadelphia three weeks later, Obama told me, 'I think that people always appreciate those moments where a politician's not talking in sound bites but trying to speak honestly about a question. So I don't know what the political effect of it may be . . . But I think what people want is common sense.'"

Jackson referred to the Philadelphia speech as Obama's speech of a lifetime.[1] Meanwhile, however, another reporter, this one for the *Daily News*, wrote that Obama's acceptance speech at the Democratic Convention in Denver was really his speech of a lifetime.[2] Two speeches of a lifetime and he hadn't even been elected president yet. But that's OK, because according to Fred Soto of Whitehouser, Hillary Clinton also gave the speech of her lifetime at the same Democratic convention.[3] And not to be outdone, Presidential candidate John McCain was preparing his speech of a lifetime, which he was planning to present to the Republican Convention a few weeks later. If you happened to miss McCain's speech don't worry, because according to yet another website, his vice presidential running mate Sarah Palin was also giving her speech of a lifetime to the same Republican conclave.[4] This may seem like a lot of speeches for a lifetime, but it doesn't end there. Rush Limbaugh gave the speech of a lifetime when Paul Harvey died.[5] And the then Prime Minister of England, Gordon Brown, delivered his political speech of a lifetime while his Labour Party trailed in the polls by 15 points.[6] I guess that one didn't go too well, because Brown eventually lost. But, if British politics doesn't suit your fancy, well then how about Palestinian politics? Hassan Nasrallah gave his speech of a lifetime when he asserted that the Israeli government was involved in the death of Prime Minister Rafiq Hariri.[7] I could go on. Illinois Governor Rod Blogojevich's speech of a lifetime was not enough to save his political career.[8] Michelle Obama's so-called "Sista from the South Side" of Chicago was her speech of a lifetime.[9] Lest I go on interminably let me just point out that if you Google "speech of a lifetime" you will get about 64,500,000 possible responses. Even if many of these links are redundant, that is an awful lot of speeches of a lifetime.

What accounts for this proclivity to give this all-important speech? There are two possibilities. Politicians talk a lot more often than they used to, so they are bound to give an important speech every now and then. It is like a monkey at a typewriter. Give them enough time and they are bound to type something profound! Or it is possible that the bromide "speech of a lifetime" has, like many other phrases in our popular political vernacular, been repeated so often that it now is essentially meaningless. Any important speech that a politician gives, and many mundane ones as well, suddenly are elevated to the status of the speech of a lifetime, that is, until they give their next speech.

So, if a speech of a lifetime is really just overblown hype why am I writing about it at all? I could be pretentious and call this the chapter of a lifetime. But, the real reason is that for all the hyperbole that is associated with speeches, and all of the droning phrases included in most speeches—phrases that history quickly forgets—speech is important. Why else in 2011 would the Motion Picture Academy give their most prestigious award, the Best Picture Oscar, to a film about a man who stuttered: it is because "The King's Speech" was his speech of a lifetime and, as the British would no doubt say, it bloody well mattered what the King said and how he said it, as the world teetered on the brink of the Second World War. And Obama's speech in Philadelphia mattered, not just to his political career, but as an important statement about race politics in America. Pundits have called Martin Luther King's "I have a dream speech" the speech of his lifetime and it was. So was Abraham Lincoln's brilliant Gettysburg Address, a speech that took just over two minutes to deliver, a lesson in succinct delivery that Bill Clinton might have paid closer attention to, for he was a politician with a propensity to speak *ad nauseam*. In his first appearance at the Democratic National Convention, Clinton was supposed to speak for only 15 minutes but went on for over 30 minutes while the crowd booed.[10]

The long and short of it, then, is that speech does matter, and if the pundits want to trivialize this all by referring to every major and many minor speech as the speech of a lifetime then so be it. President Trump has attempted to employ speeches to stabilize his presidency early in his term, and with some success. But to be successful, an effective speech must be followed with successful action, and it remains to be seen whether Trump can be successful in following up. While politicians speak a great deal today, it was not always so.

POLITICAL SPEECH AT THE FOUNDING

The Founders did not foresee a close political relationship between the public and the presidency, and the early presidents did not see popularity as an important political resource. As a result, public speaking was not a major expectation of the early American presidency. As Stuckey (1991, 14–15) writes,

> "George Washington maintained a low public profile. He spoke only rarely and then only on ceremonial occasions and in muted tones. John Adams . . . was also a reluctant public speaker. The only speeches recorded during his presidency are the annual addresses required by the Constitution . . . Partly this may have been a result of his shyness, and partly a reflection of his lack of oratorical ability. . . . Jefferson is said to have been 'one of the least effective public speakers to hold the nation's highest office' . . . In fact, Jefferson thought so little of his oral persuasive abilities that he discontinued the practice of reading his annual address

to Congress personally and had them delivered by someone else . . . Clearly, Jefferson's prose was better read than heard . . . The same might be said of James Madison, who 'rated rather poorly as a platform orator' . . . All of which reveals an interesting trend among the first presidents—none of them was an able speaker. This is a reflection of the low premium the founders placed on popular rhetoric and the 'popular arts.'"

Few of our early American presidents were gifted public speakers. Washington often spoke in a hushed whisper, difficult to hear even for those who stood nearby. John Adams was pompous and his speaking style reflected his sense of righteousness. Yet it did little to advance his political popularity, nor did he want it to. After his election to the presidency in 1796, John Adams wrote to his daughter, "If the way to do good to my country were to render myself popular, I could easily do it. But extravagant popularity is not the road to public advantage" (McCullough 2001, 471). In fact, few nineteenth-century presidents cultivated a close relationship with the American public. While Washington and Jefferson were popular presidents, in part because of their past achievements (Washington as the hero of the American Revolution and Jefferson as the author of the Declaration of Independence), neither curried public favor during their terms of office and neither had a talent for public speaking. Jefferson spoke in a slight voice with an occasional stutter.

Likewise, while by all accounts James Monroe was popular—he governed during what became known as the "Era of Good Feelings"—his popularity was not advanced by the art of public speaking. Since public speaking was not a treasured political commodity, presidents such as James Polk, who has been rated as a successful president by historians, were generally nominated. Polk had served as Speaker of the House and was a capable if not outstanding speaker, but he was a rather "[d]rab, secretive, hard-working" man who "was not a popular president" though he "left behind him a record of accomplishing every one of his major objectives" (Roseboom and Eckes 1979, 60).

The man usually ranked as our greatest President, Abraham Lincoln, also spoke relatively seldom during his presidency. Vilified by the press and virulently scorned by other politicians and even members of his own Cabinet, literally portrayed in cartoons as a man of great physical awkwardness and limited intelligence, many Americans apparently thought that Lincoln was not qualified to be president. Yet Lincoln is rated by most historian polls as our greatest president and unlike his predecessors he did leave behind a few great presidential speeches, including perhaps the greatest of them all—the Gettysburg Address, which I will examine in more detail later.

Presidential speaking ability did not improve much throughout the nineteenth century. As Stuckey (Ibid., 24) writes, "The speeches of [the post–Civil War presidents] are colorless, terse, and without vision. None of the presidents of this era earned a reputation for their oratorical skills." As can be seen from Table 1, nineteenth-century presidents made little attempt to speak directly to the American public. Only eight out of the twenty-four presidents (33%) averaged more than ten speeches per year. Only one of the first fifteen presidents, Zachary Taylor, averaged more than ten speeches per year. Eight presidents averaged fewer than two speeches per year, seven if we drop William Henry Harrison, who lived only one month after taking office, from the analysis. There was, however, an increase in public speaking from Lincoln's presidency onward, with Hayes delivering 31.5 speeches per year; Benjamin Harrison, 74; and William McKinley, 32.5. Yet while presidents were beginning to speak more often in public by the end of the century, they were not using these speeches for policy purposes. As Tulis (1987, 67) notes, only four of the twenty-four presidents "attempted to defend or attack a specific bill or law" in their speeches (see Table 1).

The presidents of the nineteenth century, then, were neither overly concerned with public approval nor with public speaking. Stuckey (1991, 133) writes, "During the early days of the Republic, the president's role was purely administrative. The president was less of an active participant in public debates, but communicated primarily to other elites." Hence, there was little incentive for presidents to curry favor with the public. Rather than worrying about communicating with the public, these early presidents aimed their written

Table 1. Speeches Delivered by Eighteenth- and Nineteenth-Century Presidents

President	Total Number of Speeches	Average per Year
George Washington	25	3.1
John Adams	6	1.5
Thomas Jefferson	3	0.4
James Madison	0	0.0
James Monroe	42	5.3
John Quincy Adams	5	1.3
Andrew Jackson	9	1.1
Martin Van Buren	27	6.8
William Henry Harrison	0	0.0
James Tyler	5	1.3
James Polk	15	3.8
Zachary Taylor	22	16.9
Millard Fillmore	20	7.4
Franklin Pierce	20	5.0
James Buchanan	9	1.1
Abraham Lincoln	78	19.5
Andrew Johnson	70	17.5
Ulysses S. Grant	25	3.1
Rutherford B. Hayes	126	31.5
James Garfield	10	14.0
Chester A. Arthur	40	12.1
Grover Cleveland*	51	6.4
Benjamin Harrison	296	74.0
William McKinley	130	32.5

*Both nonconsecutive Cleveland administrations are included here.
Source: Tulis (1987, 64).

communication skills upon those they considered most important to their election: the political parties and members of Congress. Consequently, due to "the nature of the presidential selection process," presidents "communicated with those by whom they were held accountable" (Ibid., 133–34).

All of this changed with the elevation of Theodore Roosevelt to the presidency in 1901. Before Roosevelt, presidents occasionally reached out to the public, but usually tentatively. Theodore Roosevelt (though the public affectionately called him Teddy, a nickname he did not fancy) understood that the power of the presidency depended far more on public approval than it did on a strict constructionist reading of the Constitution. As Grossman and Kumar (1981, 3) write, "A president requires popular support to obtain political influence because his office's constitutional and institutional prerogatives are insufficient for him to achieve many important objectives." Roosevelt understood this point better than any president before his time and arguably better than many since then. The connection he created between the presidency and the American public went beyond even Andrew Jackson's idea of the president as "tribune of the people." Under Roosevelt, the public began to emerge as a constituency.

Roosevelt understood that not only did the president derive authority as the "tribune of the people" (because he was the only politician elected by the entire nation), but he also derived authority continuously over time as a result of popular support from the people. Roosevelt recognized the relationship between the presidency and the public, which in turn changed—one might even say revolutionized—the presidency. As Cornwell (1965) notes, from Roosevelt's presidency onward, one of the primary goals of all presidents would be to find new ways to reach out and communicate with the public.

One major innovation was combining rhetoric with policy-related appeals. Tulis (1987, 85) writes, "Teddy Roosevelt doggedly pursued a strategy of appealing to the people regarding specific legislative matters." When Congress appeared ready to oppose the Hepburn Act, which gave the Interstate Commerce Commission authority to fix limits on railroad rates, Roosevelt attempted to "influence public opinion with speeches" (Miller 1992, 457). An expert on presidential speechmaking, Tulis (1987, 19) writes, Roosevelt was the "first president" to reach over the heads of Congress to secure legislation. As a result, "Roosevelt can lay some claim to being the father of the **rhetorical presidency**." Not only did he endorse the Hepburn Act, the "core of his argument was that a change in authorized practices was necessary to fulfill the purposes of the underlying founding theory of governance."

In this regard, Roosevelt had a unique interpretation of the president's constitutional powers. This view, often referred to as the **stewardship theory of presidential power** states that the presidency was is limited to the powers specifically delineated in the Constitution. Rather, Roosevelt (1913, 357) wrote in his autobiography, "My belief was that it was not only his [the president's] right but his duty to do anything that the needs of the Nation demanded unless such action was forbidden by the Constitution or by the laws." By combining that expansive constitutional philosophy with a new constituency, the public, Roosevelt provided a new rationale for presidential power. It is a rationale that has become familiar to his presidential successors, but it was a radical break from the past. It succeeded because the American public embraced Roosevelt as they had few other presidents. Other politicians took notice of Roosevelt's popularity and influence. While many, no doubt, feared him, others saw the political benefits of this new governing approach and sought to emulate it.

Speaking about Roosevelt's revolution in public speaking, historian Tulis (1987) notes,

"If popular rhetoric was proscribed in the nineteenth century because it could manifest demagoguery, impede deliberation, and subvert the routines of republican governance, it could [by the dawn of the twentieth century] be defended by showing itself necessary to contend with these very same political difficulties. Appealing to the founders' general arguments while abandoning some of their concrete practices, Roosevelt's presidency constituted a middle way between the statecraft of the preceding century and the rhetorical presidency that was to follow."

Roosevelt's model for public speaking was followed by most of his successors. For example, Woodrow Wilson not only used presidential rhetoric to promote his policy agenda, as Roosevelt had done, but he also created new venues for presidential communication. One of the most prominent and controversial was his use of the **State of the Union address** as a public forum to promote the president's policies. Importantly, turning the State of the Union address into a major event also became a tool for the president to set the public agenda for the nation in the year to come. On April 6, 1913, the White House announced that the president himself would deliver the State of the Union address in person before Congress and would use the address to talk about tariff reform. Though Washington and Adams had delivered this speech in person, Jefferson (who was shy and had a stutter) had ended the practice. All of Jefferson's successors followed the new precedent and sent a written transmittal to Congress, which was then read to the members by a clerk.

Confronted with Wilson's announcement, more than a dozen senators voted to adjourn the Senate in an attempt to prevent the new president from delivering the speech in person. When that attempt failed, Senator John Sharp Williams of Mississippi, who was a Wilson supporter, hoped the tariff message "would be the only instance of the breach of the perfectly simple, democratic and American custom of messages in writing which Thomas Jefferson instituted" (quoted in Milkis and Nelson 1994, 241). It was not, and for good reason: The reaction to the speech was immediate and positive. "Newspapers across the country carried the speech, whereby millions of Americans also 'heard' what Wilson had said. No previous speech had reached so many people" (Gelderman 1997,7). On a personal level, Wilson and his wife were also secretly pleased that he had thought of presenting the State of the Union address in person, while Theodore Roosevelt had not.

With one speech Wilson mightily contributed to the transformation of presidential rhetoric. Wilson joined rhetoric with policy making, something that Theodore Roosevelt had initiated, but that Wilson and his successors would do with increasing regularity. According to Tulis (1987, 133), "Wilson altered the two principal nineteenth century prescriptions for presidential speech. First, policy rhetoric, which had formerly been written and addressed principally to Congress, would now be spoken and addressed principally to the people at large." Furthermore, from now on, really "important speeches would be delivered orally, where the visible and audible performance would become as important as the prepared text."

While Harding and Coolidge were the first presidents to use the radio, it was Franklin Roosevelt who mastered the new technology. Another Roosevelt, Franklin Roosevelt, could now talk directly to the American people, tell them of his programs and, more importantly, of his vision for the country. In his inaugural and State of the Union addresses, and then through a series of **fireside chats**, Roosevelt communicated directly with the public, talking to them as individuals in their homes and building a personal bond with them. Roosevelt was so effective with the radio that, like Teddy Roosevelt and Woodrow Wilson before him, he contributed in a major way to a re-invention of both presidential practices and public expectations. Public speaking now became a central tool of the presidency. Those who excelled at it would have advantages over those who could not. As Stuckey (1991, 35) states, "Presidents through [Franklin] Roosevelt were able to choose whether they would engage in mass appeals, and such appeals were generally confined to election years. No president after Roosevelt had such a choice: Presidential leadership became, by definition, public leadership." Yet there was a cost to this new public leadership. As Stuckey (Ibid., 36) continues, "while Roosevelt reaped many benefits from this style of leadership, it also put a certain amount of pressure on him to perform up to expectations."

Since this time a number of presidents have become well known for their speaking abilities. John Kennedy was the perfect president for the television age, giving memorable speeches about racial politics and the race to the moon. Ronald Reagan became known as *The Great Communicator*. As a former actor, he brought a heightened sense of elocution to the Theodore Roosevelt's **Bully Pulpit**. And while his speeches were often long and lugubrious, Bill Clinton was a masterful politician who could hold an audience's attention for more than an hour with his State of the Union addresses. Barack Obama was but the latest then in a series of great public speakers to live in the White House. But, while public speaking can prove beneficial to a politician's career, it also has had far less positive consequences. Such is the sad case of a presidential pretender whose speech of a lifetime ended in ignominy.

THE SAD CASE OF ROBERT LA FOLLETTE

The year was 1912. Senator Robert La Follette of Wisconsin strode to the podium with an earnestness that underscored the importance of the present occasion. The venue was the annual Periodical Publishers Association dinner in Philadelphia, an unparalleled opportunity for La Follette to demonstrate his presidential credentials, for the ambitious senator already announced his intention to challenge William Howard Taft for the 1912 Republican nomination. As the head of the progressive wing of the Republican Party, La Follette would have no better opportunity to demonstrate his political bonafides to the powerful Republican establishment. It was his one chance to demonstrate that he was a legitimate force capable of dethroning both an incumbent president and then defeating an apparently resurgent Democratic Party. All eyes were therefore determinedly fixed on La Follette as he mounted the podium.

Just moments before, at the very same venue, the remarkable oratory of the expected Democratic nominee, Governor Woodrow Wilson of New Jersey, made La Follette's task infinitely more difficult. Wilson delivered "a short, urbane, perfectly pitched address, leading journalist Ray Stannard Baker to scribble that Wilson possessed "unlimited reserves of power" (Morris 2010, 165). Still, if the stakes had been raised, a successful speech would only add to La Follette's gravitas, a sure demonstration that he also belonged on the presidential stage. It was indeed La Follette's speech of a lifetime!

Yet from the very beginning La Follette's address fell disastrously short of expectations. In the words of Theodore Roosevelt's pre-eminent biographer, Morris (2010, 165), La Follette:

> . . . behaved like a candidate, not for office, but for a psychological breakdown. He was weak from a recent attack of ptomaine poisoning, starved for sleep, and possessed by the notion that Roosevelt wanted to destroy him. Before standing up he swigged a glassful of whiskey. He began to speak at 10 P.M. and was still at it long after midnight, at times rereading whole chunks of text without noticing, at others rambling so incoherently that Baker left the room in an agony of embarrassment . . . Magazine magnates boggled as his language grew personal, then, when it degenerated into yells of abuse, went to collect their hats and coats. The senator continued to rave, in a virtually empty hall, before slumping forward onto his script.

Even after this disastrous speech La Follette refused to surrender his presidential dream that year, though in reality his presidential ambitions died on the very podium upon which he literally slumped. This one speech encouraged progressives to renew their efforts to woo ex-President Theodore Roosevelt into making one more, grand race for the White House. Had La Follette delivered the great speech that he intended, perhaps history would read differently today. Perhaps he alone would have challenged Taft for the Republican nomination or served as the head of the Progressive ticket that fall. Instead, what La Follette learned the hard way is that not everyone who is called upon to make the speech of a lifetime lives up to that charge. Yet, in a political world dominated by often harsh, and far too frequently poetic rhetorical images, speech has become as important as action. In fact, it is often mistaken for action. For most successful presidents and presidential candidates, then, it is necessary to deliver what partisans of the day, if not history's long-term judgment will celebrate as the *Speech of a Lifetime*.

A SPEECH TO DIE FOR

Theodore Roosevelt took the term "speech of a lifetime" and made an almost literal fact of it when he delivered an address during the closing days of the 1912 presidential campaign. At the time, Roosevelt, a former president, was the nominee of the insurgent Progressive or Bull Moose Party. Roosevelt was politically savvy and he fully understood that he had no chance of winning the upcoming election, but he marked October 14th on his calendar for a major address, an opportunity to restate his commitment to progressive principles and politics. His candidacy might be over, but not his movement. It would live on. But, as the date for his speech neared, Roosevelt succumbed to severe laryngitis. He was capable only of speaking in a hoarse voice, at times no more than a peep or a mere whisper, hardly the forceful voice that Americans had come to know and expect from the man that historians credit with creating the "Bully Pulpit."

So, on the morning of October 14th Roosevelt spoke for but four brief minutes to a gathering in Chicago. Yet even these few words were "enough to fray his voice"

(Morris 2010, 242). Still, determined to give his major address, like a high-powered steam engine or a raging bull moose, Roosevelt continued on to Milwaukee, intent on fulfilling his obligation. As he did so, his advisers wondered if he even would be able to speak at all. All looked hopeless.

Upon his arrival in Milwaukee the ex-president was escorted to a car that was to take him to the arena where a boisterous crowd already was gathered to hear what they knew would be a historical event. What they did not know was how historical it actually would be. As the Colonel, as Roosevelt like to be called, sat in "his customary right-hand seat [in the car] while his escorts fanned out to take theirs," one of Roosevelt's entourage, Elbert Martin, saw "the gleam of a revolver that was no more than seven feet away." He leaped through the air, but as he did the assassin—John Schrank—fired a single shot. The bullet tore through Roosevelt's chest, tearing through sinew and even a copy of the speech, which the ex-president kept in his coat pocket. "He pinked me," Roosevelt told one of his compatriots. Schrank was quickly subdued and Roosevelt called out, "Don't hurt him. Bring him here. I want to see him." When Schrank was brought before him Roosevelt asked, "What did you do it for?" (Morris 2010, 244). Schrank's answer did not satisfy Roosevelt, but later, on his way to prison, after his conviction for attempted assassination, a sheriff asked Schrank if he enjoyed hunting. "Only bull moose," he is alleged to have answered (see Morris 2010).

With a gunshot wound to the chest, Roosevelt remained unnaturally calm, though it was quickly determined that he has lost and was still losing a great deal of blood. When the ex-president's driver was told to go immediately to Milwaukee's Emergency Hospital, Roosevelt tersely demanded that he be taken to the auditorium for his pre-arranged speech. His advisers were dumbfounded, but Roosevelt was so adamant and had such a powerful personality that they meekly acquiesced. Ignoring his doctor's advice, Roosevelt placed a clean handkerchief over the wound and strode onto the stage. As he did the audience was informed that the ex-president had been the subject of an assassination attempt. Angrily, someone from the crowd yelled out, "Fake! Fake." In response, Roosevelt "unbuttoned his vest and exposed his shirtfront. The spreading bloodstain, larger than a man's hand, caused screams of horror." Meanwhile macabre voices called out, 'Turn this way—turn this way," so that the many gawkers in the crowd could get a better look at the president's wound (Morris 2010, 245).

Remarkably, the president removed his speech from his coat pocket intent on continuing with it. Only then did he notice that the bullet had cut through his speech, as well as his chest. With a hollow, husky voice Roosevelt "proceeded to half-read, half-improvise a rambling rationale of his trust-control and labor policies. . . ." As he spoke, he occasionally teetered. When an aide, afraid that Roosevelt was dying, tried to stop the speech, Roosevelt shot "such a steel-gray stare that the young man retreated, helpless" (Ibid.).

His speech continued until Roosevelt finally asked how long he had been speaking. When told that it had been fully 45 minutes, he responded, "I'll speak for a quarter of an hour more." He then proceeded to speak for more than an additional half hour. "Although his voice remained forceful, he was clearly losing strength as well as blood. Aides stationed themselves below the footlights to catch him in case he fell forward, while others sitting onstage prepared to do the same behind." On and on he spoke, past the 80-minute mark, his face now devoid of all color. As he finally finished his oration he turned to his doctor and said, "Now I am ready to go with you and do what you want" (Morris 2010, 246). The surreal nature of the scene continued, however. Members of the audience now crowded forward, some slapping his back, while others tried to shake his hand as if they were intent on being the last person to touch the great man's hand (Ibid., 246–7).

Why had Roosevelt refused medical attention? Why had he gone on with a speech for almost an hour and a half as he slowly bled nearly to death, the bullet still lodged precariously in his body? One of Roosevelt's biographers, Brand (1998) surmises that Roosevelt was a romantic in the Elizabethan sense of the word. He knew that he was going to lose the election to Woodrow Wilson, a defeat that likely would spell the end of his political career. What grander way could the great man leave the political stage than by dying while delivering the most important address of his presidential campaign? Brand's theory is given credence by Roosevelt's later desire to be sent to France with a cavalry unit in 1917, there (at nearly 60 years of age), to do glorious battle against the German war machine, and if necessary to die heroically on the field of battle. Roosevelt knew that he would die someday, and probably soon, so why not today, and why not while literally giving the speech of his lifetime?

THE GETTYSBURG ADDRESS

Not all speeches are as dramatic as Roosevelt's address, but other speeches have come at critical moments in our nation's history. None came at a more difficult time than Abraham Lincoln's Gettysburg Address. Delivered on November 19, 1863, it was not even supposed to be the main address: Edward Everett delivered that speech.

Lincoln's address was a bit of an afterthought, as in someone thought, shouldn't we invite the president to this event commemorating the many soldiers who died at Gettysburg, after all he is the Commander in Chief. So, more out a sense of duty than anything else Lincoln was invited and like everyone else he dutifully sat for more than two hours while Everett droned on and on about the import of this great battle and of the ongoing Civil War. And then Lincoln strode to the podium, his long gangly body, his oversized stove top hat, with his handwritten speech in his pocket. If Everett had spoken for two hours surely the president could be counted on to speak for at least that long. The cameraman thought so. He slowly and methodically set up his camera, sure that he would have plenty of time to get a good shot of the president. Instead, the only image of Lincoln that we have is of the great president returning to his seat, for the entire Gettysburg address is so concise that I can cite it in full here:

> Four score and seven years ago our fathers brought forth on this continent, a new nation, conceived in Liberty, and dedicated to the proposition that all men are created equal.
>
> Now we are engaged in a great civil war, testing whether that nation, or any nation so conceived and so dedicated, can long endure. We are met on a great battle-field of that war. We have come to dedicate a portion of that field, as a final resting place for those who here gave their lives that that nation might live. It is altogether fitting and proper that we should do this.

But, in a larger sense, we can not dedicate . . . we can not consecrate. . . . we can not hallow . . . this ground. The brave men, living and dead, who struggled here, have consecrated it, far above our poor power to add or detract. The world will little note, nor long remember what we say here, but it can never forget what they did here. It is for us the living, rather, to be dedicated here to the unfinished work which they who fought here have thus far so nobly advanced. It is rather for us to be here dedicated to the great task remaining before us . . . that from these honored dead we take increased devotion to that cause for which they gave the last full measure of devotion . . . that we here highly resolve that these dead shall not have died in vain . . . that this nation, under God, shall have a new birth of freedom . . . and that government of the people, by the people, for the people, shall not perish from the earth.

Well the audience was startled, not by the content of the speech, but by its brevity. Lincoln sadly returned to his seat convinced that his speech had been a dismal failure. Everett consoled the president, noting that the president had gotten to the point of the matter more incisively in two minutes, than Everett had in two hours, and for once Everett was correct.[11] Lincoln not only commemorated the dead he also gave meaning to the entire Civil War. In these few words, Lincoln said these people did not die in vain. They died to create "a new birth of freedom." In just a few words, scribbled on a piece of paper that Lincoln kept in his pocket, with his own handwritten corrections still on it, Lincoln gave meaning to a dreadful war that had exhausted a nation and destroyed an entire generation of young men. It was the worst cataclysm in American history and in a few words Lincoln had made it all make sense. The nation would be better because these men had died on this battlefield. By giving purpose to the war, Lincoln also gave purpose to the nation. Why had America been created in the first place? Was it not the so-called great experiment in democracy? How could such an experiment end so ignominiously, with brother literally pitted against brother on blood stained fields in places that people had never heard of, such as Gettysburg? Didn't the very fact that America was at war with itself demonstrate to the entire world that the great experiment had been a complete, dismal failure? That is what many people thought. But now, they could consider Lincoln's few words. "A new birth of freedom!" It meant an end to slavery. It meant a renewal of the democratic ideal! It meant, that despite all the bloodshed, all the waste of precious human life, that it had all meant something. Despite the horror, America would be a better country. Lincoln's optimism redefined the war and helped to elevate him to the forefront of every subsequent historian poll on the subject of presidential greatness. Words did matter! This was indeed the speech of a lifetime, without all the hyperbole.

FEAR ITSELF

Words also mattered when Theodore Roosevelt's cousin (FDR) took the center stage 70 years after Lincoln delivered his Gettysburg Address. Again, the very future of the nation was at risk. Would America survive the worst economic depression in its history? Other nations around the globe were teetering. Hitler had used the occasion to rise to power in Germany and in America there were those who advocated dictatorship over democracy (Alter 2007).

In a strange movie that was released toward the end of the presidency of Herbert Hoover, called "Gabriel Over the White House," a weak and ineffectual president plays with a child as the world falls apart. This president is oblivious to the nation's collective pain. When he is suddenly struck ill he is possessed by the angel Gabriel, who transforms him into the kind of president the people really want. What does this ideal president do? He declares martial law, which induces the legislative branch to give him broad, one might say dictatorial emergency power. He then forces the nations of the world to come together, under the threat of mutual annihilation, and in the end, saves the world. Happy ending? Well, yes, if you don't mind searching for a benign dictator who will set things right, then die and go to heaven. As far as I can tell there is a short supply of such dictators.

What America got instead was a man that Herbert Hoover disparaged as being just half a man (Alter 2007). Franklin Delano Roosevelt, the cousin of Teddy Roosevelt, could not walk. Polio had stripped him of this simple power. To do that simple task, he had to strap on heavy braces and then lean on someone, often his son, just to appear to walk a few tenuous steps to a podium. Of course, he could have rode to the podium in a wheelchair, but at that time in American history, being physically challenged meant that you were no longer fit for society, never mind political office. People hid relatives with physical impairments. There was no such thing as mainstreaming the differently abled. If you could not walk, then to many people you were not capable of doing any job worth doing, especially the presidency.

This prejudice may be hard for us to comprehend. But Roosevelt, like his cousin, was not about to surrender to such prejudices. After all, cousin Teddy had been diagnosed with asthma as a child, an illness that was so devastating that doctors told his father there was nothing they could do for the poor boy. He would live out his life as an invalid. But, Teddy did no such thinking and neither would cousin Franklin.

Roosevelt found hot springs in Warm Springs, Georgia and there opened the world's first institution providing care for people with polio. There he worked directly with the young and old alike, often raising funds so that even the poorest could enjoy Warm Spring's healing waters. In the process, Franklin Roosevelt, a spoiled, aristocratic glad-hander, a man Oliver Wendell Holmes would famously declare had "a first class temperament" even though he also had a second class intellect, became, in the words of his admirers, Dr. Roosevelt, an unofficial title but one that the future president loved. It was during this time that Roosevelt learned not to walk, for he would never regain that ability, but to understand what it was like to be disadvantaged. For a man who was born with a silver spoon in his mouth, this was quite a revelation.

And this brings us to Inauguration Day, March 4, 1933. One of the great ironies of American history is that a man who could not walk, a cripple in the cruel parlance of the time, helped a nation to walk. For if you think about it, what was America in 1933? The Depression had left the United States weak, like an invalid, unable to walk, teetering on the brink of a revolution! The economy was failing and there was a question as to whether this revolution marks the end of capitalism? Would America follow Russia's path toward communism? Or would it move to the right, behind a dictator like Hitler? Hard as it is to imagine, these were very real possibilities in March 1933 when Franklin Roosevelt, with braces on his legs took the oath of office and delivered the most important speech in American history since Lincoln's Gettysburg address.

Do words matter? You bet! If Franklin Roosevelt miscalculated, like La Follette, the nation might have been ruined. Imagine what it would have been like if the newly elected president had delivered a meandering address, insulted his audience, and then slumped insensibly onto the podium? The American people would have been left without faith in their leader and lacking a sense of national direction. We would now be living in an entirely different world! But, luckily for us FDR was no La Follette.

Instead, like Lincoln, in a few carefully chosen words, Franklin Roosevelt gave hope to a nation. Imagine then how Americans felt as they leaned anxiously forward toward their radios and heard the new president declare these first words:

> I am certain that my fellow Americans expect that on my induction into the Presidency I will address them with a candor and a decision which the present situation of our Nation impels. This is preeminently the time to speak the truth, the whole truth, frankly and boldly. Nor need we shrink from honestly facing conditions in our country today. This great Nation will endure as it has endured, will revive and will prosper. So, first of all, let me assert my firm belief that the only thing we have to fear is fear itself—nameless, unreasoning, unjustified terror which paralyzes needed efforts to convert retreat into advance. In every dark hour of our national life a leadership of frankness and vigor has met with that understanding and support of the people themselves which is essential to victory. I am convinced that you will again give that support to leadership in these critical days.

He ended his speech with the following refrain:

> We do not distrust the future of essential democracy. The people of the United States have not failed. In their need they have registered a mandate that they want direct, vigorous action. They have asked for discipline and direction under leadership. They have made me the present instrument of their wishes. In the spirit of the gift I take it . . .

It was a remarkable speech and people responded to it literally overnight. The White House was inundated with letters from average Americans thanking the president and asking him for their help. It was a moment that transformed not only the nation, but also the presidency itself. From this moment on Americans would look first to the presidents for leadership and presidents speeches will forever been seen as the mechanism for their **agenda setting** efforts. It was all due to Franklin Roosevelt's carefully chosen and masterfully delivered inaugural address.

CONCLUSIONS

On November 9, 2010 Paul Waldman wrote,[12]

> " . . . I keep returning to Mario Cuomo's famous dictum that you campaign in poetry but govern in prose. The poetry of campaigning is lofty, gauzy, full of

possibility, a world where problems are solved just because we want them to be and opposition melts away before us. The prose of governing is messy and maddening, full of compromises and half-victories that leave a sour taste in one's mouth."

This may be true, but governing requires poetry as well as prose. Lincoln's words are expertly expressed. He chose just the right words to express just the right sentiment. Change the speech and you may very well change the nation's entire history. The same is true of Franklin Roosevelt. His speech provided needed succor for a starving nation, gave hope to the hopeless, ended all talk of the need for dictatorship, and though the depression would not end until nearly a decade later, restored our nation's faith in ourselves and our democracy.

In sum, to put it as bluntly as possible, words matter! We may trivialize them with phrases like "the speech of a lifetime," but the reality is that without two very prominent speeches America would be a very different nation today. It may be difficult in a world so defined by social media for a president to replicate the impact that Abraham Lincoln and Franklin Roosevelt had. President Trump, for example, has found communicating through Twitter an effective communication tool. But, it's hard to imagine that tweets will be able to inspire a nation in the manner that great oratory did in the past. Replicating the lessons of great leaders is a major challenge in the modern era.

Key Terms

Agenda Setting—the ability of the president to determine or influence the major issues to be addressed by government.

Bully pulpit—the idea that the presidency provides a unique opportunity for expressing and promoting the president's agenda due to the access the office provides to the American people.

Fireside chats—a series of radio addresses given by President Roosevelt throughout the 1930s, which are credited with creating the perceived personal connection between the president and the American people.

Rhetorical Presidency—the idea that direct popular appeal to the American public is an important tool regularly used by the president.

State of the Union address—constitutionally mandated communication by the president to Congress in which the president lays out his political agenda.

Stewardship theory of presidential power—the idea that the presidency is not limited to powers and duties listed in the Constitution but rather can do anything not expressly forbidden in the Constitution.

Multiple Choice Questions

1. The rhetorical presidency is the idea that:
   a. The words and speeches of the president are irrelevant.
   b. The ability of the president to appeal directly to the American public in his or her speeches is a source of influence or power.
   c. The words or rhetoric of the president must align with his or her actions to be believable.
   d. Presidential speeches are key indicators of the president's agenda.
   e. The speeches given by presidents shape the outcome of political events.

   Answer: B

2. Presidential speeches have changed over time by:
   a. presidents giving the speeches in person as opposed to having them given by someone else.
   b. president using developing technology like radio to reach out to larger audiences
   c. presidents beginning to give more speeches directly to the public.
   d. president's using the State of the Union address as an opportunity to advance their agenda.
   e. All of the above.

   Answer: E

3. The idea that the powers of the presidency include all things not expressing forbidden in the Constitution is known as:
   a. The constitutional theory of the presidential power.
   b. The expansive theory of presidential power.
   c. The stewardship theory of presidential power.
   d. The imperial presidency.
   e. All of the above.

   Answer: C

4. The idea that the presidency provides a unique opportunity for promoting a political agenda because it gives access to the American public is known as:
   a. The public presidency.
   b. The power of presidential speech.
   c. The bully pulpit.
   d. The Roosevelt influence.
   e. The power of the public.

   Answer: C

5. Roosevelt's use of fireside chats was an important development in presidential speeches because:
   a. they changed the way people viewed the president.
   b. he used them as opportunities to share his vision for the country.
   c. their success solidified the importance of public speaking as tool of the presidency.
   d. In them the president spoke to the public directly as individuals in a very personal way.
   e. All of the above.

Answer: E

Discussion Question

1. Explain the importance of presidential speeches as a leadership tool. How has this tool developed over time?

References

Alter, Jonathan. 2007. *The Defining Moment: FDR's Hundred Days and the Triumph of Hope.* New York: Simon and Schuster.

Boorstin, Daniel J. 1992. *The Creators: A History of Heroes of the Imagination.* New York: Random House.

Brand, H. W. 1998. *TR: The Last Romantic.* New York: Basic Books.

Cornwell, Elmer E. 1965. *Presidential Leadership of Public Opinion.* Bloomington, IN: Indiana University Press.

Gelderman, Carol. 1997. *All the President's Words: The Bully Pulpit and the Creation of the Virtual Presidency.* New York: Walker and Company.

Grossman, Michael Baruch, and Martha Joynt Kumar. 1981. *Portraying the President: The White House and the News Media.* Baltimore: John Hopkins University Press.

McCullough, David. 2001. *John Adams.* New York: Simon and Schuster.

Milkis, Stanley M., and Michael Nelson. 1994. *The American Presidency: Origins and Development.* Washington, D.C.: Congressional Quarterly Press.

Miller, Nathan. 1992. *Theodore Roosevelt: A Life.* New York: William Morrow and Company.

Morris, Edmund. 2010. *Colonel Roosevelt.* New York: Random House.

Roosevelt, Theodore. 1913. *An Autobiography.* New York: Scribners.

Roseboom, Eugene H., and Alfred E. Eckes, Jr. 1979. *A History of Presidential Elections: From George Washington to Jimmy Carter.* New York: Collier Books.

Stuckey, Mary E. 1991. *The President as Interpreter-in-Chief.* Chatham, NJ: Chatham House.

Tulis, Jeffrey K. 1987. *The Rhetorical Presidency.* Princeton: Princeton University Press.

Notes

1 http://groups.yahoo.com/group/NatNews/message/48390.

2 http://articles.nydailynews.com/2008-08-28/news/17903038_1_senator-obama-john-mccain-speech.

3 http://whitehouser.com/elections/hillary-clinton-gives-speech-of-a-lifetime/.

4 http://www.freerepublic.com/focus/f-news/2074286/posts.

5 http://www.democraticunderground.com/discuss/duboard.php?az=view_all&address=389x5160778.

6 http://www.forexlive.com/53746/all/uk-prime-minister-gordon-browns-speech-of-a-lifetime.

7 http://uprootedpalestinians.blogspot.com/2010/08/hezbollah-to-implicate-israel-in-hariri.html.

8 http://www.lincolncourier.com/archive/x514547706/Speech-of-a-lifetime-not-enough-to-save-Blagojevich.

9 http://traceyricksfoster.wordpress.com/2008/08/26/michelle-obama-sista-from-the-south-side-gives-speech-of-a-lifetime-at-democratic-convention/.

10 http://www.vox.com/2016/7/26/12285312/bill-clinton-dnc-1988-speaker-late-night

11 The Ken Burn's PBS Civil War program provides an outstanding resource on the Gettysburg Address and is highly recommended as a companion to this essay.

12 http://www.prospect.org/cs/articles?article=campaign_in_poetry_govern_in_prose.

DON'T KNOW MUCH ABOUT THE JUDICIARY

BY JOSEPH STEWART, JR.

LEARNING OBJECTIVES

Students should be able to:

1. Understand how low levels of knowledge about the judiciary are connected to and how the media covers the judiciary.
2. Identify the means by which the media affects perceptions of the judiciary.
3. Discuss the implications of how media coverage of the judiciary has an impact on U.S. Government and politics.

In 1960, the classic soul artist Sam Cooke released a recording of a song he had co-authored with Herb Alpert and Lou Adler, "What a Wonderful World." The lyrics repeated a long list of subjects about which the singer claimed to not "know much"—for example, history, biology, science, French. Omitted from the list was something that could be included by most residents of the United States—the judiciary. For better or worse, usually worse, what most people know about the judicial system is shaped by media coverage (Yanus, 2009), and that coverage is often limited and misleading. Thus, the fact that you might truthfully sing: "don't know much about the judiciary" lumps you in with a large part of the United States' population. This brief chapter seeks to describe and explain some of the limitations of both news and popular media coverage of the judicial system and the implications of these limitations.

THE MEDIA AND THE COURTS

"The media play an important role in what we know about the courts and how we view the actions of judges, juries, lawyers, and litigants" and " . . . press coverage of what courts do, and how they do it, is limited" (Neubauer and Meinhold, 2017, 5, 204). Thus, it is understandable that the average person has, at best, a distorted view.

Media coverage of the judiciary is affected by all the influences on media, both good and bad. As a market driven industry, the media have to sell advertising. Thus, media outlets of all sorts seek to present stories that are "accessible, intriguing, even entertaining"

Contributed by Joseph Stewart Jr. Copyright © Kendall Hunt Publishing Company.

(Haltom and McCann, 2004, 19). What attracts readers or viewers takes precedence over what is representative of the legal system. Drama supersedes the typical.

Criminal law appears as a topic more frequently in media coverage than does **civil law**, yet a majority of trial court caseloads involve litigation between private parties or litigation between private parties and a government acting in a nonprosecutorial role. The focus on criminal law is a natural follow-up to a focus on crime in the news. The adage "If it bleeds, it leads" is not untrue. Violent or particularly gruesome crimes capture more media space than their incidence would suggest is warranted. Thus, even though the crime rate began declining in the 1990s, "[n]ewspapers headline major drug busts. Local television news programs show graphic footage of the latest murder scene" (Neubauer and Meinhold, 2017, 214–215).

The degree of violence can be replaced or supplemented as an attractor by the personalities involved. A high-profile civil case divorce, such as the recent divorce of Brad Pitt from Angelina Jolie, can bring excessive media attention. If the activity involves a public official or well-known public figures, so much the better—it will get coverage. Or, if the crime involves wrongdoing by government officials, it is attention worthy.

This is not to argue that all such media coverage is devoid of public policy content. Controversial issues or crimes that involve victims who can be portrayed sympathetically or situations which raise salient policy questions will receive coverage. For example, in whatever venue, a story that touches on the issue of abortion will receive media attention. Likewise, allegations of domestic violence or child sexual abuse will invariably attract media attention. Moreover, free speech cases by definition fit the criteria for media coverage because they involve unpopular speech. Part of free speech is **"symbolic speech,"** and that issue often attracts a great deal of media attention, such as when Gregory Johnson burned an American Flag in protest during the 1984 Republican Convention (*Texas v. Johnson*, 1989). If the speech at issue is not unpopular, the case does not arise so we only see coverage of issues of free speech which are controversial.

Media coverage also over-represents trials. Whether it is popular TV programs or news coverage, most presentations of the legal system focus on trials. Again, this is understandable. A trial gives a media representative an event on which to focus and report. Furthermore, the adversarial system of justice used in the United States is inherently confrontational and dramatic. In a criminal case, it is easy to cast the characters as "good" versus "evil." The reality is, however, both as a proportion of total cases and in terms of the absolute number of cases, trials have been declining (Galanter and Frozena, 2014). Criminal cases are typically resolved by **plea-bargains** in which the defendant pleads guilty to a charge in exchange for a reduced sentence, the dropping of other charges, or some other consideration. Civil cases, likewise, are generally settled by the disputants, often just before a trial is scheduled to begin. The "death of the American trial" (Burns, 2009) does not necessarily mean that the threat of a trial does not have an influence on the judicial process. It does, however, mean that a media focus on these events distorts how the judicial system operates.

Parallel to the overrepresentation of trials by the media is the overrepresentation of juries. By definition, the proportion and number of cases resolved by trial has been declining, thus the resolution of cases by juries would almost necessarily be diminished. This is not a new phenomenon. Almost a century ago a law review article announced "The Vanishing Jury" (Moley, 1928). Again, when there are trials, charging shocking crimes or if the defendant is notable, it is likely to be a jury trial, so the public perception of their frequency is likely to be inflated. Most cases are simply not resolved by using juries. (It is worth noting that 90% of all jury trials of the world occur in the United States [Neubauer and Meinhold, 2017, 368]).

Trials and juries are the place where fact and fiction may be blended. Themes such as the "sinful rich," "the abuse of trust or power," or "evil strangers" can be found in newspaper headlines or TV stories and lend themselves to fictionalization or "docudramas." These "media trials" may, but should not, be taken as accurate portrayals of typical judicial processes. In television stories, the drama of a trial makes for far better drama that a plea bargain.

The depiction and communication about the judicial process by the media and its potential and pitfalls are issues of long concern. Those who amended the Constitution soon after its adoption specifically included freedom of the press in the First Amendment and the right to a speedy and public trial before an impartial jury in the Sixth Amendment. These two amendments were added to the Constitution as a means of letting the public monitor their government and political leaders. If trials were to be speedy and public, there was less chance that government could use the legal system to persecute their opponents or treat some people unequally/unfairly. If the media was to be free and unregulated, they would have the ability to report on actions of government so that the public could evaluate said actions and hold their government accountable. While the forms of the media have changed since the days of our framers, the underlying issues are the same. Whether it be print media, TV, the Internet, or social media, the possibility of representing and the danger of misrepresenting the judicial process have only grown more complicated.

As coverage of trials has long been a focus on the media, attempts to block media access to trial proceedings are invariably met with a united media challenge. The Supreme Court long has understood that media coverage can affect the outcome of a case, as in the famous example of Dr. Sam Sheppard in a 1954 case where Dr. Sheppard was accused of bludgeoning his wife to death. The court observed that: "The fact is that bedlam reigned at the courthouse during the trial and newsmen took over practically the entire courtroom, hounding most of the participants in the trial, especially Sheppard (*Sheppard v. Maxwell*, 1966)." Based upon that observation, the court ruled that Sheppard had not received a fair trial under the due process clause of the Fourteenth Amendment. But to deny the media the right to cover would compromise the intent of a "public trial." Therefore, as with other issues relating to trial, there is a balancing act between shining light on a trial and making the trial into a media circus.

While the courts have been clear that trials should be open to public scrutiny, such access can also be problematic. One only has to think of the publicity surrounding cases like the O.J. Simpson or the Casey Anthony murder cases to recognize that too much media access can hinder the process. Both cases, captivated the American public, were labeled as the "trail of the century" as they played out, and were given untold amounts of coverage. But perhaps more importantly, the ability of the defendant to receive a fair trial and the eventual verdict handed down was called into question due to the publicity surrounding the case. Therefore, the challenge for our legal system is to balance the need for cases to be conducted in an open and public sphere while simultaneously protecting the rights of the accused and the integrity of the process in what can be called the "media circus."

U.S. Supreme Court decisions also receive a great deal of media coverage (Slotnick and Segal, 1998) particularly if they are not unanimous. An interesting fact is that approximately 8,000 cases are appealed to the Supreme Court every year and fewer than 80 are actually heard. This points to the fact that the overwhelming majority of cases appealed to the Supreme Court involve "settled law" where the judges, liberal and conservative alike, agree on what the law is. On many other issues, both liberals and conservatives agree on the merits of a case—a majority of the 80 cases the court hears each year are unanimous decisions. That isn't to say there isn't disagreement between judges, but it does suggest that media emphasis on disagreement vastly overstates conflict on the court and vastly understates agreement.

The opening on the Supreme Court caused by the death of Antonin Scalia in 2016 became a huge political issue as President Obama's nomination of Merrick Garland was not acted on by the Senate and then after the election, the nomination of Neil Gorsuch by President Donald Trump was vilified by Democrats in the Senate. The Republican majority had to abolish the right to use a filibuster to block a judicial appointment in order for Gorsuch's confirmation to be accomplished. Clearly, appointments to the court are important and the focus of much political attention and there are significant landmark cases each year. But in most cases, ideology is less important than the clear meaning of the Constitution and law passed in pursuance thereof.

When a verdict is rendered, either by judicial decision, a jury, or a judicial endorsement of a plea bargain (in a criminal case) or by a negotiated settlement (in a civil case), the media presentation of this judicial output fits within our framework often failing to contribute to public knowledge about the judiciary. Both judicial and jury deliberations are largely conducted in private and therefore cannot be effectively communicated to the public. Juries sometimes reach decisions that appear to be at odds with the evidence as known by the public (jury nullification). While occasionally, individual jurors may comment on influences that affected their decision making or the dynamics within the jury room but this is fairly rare. Moreover, judges are loathe to reveal their deliberations. Judges generally see it as beyond their role to educate citizens about the judiciary, and perhaps even improper. As well summarized by long-time reporter of the Supreme Court, Linda Greenhouse (1996, 1537), "[J]udges for the most part, speak only through their opinions, which are difficult for the ordinary citizen to obtain and understand."

Thus, how do the media portray the outputs of the judicial system? In criminal cases, outputs that are unexpected or that deviate from normal patterns get news coverage but do little to educate anyone about how the judicial process operates nor do they explain why such an output might come about. Thus, a judge's order to a young man convicted of producing obscene comic books to "stop drawing" such books gets coverage in the *St. Petersburg (FL) Times*. An order in juvenile court strapping miscreant kids to their parents or an order of chemical castration to a convicted sex offender will merit media coverage. Any kind of silly action by a defendant or a plaintiff in a civil case will likewise merit coverage.

On the civil side of the judiciary, there is perhaps no better example of "distorting the law" than the coverage of civil judgments. Media coverage creates the impression that there are an almost never ending number of civil cases being filed. At the extreme, this distortion supports the "common knowledge" that there is a "litigation explosion" that has all sorts of negative effects for the society and economy. Haltom and McCann (2004) have undertaken extensive analysis, concluding that the media routinely misrepresent the law and have contributed to popular "knowledge" about law. For example, over half of the nation's population incorrectly believes that litigation rates are rising faster than the population. Relatedly, Baker (2005) empirically shows that medical malpractice insurance rates, one of the common *bêtes noires* of the litigation explosion and a common rationale for tort reform, are unrelated to the incidence of medical malpractice but strongly related to the performance of the stock market. In other words, the common media notion that high jury awards in medical malpractice cases causes insurance rates to be unreasonably high, but the reality is that insurance rates are set by what the market rate will bear.

SO WHAT?

None of the preceding text is meant to suggest that the events the media choose to cover are not worth covering. Given the dramatic shrinkage in print media markets and consolidation in various other media, one cannot criticize reporters for responding to economic forces. They have to cover that which sells. One can, however, note that one trying to learn about the judiciary is not well served by limiting oneself to stories from either the news media or the popular media or both.

While it is true that the United States' judicial system is established in an adversarial form, if one is to understand how the system operates, it is important to understand that the important actors within any given court are people who know each other, who interact with each other on a repeated basis, and who were working to process cases as expeditiously as possible. Scholars who study the operation of courts refer to these people as a **"courtroom work group"** (Eisenstein and Jacob, 1977). The most heavily publicized manifestation of the courtroom work group's work is the plea bargain. What is heavily publicized is that plea bargains exist; what is not publicized is **how** they are achieved. Plea bargains are generally negotiated between the prosecutor and the defense attorney in a private meeting, without judicial supervision, and ratified by a judge who accepts a sworn statement by the defendant that no bargain has been struck.

Without a thorough knowledge of the United States' judiciary and its operation, one is ill-equipped to evaluate critically alternatives to how "we do things." In the United States, if a judge determines that pretrial publicity by the press exercising their First Amendment Free Press rights has potentially prejudiced the rights of the defendant's Sixth Amendment right to a fair trial by an impartial jury, the remedy is a change of venue. For example, when Timothy McVeigh was on trial in federal court for the bombing of a federal building in Oklahoma City which killed 168 people and injured many more, the trial was moved to Denver, Colorado to enhance the chances of impaneling a jury which could render a verdict based solely on the evidence presented in court, not one influenced by media coverage of the worst act of domestic terrorism in U.S. history. In other countries, such as Canada or the United Kingdom, once the suspect had been charged, only official court proceedings can be printed by the press, and violators could be prosecuted under contempt laws. These official documents are the dry stuff of legal proceedings rather than the dramatic, sensational recounting of events. Therefore in these countries, the media coverage of judicial actions may be less dramatic but it also runs less of a risk of distorting the public understanding of the issues of the case.

It is worth your while to go beyond what the media did not to learn about the judiciary. Law is not just black letters written in long combinations in heavy books or big files. Law is one of the instruments by which governmental authority is used to settle disputes, structure social arrangements, and make public policy in our political system. It is comparable to other social institutions—the family, the religion, the market—that attempt to achieve these ends. Whether one is interested in law from a conceptual perspective, that is concerned, for example, with justice, equity, fairness, or from a vocational perspective, that is how to practice law effectively, pursuing that interest requires a knowledge of the actors who mobilize and the institutions which "administer" law throughout the U.S. federal system—"courts"—and what difference all of these make.

Even if you have no specific interest in law, as a resident of the United States, the odds are high that you already have had or will have contact with some part of the legal system, either as a plaintiff or as a defendant in a civil suit, as someone who has been a victim of a crime, as a party in a contract, or as a juror. One cannot gain a very deep understanding of either the substance or the importance of law in the U.S. political system without an understanding of who works within the system, how the institutions are structured and function, and going beyond what you can learn from the media.

Key Terms

Civil law—law related to relations among private individuals and/or corporations.

Courtroom work group—this refers to a common practice of prosecuting attorneys, defense attorneys, and judges meeting before trial to settle the outcome of a case as a common work-a-day practice.

Criminal law—law defining actions or in actions as offenses against society as a whole and prescribing punishment if one is convicted by the state.

Plea bargain—a deal between a prosecutor and a defendant's attorney which some form of leniency is promised in exchange for a guilty plea.

Symbolic speech—actions that purposefully and discernibly convey a message to those who observe them.

Texas v. *Johnson*, 491 *U.S.* 397 (1989)—this is a court case that flag burning is a protected form of political symbolic speech. The court ruled that the First Amendment protected Johnson's right to express displeasure with American government by burning a flag.

Multiple Choice Questions

1. The general level of knowledge of how the judiciary works is
   a. high, because of so many police shows on television.
   b. high, because most people have served on a jury or been arrested.
   c. low, because media coverage of the judiciary is distorted.
   d. low, because it is illegal for reporters to reveal what is going on and the courts.
   Answer: C

2. The most important and common way the judiciary operates is through a
   a. trial.
   b. presidential appointment.
   c. negotiated agreement between the parties.
   d. legislative veto.

   Answer: C

3. The Constitution includes a right to
   a. plea-bargain.
   b. televise all judicial proceedings.
   c. press coverage of judicial proceedings.
   d. educated judges.

   Answer: C

4. The idea that there is a "litigation explosion" is
   a. backed by our data.
   b. popular in the media.
   c. unconstitutional.
   d. true for the Supreme Court, but not for lower courts.

   Answer: B

Discussion Question

1. How is the growth in social media—for example, cameras on cell phones, use of the Internet, social networking, Facebook— likely to affect people's knowledge of and perceptions of the judiciary?

References

Baker, Tom. 2005. *The Medical Malpractice Myth*. Chicago: University of Chicago Press.

Burns, Robert P. 2009. *The Death of the American Trial*. Chicago: University of Chicago Press.

Eisenstein, James, and Herbert Jacob. 1977. *Felony Justice*. Boston: Little, Brown.

Galanter, Marc A., and Angela M. Frozena. 2014. "A Grin Without a Cat: The Continuing Decline & Displacement of Trials in American Courts," *Daedalus* 143: 115–28.

Greenhouse, Linda. 1996. "Telling the Court's Story: Justice and Journalism at the U.S. Supreme Court." *Yale Law Journal* 105: 1537.

Haltom, William, and Michael McCann. 2004. *Distorting the Law: Politics, Media, and the Litigation Crisis*. Chicago: University of Chicago Press.

Moley, Raymond. 1928. "The Vanishing Jury." *Southern California Law Review* 2: 97.

Neubauer, David W., and Stephen S. Meinhold. 2017. *Judicial Process: Law, Courts, and Politics in the United States*. Boston: Cengage Learning.

Slotnick, Elliott E., and Jennifer A. Segal. 1998. *Television News and the Supreme Court: All the News That's Fit to Air?* New York: Cambridge University Press.

Yanus, Alixandra. 2009. "Full-Court Press: An Examination of Media Coverage of State Supreme Courts." *Justice System Journal* 30: 180–94.

Note

1   The song was subsequently recorded by Otis Redding (1965), Herman's Hermits (1965), and Art Garfunkel (1977).

THE PROGRESS PROBLEM IN CONGRESS: THE GENDER GAP IN CONGRESSIONAL FEMALE POLITICAL REPRESENTATION

ONE IDEA FOR A GENERATION

BY JENNIFER HORAN
University of North Carolina, Wilmington

LEARNING OBJECTIVES

Students should be able to:

1. Develop an understanding of women's historical and contemporary political representation in the U.S. political system.
2. Think critically about how "representative" democracies do or do not reflect their populations.
3. Analyze the implications of various explanations for the underrepresentation of women in the U.S. political system.

INTRODUCTION

In the United States today, women make up an estimated 50.8% of the population.[1] Yet, in the most powerful representative body in the world, the U.S. Congress, there were 99 women out of 535 seats (18.5% of the total) in 2014. In 2017, that number increased by 5 to 104. Of the 2017 total, 83 women serve in the House of Representatives (62 Democrats and 21 Republicans, 19.3% of the 435 available seats) while 21 women serve in the U.S. Senate (16 Democrats and 5 Republicans, 21% of the 100 seats).[2] Since the election of the first woman to serve in the U.S. Congress in 1917, only 324 women have served in Congress. Over this 100-year period, the pattern of increase averages out to approximately 3 women a year and it is not representative of women in proportion to their population.

In sharp contrast, female representation in national legislatures in other countries is frequently higher. In Rwanda, women comprise 61.8% of the national legislature. In Bolivia, they are 53.1%. In Sweden, they are 43.6%. In Iceland, women comprise 47.6% and in Germany they are 37% of the national legislature. Between 2000 and 2015, Mexico increased its female representation in its national legislature from 16% to 42.4%. Today, in international rankings of female representation in legislatures, the United States ranks 104th in the world and this number is down from 84th in 2014.[3]

When we think about representative democracy, it is also important to look to the lower levels of government to see what is going on with women's representation and leadership throughout a political system. Women in the United States are not significantly better represented at lower levels of our political system than they are in Congress. Currently, women are approximately 24.9% of the representatives in the state legislatures (in 2014, women had 24% of the seats in state legislatures). Today, only four states are led by female governors. In the United States, we have never had a female president but Chile, Argentina, Brazil, Costa Rica, Germany, Great Britain, India, Liberia, New Zealand, the Philippines, and Australia have all had democratically elected female heads of government and in some of these countries women have served as the nation's chief executive on multiple occasions and for more than one term.

The right to vote and to be represented in approximate proportion to your population are the twin elements of representative democracies. John Stuart Mill is one of the earliest thinkers to argue that government needs the participation of all of its citizens (including women whom he viewed as equal to men) and that this participation should encompass both voting and being elected as a representative. For Mill the best form of government was representative democracy because this form was one " . . . in which the sovereignty . . . is vested in the entire aggregate of the community." Mills also argued that citizens should have a voice in the government via voting and elections as well as being "called on to take an actual part in the government, by the personal discharge of some public function, local or general" (Mill 1861). This chapter examines the historical roots of female representation in the American democratic system. It will explain why it is the case that women in the United States of America are not serving in elective office in proportion to their population at any level of government in the middle start of the second decade of the 21st century and discuss why that is a problem for representative democracy in the United States.

BRIEF HISTORY OF WOMEN'S POLITICAL PARTICIPATION

Women in the United States have struggled against multiple factors that have limited their access to the political system and their willingness to engage in electoral competition. First, American women did not enjoy basic legal access to the U.S. political system, the vote, from the 1789 ratification of the U.S. Constitution until the addition of the 19th Amendment in 1920. Between 1848 and 1920, women fought to attain suffrage. The women's rights movement spanned 72 years of American history (1848–1920) and began as a multi-issue movement but was eventually distilled into a single-issue campaign, the vote. This goal was achieved in 1920 as a direct consequence of women's political organization and dedication to the cause.

Elizabeth Cady Stanton organized the first meeting about women's access to power and the U.S. political system in 1848 in Seneca Falls, New York. For Stanton, gaining the right to vote was the most important step for women in a democratic system. Without the right to vote, basic democratic accountability of elected officials was impossible. Without equal access and equal participation in the American political system, women's citizenship was constrained. Women's interests could be ignored by elected officials. When Stanton organized the Seneca

Falls meeting, women had none of the rights they enjoy and take for granted today. They had no right to own property, no right to control money either earned or inherited, no right to divorce, and no right to custody of their children. They were nonpersons in the eyes of the law and although not explicitly identified as property by the legal system as were black slaves, their informal status was similar. In a country governed by rule of law, this means they figuratively had no power and no access to fundamental tools of empowerment. This powerlessness became literal if they were not part of the traditional housewife model. Women whose parents died while they were young, whose husbands died or abandoned them, who were indentured servants or slaves had no rights in the American political system according to the legal structures created by the Founding Fathers. This meant that a woman whose family (father, husband, brothers) were deceased, incapable, or unwilling to support her was alone and without recourse. Women in such a situation were wholly dependent on the charity of others or on the street homeless. It is important to note that the omission of women from the legal system created by the founders is a well-documented, purposeful omission.

During the struggle for suffrage, women organized and attended conferences, made public speeches, protested, lobbied state and federal legislators, and negotiated with other interest groups for political support. They participated in all of the possible types of political action up to and including registering to vote and voting (in violation of the law).[4] For these and other behaviors, some women were tried and, in the case of Susan B. Anthony, convicted and fined $100.[5]

The importance of the women's movement for other groups yet to come cannot be overstated. Women's political action shaped the American system in many important ways. Female textile workers started the union movement and suffragettes began the tradition of protest, and civil disobedience. Eventually, these efforts began to pay off first at the state level. One example can be seen in Montana, which allowed women to vote and subsequently elected the first woman to Congress, Jeanette Rankin in 1917, 3 years before the ratification of the 19th Amendment in 1920.

The commitment of this movement and the obstacles faced by its members over time created enormous frustration for individuals such as Elizabeth Cady Stanton. Stanton believed and argued that there would be universal suffrage or incremental suffrage and the latter would be detrimental to all. Looking at the course of U.S. history, we can see that indeed she was correct. If women had gained suffrage in the 1800s with black men, the American political system would have moved forward in the context of universal suffrage. True democracy would have been achieved a 100 years earlier making it more difficult to discriminate based on gender or race.

In 2020, women in America will celebrate 100 years of suffrage. It is important to note that suffrage is a basic right of citizenship in electoral democracies because it is through the vote that we select our representatives. Political representation is "democratic" because those elected reflect and represent the will of the people. When Elizabeth Cady Stanton ridiculed Wendell Phillips about his generational approach to political change,[6] she complained that without universal suffrage you cannot claim equality, only hierarchy, which is not democratic. Finally, when we think about voting we also think about elections and who wins and goes on to represent "the people." Democracies focus power in their legislatures because this branch of government is considered the branch closest to the people and best able to represent the popular will. Thus, in situations in which 50% of the population has only 17% of the representation the questions we should ask are why is this the case, is it fair, and can election rules be adjusted to accommodate the related goals of fairness and representativeness?[7]

EXPLANATIONS FOR THE UNDERREPRESENTATION OF WOMEN IN ELECTORAL DEMOCRACY

The literature on women and elections is extensive. The subset of this literature focusing on women's political representation has long sought to provide systematic explanations for the dearth of women in elected legislative positions. The earliest research focused on testing multiple hypotheses. Some were about discrimination, are women candidates discriminated against by voters or by political elites? Other hypotheses examine the presence of women in the pool of candidates, their ability to fundraise, and whether or not women are politically ambitious (Darcy, Welch, and Clark 1994)

Elite (recruitment) and Voter Discrimination

According to this hypothesis, voters and elites may discriminate against women because they are women. So voters who discriminate against women go to the voting booth and simply refuse to vote for any female candidates. Elite discrimination is hypothesized to work in a similar manner, however elites are more uniquely positioned to "recruit" and help develop women as political candidates in the first place. Today, there is scant evidence of voter discrimination. If voters continue to discriminate, those individuals are likely to be voting on the extremes of the voter spectrum and their numbers are so small as to be undetectable, which means that they also do not have an impact on election outcomes (Conover 1988, 333).

Testing the idea that elites do not recruit women has been difficult as empirical data on elites and whether or not they discriminate against women would require that researchers actually ask and have answered by political party officials the question, "Do you discriminate against women when you are recruiting candidates for office?" It seems pretty obvious that no one is going to admit such a thing. This leaves researchers with only indirect methods for determining whether or not elite discrimination (the failure of political party leaders to recruit women to represent the party in an electoral competition) has occurred. The most common method of doing this is to ask women candidates if they experienced discrimination. When employing this tactic, researchers found that some women indeed claimed that they were ignored, not aided, not recruited by party officials, while party officials claimed that they indeed treated candidates equally. In the end, researchers found little systematic, replicable evidence of elite discrimination. Recently, some elite discrimination has been quantified by Lawless in her work and what she finds is that women are 14% less likely than men to be recruited to run for office. She concludes that women who have the same objective qualifications to run for office as do men are "not equally sought by electoral gatekeepers" (Darcy, Welch, and Clark 1994; Lawless and Fox 2005, 89).

Pipeline/Qualifications/Fundraising Hypotheses

Another possible explanation for the lack of women in power is what has been referred to as the pipeline hypothesis. This hypothesis suggests a relationship between women's achievement of the informal requirements for political office in the United States and their underrepresentation at all levels of government (local, state, and national). It is generally accepted that there are three informal requirements for office in the U.S. political system. They are high levels of education (college degree), job prestige (such as the legal profession), and high income. As recently as the 1980s, *most* women did not have college degrees, they were not working in prestigious professions and they therefore did not have high levels of earned income.[8] This research suggests that once women closed the gap in the area of higher education their candidacies and electoral fortunes would shift and female political representation would climb. Unfortunately, that has not been the case. In fact, today women earn well over 50% of all undergraduate degrees, 50% or more of most graduate degrees, and constitute 50% of the U.S. workforce. Female political representation however has not increased at the same pace as educational attainment. Another component of this issue is the fundraising question. Successful fundraising is instrumental to electoral success. Are female candidates for office able to raise as much money as male candidates? The answer is yes. Today, female candidates for political office raise their own money and raise what they need and more. They have the benefit of their own interests groups, such as Emily's List, dedicated to fundraising for female candidates. So, not only do women enjoy fundraising parity with men today, they have long since closed this particular gap (Darcy, Welch, and Clark 1994, 100; Burrell 1998). So, that is not the answer.

Incumbency

In the American political system, it is widely understood that the individuals who currently hold an elected position are 95% likely to retain or "hold" that position should they seek to run for reelection (Jacobson 1997; Palmer and Simon 2006). The reasons for this are many but they boil down to two things: superior access to many types of financial resources and name recognition (see Palmer and Simon 2006, 35–36 for a lengthy discussion). In the last 50 years of congressional elections, incumbents have been returned to office 95.3% of the time in House elections. Senators in contrast have lower reelection rates of only 84.7% over the past 50 years (Palmer and Simon 2006, 38–39). Therefore, one of the most important explanations for the underrepresentation of any group in the U.S. Congress is that white men already dominate the body and they do not give up their seats. They run over and over again, utilizing the advantages that incumbency brings. These individuals are the ones people refer to when they talk about "career" politicians. Not only do incumbents get reelected, this significantly deters other candidates from challenging the incumbent either in the party primaries or, with increasing frequency, in the general election (Palmer and Simon 2006; Lawless and Fox 2005). Incumbency and careerism (holding elected office for 20 years or longer) have combined to decrease turnover in the American legislature since the 1970s. This means that just when women were increasing their educational attainment, coming into the workforce in significant numbers and becoming qualified to enter electoral office, the most common opportunities (open seats) were decreasing.[9]

Despite these constraints, there are still opportunities to compete for and win public office. But if they get into office, will women also enjoy the benefits of incumbency? Overall, it is the case that incumbent women running for reelection are enjoying the benefits of incumbency, retaining their seats at similar and occasionally better rates than male incumbents (Palmer and Simon 2006, 123). There is however, a different pattern for female incumbent retention compared to male incumbent retention. Male incumbents are more likely than female incumbents to enjoy the "free pass" (where there is no opponent) primary or general election (or both). Female incumbents are usually challenged and increasingly the challengers are other female candidates. This is a striking difference. So, women officeholders who run for reelection typically must work harder and raise more money than their male incumbent counterparts to stay in office. And, sometimes these women are defeated. Men who regularly do not face a challenger have an obviously easier path to remaining in office (Palmer and Simon 2006, 123).So, why are women more likely to face an opponent? There are two factors working to increase the number of challengers women incumbents face. First, a district that has elected a woman may be a "woman-friendly" district. "Women friendliness" makes it more likely that women can get elected and encourages candidacies. Democratic "women-friendly" districts are typically more liberal, urban, diverse, educated, and wealthy. Republican "women-friendly" districts are typically less conservative, more urban, and more diverse. Second, other women in that district see examples of successful female leadership. We are influenced by the political environment around us and seeing women in office normalizes women officeholding for other females and encourages female candidacies.

Table 1. General Elections in House and Senate Races with Female Incumbent and Female Challenger 1992–2014.

Year	Female incumbent defeats female challenger	Female challenger defeats female incumbent	Open seats	Total
1992	2	0	4	6
1994	9	2	0	11
1996	3	0	1	4
1998	14	0	1	15
2000	10	0	1	11
2002	9	1	2	12
2004	8	0	3	11
2006	10	0	1	11
2008	7	3	1	11
2010	10	2	0	12
2012	10	0	2	12
2014	11	0	4	15
Total	103	8	20	131

Source: Table adapted from Palmer and Simon 2006, 125. Table 5.1 and extended data collected by the author and from the Center for American Women and Politics, Rutgers University, Woman versus Woman Fact Sheet 2012 http://www.cawp.rutgers.edu/sites/default/files/resources/womvwom.pdf (accessed April 28, 2017).

Political Ambition

Although it is clear that incumbency is extremely important, even when we account for it, the fact remains that all incumbents eventually leave Congress, John Dingle's 55 years of continuous service is impressive but not the norm and seats do open up or could be challenged. If the barrier of incumbency was the full explanation for women's underrepresentation in the U.S. Congress, then the rates of representation would be higher than they are today. It's just simple math. For example, what we know about open seats is that women candidates win open seat elections half of the time. They have a 50/50 chance of defeating a male candidate. If the House of Representatives had no incumbents in an election and if women and men candidates competed in equal numbers, then the likelihood of women winning half of the 435 seats is 50%. Could it be that political ambition may be different for women compared to men?

The political ambition hypothesis is that women are less interested in acquiring and holding political power than are men.[10] The consequence of lower ambition in women is that fewer women are choosing to pursue elected office. This reduces the pool of eligible woman candidates and keeps the numbers of women officeholders low. The Citizen Political Ambition Study, a national survey of 3,800 individuals qualified to run for political office but who did not currently hold elective office (Lawless and Fox 2005) allowed political scientists to document real gaps in political ambition between men and women. This research indicates that political socialization[11] is different for women compared to men. A primary consequence of this difference is that fewer women develop political ambition and subsequently decide to run for office.

An additional element of the political ambition hypothesis entails the idea of elite recruitment. The apparent reluctance of women to consider becoming candidates raises the question, why does it appear that women do not choose to enter electoral politics? Women do everything else: play sports at elite levels, work in professions at all levels, participate in elections, they are activists in the political arena—creating and running many important interest groups, so why don't they choose to run for office. Lawless and Fox (2005) suggest a complicated relationship between women's individual levels of political ambition and what they term the candidate emergence process. While men seem to take for granted the idea that someday they might consider a run for elective office, most women do not. In fact, women seem to perceive that there is an extremely high threshold of qualifications necessary to achieve before they run for office. This is very different from men's view of the necessary qualifications. Add to this the fact that even today American women, 80% of whom will have children, bear the majority of the responsibility in the area of parenting. The acceptance of this gender role by women moves them away from elections. It is hard to envision running for office while working, getting the kids to day care, cooking dinner, and all the other things most women do in a day.

This also means that women are self-selecting themselves out of electoral politics at rates higher than those experienced by men. What can change this? Potentially, this can be changed by the experience of being recruited and by an expanding climate of female political leadership. First, when political elites target women and recruit them to run for office, these women are more likely to be persuaded and under these circumstances will become candidates. There is no systematic evidence that when women run for office they are defeated because of gender. Women lose for the same reasons men lose, their partisanship doesn't match with the voters or they are confronting an incumbent. Second, the expansion of the climate of female political leadership is moving to encompass the political right much more slowly than the political left. Two pieces of evidence about each of these claims are important; first the Hillary (Clinton) candidacies for the presidency in 2008 and 2016, both resulted in large voter turnout for her especially in the 2016 presidential election when Mrs. Clinton defeated Mr. Trump in the popular vote 65,844,610 to 62,979,636.[12] Second, when it comes to female representation the Democratic Party has a standing tradition of working toward gender parity while the Republican Party does not.

CONCLUSION

The evolution of the American experiment with democracy has one fundamental theme—access by the citizens, to government. We see this theme in the founding of the nation where more citizens than in any nation in history at the time were granted the right to vote, to participate in the leadership selection process. The thread of U.S. history continued in this vein; through the original women's movement, the onset of the Civil War, the debate about suffrage for black men versus universal suffrage, the resumption of the women's rights movement and its transformation into a women's suffrage movement, the start and development of the civil rights movement, all of these elements of our past demonstrate a clear commitment over time by citizens to the ideal that they should participate in and be represented by their government. Candidates who run effect who can win, which effects representation, which is key to democracy.

Why does the representation of women matter in representative democracy? John Stuart Mill thought that "human beings are only secure from evil at the hands of others in proportion as they have the power of being, and are, self-protecting; and they only achieve a high degree of success in their struggle with Nature in proportion as they are self-dependent, relying on what they themselves can do, either separately or in concert, rather than on what others can do for them." In other words, the most effective government, least corrupt or corruptible government represents and leads by reflecting its citizens and their interests, and because citizens may be different from one another, those differences should be incorporated into government via the individuals who serve.

Key Terms

Representative democracy—type of democracy based on the idea that elected officials represent groups of people.

Seneca Falls—the 1848 location of the first woman suffrage conference in New York State.

Candidate emergence—the process by which individuals emerge as candidates for public office.

Political socialization—the process by which citizens acquire their beliefs, values, and attitudes about their political system.

Woman-friendly district—a district that elects women leaders. Democratic women-friendly districts are typically more liberal, urban, diverse, educated, and wealthy. Republican "women-friendly" districts are typically less conservative, more urban, and more diverse.

Multiple Choice Questions

1. The process by which citizens acquire their beliefs, values, and attitudes about their political system is:
   a. political culture.
   b. political contacting.
   c. political socialization.
   d. political agency.

   Answer: C

2. Women friendly districts are more:
   a. rural and homogeneous.
   b. urban and diverse.
   c. politically conservative.
   d. dominated by the Republican party.

   Answer: B

3. One of the most significant barriers to congressional turnover is:
   a. incumbency.
   b. partisanship.
   c. ambition.
   d. elections.

   Answer: A

4. The idea the lack of women in elected office is because women do not acquire the informal requirements to run for office is known as:
   a. the elite discrimination explanation.
   b. the fundraising hypothesis.
   c. the attributes explanation.
   d. the pipeline hypothesis.

   Answer: D

5. Compared to many other nations in the world, the United States has:
   a. about the same level of women in elected office.
   b. about the same level of female representation.
   c. significantly more women in elected office.
   d. significantly fewer women in elected office.

   Answer: D

Discussion Question

1. Explain and discuss the political ambition theory and how it explains the number of women in elected office in the United States.

References

Burrell, Barbara. 1998. "Campaign Finance: Women's Experience in the Modern Era." In *Women and Elective Office*, edited by S. Thomas and C. Wilcox. New York: Oxford University Press.

Center for American Women and Politics. "Fact Sheets, various years." Eagleton Institute of Politics, Rutgers, The State University of New Jersey. New Brunswick, NJ. Retrieved from http://www.cawp.rutgers.edu/fact-sheet-archive-women-congress.

Conover, Pamela Johnston. 1988. "Feminists and the Gender Gap." *Journal of Politics* 50 (4): 985–1010.

Cook Report. 2016. "National Popular Vote Tracker." Accessed April 28, 2017, https://docs.google.com/spreadsheets/d/133Eb4qQmOxNvtesw2hdVns073R68EZx4SfCnP4IGQf8/htmlview?sle=true#gid=19.

Darcy, Robert, Susan Welch, and Janet Clark. 1994. *Women, Elections and Representation*. 2nd ed. Lincoln: University of Nebraska.

Interparliamentary Union. 2014. "Women in National Parliaments." Accessed July 7, 2014, http://www.ipu.org/wmn-e/classif.htm.

Jacobson, Gary. 1997. *The Politics of Congressional Elections*. New York: Harper Collins.

Lawless, Jennifer and Richard L. Fox. 2005. *It Takes a Candidate: Why Women Don't Run for Office*. New York: Cambridge University Press.

Mill, John Stewart. 1861. *Representative Government*. Accessed May, 2017, http://www.constitution.org/jsm/rep_gov.htm.

Palmer, Barbara and Dennis Simon. 2006. *Breaking the Political Glass Ceiling Women and Congressional Elections*. New York: Routledge.

Swers, Michelle. 2001. "Research on Women in Legislatures: What have we learned? Where are we going?" *Women & Politics* 23 (1/2): 167–185.

Notes

1. Source: U.S. Census 2012 data.
2. Source: Interparliamentary Union (2017), "Women in National Parliaments"; Center for American Women and Politics (2016) "Women in Congress" Fact Sheet.
3. Source: Interparliamentary Union 2014 and 2017 data lists. See http://www.ipu.org/wmn-e/classif.htm accessed July 7, 2014 and April 28, 2017. This figure changes with virtually every election in the world. For up to date figures one must check the IPU after any country has a national legislative election.
4. Virginia Minor attempted to vote in the state of Missouri during the 1872 presidential election. At that time, the registrar of voters (Happersett) refused to register her as a lawful voter. This action was upheld as constitutional by the U.S. Supreme Court in its ruling on the subsequent lawsuit (see *Minor v. Happersett* 88 U.S. 162 (1874). In the same presidential election, Susan B. Anthony was able to register to vote and then successfully cast her ballot in Rochester, New York. She was subsequently arrested and tried for voting illegally. She was tried in federal court, found guilty and fined.
5. A $1,925.08 fine in 2016 dollars.
6. Wendell Phillips famously argued that major political changes should occur in order of importance separated by a generational cohort. His order was "Negro suffrage, temperance, woman's suffrage." (ECS speech)
7. In 2000, women comprised 13.6% of the House of Representatives and 13% of the Senate; the movement in a decade of only 4% points is an exceptionally slow rate of change (Swers 2001, 168). In 2010, those numbers had again increased by a comparably slow rate with current membership at 17 members of the Senate (17%) and 73 members of the House (16%) (CAWP Fact Sheet 2010, Center for American Women and Politics, Eagleton Institutes of Politics, Rutgers University. Accessed: http://www.cawp.rutgers.edu/history-women-us-congress; http://www.cawp.rutgers.edu/sites/default/files/resources/house2010.pdf; http://www.cawp.rutgers.edu/sites/default/files/resources/senate2010.pdf.
8. There are many independently wealthy women in the Unites States which raises an interesting question about why independently wealthy men do run for office (Ross Perot, Steve Forbes, Donald Trump) while equally wealthy women do not (Oprah, none of the women of the Walton family, Abigail Johnson CEO of Fidelity Investments, or Jacqueline Mars (Mars candy fortune). So far only Meg Whitman (R), the founder and CEO of eBay has run for office. Whitman spent 141 million of her personal fortune in the California gubernatorial race but was defeated by Jerry Brown (D), whose campaign cost was $32 million.
9. The longest serving member of Congress is John Dingell (D) who has represented Michigan in the House of Representatives since 1955. The longest serving female member of Congress is Marcia "Marcy" Kaptur. Representative Kaptur has represented Ohio's 9th District since 1983. She is the 25th longest serving member of the House. The next longest serving female member of Congress ranks 36th overall and is Louise Slaughter who was elected to represent New York's 29th District in 1993.

10 Political ambition is defined as "the desired to acquire and hold political power through electoral means" (see Lawless and Fox 2005, 3).
11 Political socialization is the process by which citizens acquire their beliefs, values, and attitudes about their political system. Agents of socialization are the direct and indirect socializers. An example of a direct socializing agent is the family—they tell, teach, expect, and reinforce values directly. An example of an indirect socializing agent is the media—the media that any individual consumes is chosen by the individual, no one is "forced" to watch, read, or click on particular news presented by the media.
12 The Cook Report: 2016 National Popular Vote Tracker, accessed 4/28/2017. See https://docs.google.com/spreadsheets/d/133Eb4qQmOxNvtesw2hdVns073R68EZx4SfCnP4IGQf8/htmlview?sle=true#gid=19

WHO GETS TO HAVE A SAY IN POLICY-MAKING?: A LOOK AT HEALTH CARE POLICY

BY JUAN CARLOS HUERTA AND JO MARIE RIOS
Texas A&M University—Corpus Christi

LEARNING OBJECTIVES

Students should be able to:
1. Describe what public policy is and understand the policy-making cycle.
2. Explain the importance of pluralism in policy-making.
3. Understand the differences between institutional and noninstitutional actors.
4. Understand why health care is a public policy problem.
5. Analyze the importance of noninstitutional actors in the passage of the Affordable Care Act.

INTRODUCTION

When the citizens in the United States are having problems, many times they look to government to provide solutions. When the government offers solutions, this is known as public policy. In public policy, there are numerous policy issue areas such as education, criminal justice, environment, transportation, taxes, and health care to name just a few. If action is taken at the federal level, the solutions ultimately result in legislation that is enacted by Congress. Having said that, it is no easy task to get legislation passed given the political and policy systems that we have in the United States. This chapter will present some of the intellectual framework for understanding public policy and will use health care policy as an example. A specific focus of the chapter is the role that interest groups have in influencing public policy legislation.

What is **public policy?** It comprises government laws, regulations, and rules that affect the public.[1] Thus, providing more federal financial aid for students to attend college is an example of public policy as is the selection of weapons systems for the Department of Defense. Public policy can also mean not taking action on an issue, such as a decision to not have a national dental insurance program. Peters adds that public policy is "the sum of all government activities, whether pursued directly or through agents, as those activities have an influence on the lives of citizens."[2] Peters' definition implies that laws are enacted to change people's behavior in some way.

In our political system, there is a separation of powers within the branches of government such that each have a constitutional and institutional role. These are known as **institutional actors**. When it comes to policy-making, the United States has a pluralist policy system, which connotes that many groups, primarily interest groups, can coalesce to try to influence how policy is made, and these are referred to as **noninstitutional actors**.

PLURALISM

At the national policy-making level, Congress, the president, courts, and federal agencies (federal bureaucracy) are all important institutional actors in the process. No understanding of the policy process can ignore the role that presidents have in shaping the political agenda, congressional committees have in drafting laws, and federal agencies in implementing policy. Nonetheless, understanding public policy also means considering noninstitutional actors. Noninstitutional actors include interest groups, nonprofits, and social movements. Pluralism provides an intellectual framework for understanding the role of noninstitutional actors in the public policy process.

In a pluralist democracy, the emphasis is on the role groups have in influencing policy. On any given issue, groups can take positions and attempt to influence the outcome of legislation. Groups will also collaborate with other groups to form alliances. Tactics groups use for influencing the policy-making process include, but are not limited to, direct lobbying of public officials, providing information, testifying at hearings, mobilizing their supporters, advertisements, campaign donations, and campaign work.

POLICY-MAKING PROCESS

To understand how various institutional and noninstitutional political actors influence policy, it can help to have a model for how policy is made. Political scientists view the policy-making process as a cycle with the following steps:

1. Agenda setting: The policy issue receives attention.
2. Policy formulation: Policy-makers formulate proposals to address the issue.
3. Policy adoption: A solution is adopted.
4. Policy implementation: Government agencies take the steps to make the policy work.
5. Policy evaluation: Analysts review the policy to judge how well it is working and make any needed recommendations for improvement.[3]

These steps work as a cycle with policy evaluation informing agenda setting. Policy evaluation can also directly inform policy implementation and policy formulation. Groups have an opportunity to influence each step in the policy process. Both the institutional and noninstitutional actors are important at each stage of the policy-making process.

Actors in Policy-Making

Public policy is a dynamic process where much activity occurs before the actual bill is ever introduced as a piece of legislation. The Constitution provides institutional actors, such as Congress, the presidency, the bureaucracy, and the judiciary. In our pluralistic democracy, there are also noninstitutional actors that can try to influence certain stages of the policy cycle by lobbying the institutional actors to pose (or oppose) solutions to public problems.[4]

INSTITUTIONAL ACTORS

For the institutional actors, Congress has been charged with the constitutional role of enacting legislation. However, there is much activity between Congress, the president and the bureaucracy, and the noninstitutional actors in the early stages of the policy cycle, specifically agenda setting and formulating solutions stages.

Congress is the legislative branch, thus has a major role in public policy legislation. Bills are introduced to address public policy, and then the difficult path for the bill to become a law commences. Bills work their way through committees on their way to becoming legislation. There are numerous votes and hearings meaning that there are many opportunities to defeat, or substantially change, bills as they work their way through Congress.

The president also has an important role in policy-making. Every January, the president presents his or her agenda in the State of the Union address. In this speech, presidents state their policy goals for issues such as education, health care, welfare, and so on. Presidents, and their advisors, also work with Congress on passing the president's policy agenda. The public often looks to presidents for leadership on public policy issues, thus presidents are expected to have public policy proposals.

Federal agencies (federal bureaucracy) are not mentioned in the Constitution but rather the president is charged with the responsibility of implementing the laws. He or she accomplishes this through use of the cabinet-level political appointments and the civil service employees who work for a federal-level agency. The bureaucracy has two important roles in policy-making. First, the agency heads will provide data, expertise, and possible solutions to inform discussions of public problems. In other words, they are active players is crafting legislation. The second role of the bureaucracy is to write the rules and regulations to implement the laws once enacted. This is called regulatory policy. The rules and regulations are likely to follow the ideology of the president since he or she is the person who nominates the heads of the agencies.

The courts or judiciary have the responsibility of performing constitutional judicial review, meaning they are responsible for reviewing acts of Congress and the president. The decisions handed down by the courts can have the same effect as a law passed by Congress and as such make policy. An example is same-sex marriage. Several states had laws that forbade same-sex marriage. The U.S. Supreme Court, in *Obergefell v. Hodges*, ruled that the U.S. Constitution guarantees a right to same-sex marriage.[5] Thus, by ruling that the Constitution protected same-sex marriage, the ruling of the court impacted public policy by invalidating state laws that forbade same-sex marriage.

Noninstitutional Actors

While not specifically mentioned in the Constitution (though protected by the First Amendment), noninstitutional actors are acknowledged players in the policy process and are important for understanding pluralism. The following paragraphs identify several types of noninstitutional actors.

Interest Groups. The noninstitutional actors' participation most commonly studied deals with interest group behavior in their attempts to influence policy solutions. Political scientists identify different types of interest groups. *Economic interest groups,* such as business groups, professional associations, and labor unions, attempt to influence government for the economic benefit of their members. These business groups are often viewed as being politically powerful because of their ability to raise large sums of money for campaign donations.

Equal opportunity interest groups, such as civil rights groups, work to advance the rights of underrepresented people. Consumer groups and environmental groups are classified as public interest groups. They promote benefits that are not limited to their members.[6] For example, Consumer Union (a group that represents consumers) is unable to limit safe cars to their members even though they were instrumental in getting safety regulations, such as mandatory back-up cameras for vehicles (effective in 2018), nor can an environmental group limit clean water just for their members.[7]

Media. The role of the media is multifaceted. They are vital to our democracy and First Amendment rights. They function as a watchdog for government actions to ensure transparency and responsiveness by politicians. In terms of policy-making, the media is considered to be a noninstitutional actor that has the ability to bring attention to and provide media coverage of a problem, and thus has a role with agenda setting. They inform the public about an issue. The media also possesses the ability to affect the perception of a problem based on its coverage of an event. This perception begins to define a problem for the citizenry. In policy-making, how a problem is defined drives the proposed solutions. For this reason, the media shapes people's perceptions of problems, calls attention and helps define the problem. Finally, it is important to note that media coverage is selective (they cannot cover every possible issue) and can many times be biased as evidenced by the numerous cable network news sources that lean to the political right or left.

PLURALISM AND UNDERSTANDING HEALTH CARE POLICY

Health care policy has been on and off the policy agenda for over 60 years with numerous attempts to address health insurance coverage and access. Why have we not resolved this issue if we have been attempting to deal with it for so long? Pluralism can help explain why many efforts were unsuccessful and why President Barack Obama was able to sign the **Affordable Care Act** (ACA) into law in 2010. In 2014, as a result of the ACA, more Americans were able to purchase affordable health insurance and the percentage of Americans without health insurance declined. While there are still issues remaining and health care has not been "solved," the ACA still represents a significant public policy accomplishment.

The Problem

One of the primary problems policy-makers have attempted to deal with over the years is access to affordable health insurance that provides comprehensive coverage. In all other advanced democracies, there are government programs that work toward **universal health coverage** for all. According to the World Health Organization (WHO), universal health coverage (UHC) "... means that all individuals and communities receive the health services they need without suffering financial hardship. It includes the full spectrum of essential, quality health services, from health promotion to prevention, treatment, rehabilitation, and palliative care."[8]

Achieving UHC in the United States has been a challenge, with considerable disagreement about it being a public policy goal. In most democracies, public policies have an active role for government in making health insurance widely available and affordable, thus they are better able to come closer to UHC.

In the United States, health insurance is most often employer based, meaning people receive health insurance as a benefit of employment. Prior to 2014, when health insurance was not provided by an employer, individuals bought insurance directly from insurance companies (or did without). This is known as the "**individual market**." This individual market was problematic for many because the cost of purchasing insurance (premiums) were often very expensive. In addition, insurance companies were often reluctant to offer coverage for what are known as "**pre-existing conditions**." For example, an individual who had a history of diabetes would find themselves unable to obtain coverage because diabetes was considered a pre-existing condition.

Individuals could make it without health insurance as long as they remained healthy. The problem occurred when illness struck or expensive care was needed. Heart attacks and cancer treatments are expensive, as is maternity care. Families faced extreme financial hardship, and it was not uncommon for them to have to file for bankruptcy, because of expensive health care bills.

Insurance is a business that depends on risk pools—a large group of people who buy health insurance. Most in the risk pool are healthy and do not receive benefits greater than they paid in. A small group of people in the risk pool will get sick or need expensive care, and need benefits from insurance that exceed the amount they have paid in to the system. Insurance companies are profit-seeking businesses, and to make a profit they must collect more revenue than what they pay in benefits. Hence, they need a large pool and healthy customers and could not make a profit if only patients needing expensive care bought insurance, or they would need to charge very expensive premiums that individuals would have difficulty affording. So, the people who need/want insurance are most likely to use it and for whom it would be the most expensive. For these reasons, health insurance was considered a public policy problem.

BRIEF OVERVIEW OF HEALTH CARE POLICY SINCE 1945

Health care policy in the United States has largely focused on the role of government in expanding access to health care and providing affordable coverage. On November 19, 1945, President Harry Truman proposed a national health insurance fund administered by the federal government. The program was to be available to all, yet optional. Participants would pay monthly premiums that would cover all expenses. The American Medical Association (AMA) strongly opposed the plan, calling it "socialized medicine" (because the government would administer the program) and their opposition helped to defeat it.[9] Over the next 65 years, health care policy has been off and on the public agenda with proposals to expand coverage to more people, make it more affordable, and provide greater benefits. One important step toward the provision of health care was seen on July 30, 1965 when President Lyndon B. Johnson signed Medicare and Medicaid into law.[10] Medicare provided health insurance for older Americans and Medicaid provided insurance for those with lower incomes. These are two of the groups most subject to the challenges of the individual health care market.

While Medicare and Medicaid greatly expanded access to health care in the United States, they did not provide universal health care coverage. In 1974, President Richard Nixon made a serious effort toward universal health insurance. However, his effort faltered after his resignation resulting from Watergate. President Jimmy Carter also proposed a national health plan. Cost containment was a major feature of Carter's plan, yet it was defeated amid opposition from insurance companies in favor a voluntary plan to control costs. President Bill Clinton made the next major effort to achieve universal coverage in 1993. His plan was ultimately defeated based on opposition from the insurance industry and small business groups.[11] A common theme in the defeats of health care reform has been the opposition from powerful noninstitutional actors.

After being unable to pass a comprehensive plan in his first term, President Clinton worked to pass expansion of health care for children from families earning too much income to qualify for Medicaid, yet were financially unable to obtain health insurance. This program, known as the Children's Health Insurance Program (CHIP) became law in 1997. In 2003, President George W. Bush signed a new Medicare prescription drug benefit into law. These two laws targeted specific populations—children and the elderly. Making a case for expanding health care for children is more straightforward—they do not choose to live in low-income households. Prescription drugs for senior citizens can be costly, and seniors are a powerful voting bloc.

In summary, efforts to provide a comprehensive health insurance for all had been unsuccessful, while efforts at expanding health care for specific populations had some success. The remainder of the chapter will examine the passage of the Affordable Care Act (ACA) and the pluralism model to understand how this effort at comprehensive health care became law.

PLURALISM AND HEALTH CARE POLICY: THE AFFORDABLE CARE ACT

President Barack Obama signed the ACA into law on March 23, 2010, and with that action achieved a public policy accomplishment that had eluded many others.[12] As we have seen, opposition from powerful noninstitutional actors were factors in the defeats of previous efforts at passing comprehensive health care policies. A key to understanding why the ACA succeeded while previous efforts were unsuccessful can be seen once again in the role of noninstitutional actors, such as powerful interest groups.

But first, let's start with the institutional actors. During the 2008 Democratic primary both Hillary Clinton and Barack Obama campaigned on passing comprehensive health insurance and it was part of the Democratic Party platform. The Republicans also had health care objectives with plans to expand health care typically involved providing tax breaks for people who purchased policies, savings accounts to pay for health care expenses, and scaling back regulations that they argued kept prices artificially high.

The 2008 election produced a Democratic president and a democratically controlled Congress. Thus, the institutional actors were aligned to pass health care reform. What about the noninstitutional actors?

President Obama hosted a health care forum in March 2009 where he declared that his goals for comprehensive health care reform were to lower costs, improve quality, and expand coverage.[13] Attendees at the forum included representatives for physicians, labor unions, business groups, hospitals, insurance companies, and consumer organizations.[14] Hosting a forum for all the participants in the health care industry was an effort to engage noninstitutional actors in the process and critical to the development of a plan they would support.

Health Care Industry Groups

Among the industry groups that were included in negotiations were the America's Health Insurance Plans (AHIP) and the Pharmaceutical Research and Manufacturers of America (PhRMA).[15] They were included in the negotiations to gain their support, or at least minimize their opposition, to health care reform. Both groups were looking out for the interests of their members because neither wanted to lose money in any health care reform that might include regulations that limited what they could charge.

AHIP worked for a plan that would require all Americans to purchase health insurance (individual mandate) and opposed a government-run health insurance option (public option). They agreed to accept stricter regulations, cost controls, and to provide health insurance for those with pre-existing conditions.[16] In exchange, insurance companies stood to enjoy healthy profits as a result of the individual mandate requirement that **all** Americans purchase health insurance. Insurance companies opposed the public option because that entailed the federal government becoming a competitor in the health care market. Similarly, PhRMA was also part of negotiations and was able to reach an agreement to support health care reform. Pharmaceutical companies could earn higher profits if more people are insured and have prescription drug benefits.[17]

The Obama administration made deals with potential foes of health care reform so they would not be in opposition. These deals potentially complicated negotiations in Congress however because critics thought the president did not extract enough concessions from those who stood to benefit from the ACA.[18]

PHYSICIAN GROUPS

In December 2009, the American Medical Association (AMA) endorsed a Senate health care reform bill that eventually became the ACA. Despite having been in opposition to previous reform efforts,[19] physician groups were found to not have had as much impact in the passage of the ACA as they had during past failed reform efforts because they were not as united. Physicians were divided into specialty and interest groups—the AMA no longer represents the vast majority of physicians. For example, physicians for a National Health Program favored a single-payer health care system and wanted to eliminate the private insurance industry.[20] In contrast, the American Academy of Pediatrics, representing 60,000 pediatric care physicians, supported passage of the ACA.[21] Interests are always more influential when they are united and this time the physicians were not.

Organized Labor

Organized labor was also included in the negotiations because they are a key component of the Democratic Party coalition and because they were concerned about the long-term sustainability of employer-based health care.[22] As two of the largest representatives of labor in the United States, the American Federation of Labor and Congress of Industrial Organizations (AFL-CIO) and the Service Employees International Union (SEIU) both supported health care reform and were included in negotiations. The AFL-CIO favored a public option while the SEIU indicated support for plan that did not include a public option.[23] As the final bill was nearing completion, the AFL-CIO was concerned about a tax on health care plans, which would have raised taxes on their members who receive health care as part of their employment, but they were able to negotiate a lower tax rate making it possible for them to support the bill.[24]

Senior Citizens

The American Association of Retired Persons (AARP) is considered one of the most powerful interest groups in the United States. Representing senior citizens, their support was crucial to health care reform passage. The AARP was particularly concerned with prescription drug coverage and health care plans for seniors too young to qualify for Medicare.[25] Many of their members are old enough to have expensive health conditions, which make buying health care coverage a challenge but they are not yet old enough to take advantage of Medicare. The final bill improved prescription drug benefits and a long-term care program—issues important to the AARP.[26] The AARP's endorsement of health care reform was considered critical to the eventual passage.

Abortion Rights Groups

Abortion is one of the more polarizing issues in American politics. Even though the presidency and Congress were both controlled by the Democratic Party, there is a significant range of opinions about abortion within the party. While most consider the Democratic Party to be more liberal on the issue of abortion rights, there are factions within the party that are not supportive of abortion rights. Groups opposed to abortion rights worked to insert language that prohibited federal dollars being used to pay for abortions. The president agreed to sign an Executive Order to strengthen the provision that no federal funds be used to pay for abortions.[27] Groups in support of abortion rights were upset with the Executive Order, yet still supported passage of the bill.[28]

The Affordable Care Act

The purpose of this chapter was to examine public policy with an emphasis on the role of interest groups (noninstitutional actors), and one can see from an examination of the ACA passage that interest group agreement to the bill was a key to the passage. It took 13 months to pass the ACA and there were many times when it appeared the effort would fail.[29] Congress held numerous public hearings, negotiated multiple drafts and included interest groups in negotiations, before finally coming to an agreement.[30] The president, congressional Democrats, and key interest groups persisted and Congress passed the legislation on March 21, 2010 and then two days later the bill was signed into law.

Negotiations with noninstitutional actors and winning their support (or at least having them agree to not oppose) was a key difference from the earlier attempts at health care reform that failed. Institutional actors alone do not explain the passage. Following the 1964 and 1976 elections, Democrats had large congressional majorities and control of the White House. Nonetheless, comprehensive health care was not passed in either era. This time the institutional actors were able to negotiate a deal with key noninstitutional actors. While there were efforts to negotiate with powerful business groups, many business groups remained in opposition. The passage of the ACA came at a high political cost as the Democrats lost their House majority in the 2010 midterm elections and saw their Senate majority reduced. And the controversy over health care policy continues today.

In summary, passing public policy is a complicated process. It is not simply about having a majority in Congress or a good idea. It takes skilled politicians working and negotiating with key noninstitutional actors.

Key Terms

Public policy—government laws, regulations, and rules that affect the public.

Pluralism—a theory emphasizing the role of interest groups, competing against each together, in influencing public policy to benefit the members of their group.

Institutional actors—actors in the policy-making process that are part of government. In the United States, these include the president, Congress, and courts.

Noninstitutional actors—actors in the policy-making process that are not a part of government, including interest groups, social movements, and the media.

Interest groups—organizations with members with shared goals that attempt to influence public policy to benefit their members.

Universal health coverage—all receive needed health services that does not cause financial hardship.

Individual market—individuals purchase health insurance policies directly from health insurance companies and are not part of group plan.

Pre-existing conditions—medical conditions that individuals have that are used by health insurance companies to deny selling the individual a health insurance plan.

Affordable Care Act—health care law passed in 2010 that expanded health care coverage in the United States.

Multiple Choice Questions

1. Which of the following statements is true about public policy?
   a. Public policy is a value choice that provides solutions to public problems.
   b. Public policy involves all government actions to influence the lives of citizens.
   c. Government intervention is not always appropriate to fix all problems.
   d. All of the above.
   Answer: D

2. In a pluralist democracy, the emphasis is on the role _____ in influencing policy.
   a. Congress has
   b. the courts have
   c. groups have
   d. presidents have
   Answer: C

3. The _____ actors include Congress, the president, and the courts.
   a. noninstitutional
   b. constitutional
   c. federalist
   d. institutional
   Answer: D

4. An example of a noninstitutional actor is (are) _____.
   a. interest groups
   b. bureaucrats
   c. congressional staff
   d. the president's cabinet
   Answer: A

5. The problem in health care that is addressed in the chapter is _____.
   a. the high cost of health care for individuals without employer-based health care or a government health care program.
   b. the scarcity of physicians in rural areas.
   c. low profits for insurance companies.
   d. the proliferation of specialist physicians and the decline of family practice physicians.
   Answer: A

6. What do the authors argue was a major reason for the successful passage of the Affordable Care Act, in comparison to unsuccessful efforts from the past 60 years?
   a. Social media
   b. Support of noninstitutional actors
   c. Changes in the way Congress passes legislation
   d. Better calculations based on improved health care data

Answer: B

Discussion Question

Presidents Truman, Nixon, Carter, and Clinton all unsuccessfully attempted to pass laws that would bring the United States closer to universal health coverage. President Obama was successful with the passage of the Affordable Care Act (ACA). What are some key differences between the process of passing the ACA compared to the failures of the earlier efforts?

Notes

1. Dautrich, Kenneth, David A. Yalof, and Christina E. Bejerano. *The Enduring Democracy*, 5th ed. Boston: Cengage, 2017.
2. Peters, B. Guy. *American Public Policy, Promise and Performance*, 9th ed. Sage/CQ Press, 2013.
3. Barbour, Christine and Gerald C. Wright. *Keeping the Republic, Power and Citizenship in American Politics*, 3rd Brief Edition. Sage/CQ Press, 2009.
4. Cahn, Matthew A. "The Players: Institutional and Noninstitutional Actors in the Policy Process," In Stella Z. Theodoulou and Matthew Cahn (Eds.), *Public Policy, The Essential Readings* (pp. 201–211). Upper Saddle River, NJ: Prentice Hall. 1995.
5. Liptak, Adam. "Supreme Court Ruling Makes Same-Sex Marriage a Right Nationwide," *New York Times*, June 26, 2015, https://www.nytimes.com/2015/06/27/us/supreme-court-same-sex-marriage.html.
6. Barbour, Christine and Gerald C. Wright. *Keeping the Republic, Power and Citizenship in American Politics*, 3rd Brief Edition. Sage/CQ Press, 2009.
7. Undercoffler, David. "Backup Cameras to be Required in All New Vehicles, Starting in 2018," *Los Angeles Times*, March 31, 2014, http://www.latimes.com/business/autos/la-fi-hy-autos-nhtsa-backup-camera-20140331-story.html.
8. World Health Organization. *Universal health coverage (UHC)*. http://www.who.int/mediacentre/factsheets/fs395/en/.
9. "This Day in Truman History, November 19, 1945, President Truman's Proposed Health Program," *Truman Library*, https://www.trumanlibrary.org/anniversaries/healthprogram.htm.

10 Zelizer, Julian E. "How Medicare Was Made," *The New Yorker*, February 15, 2015, http://www.newyorker.com/news/news-desk/medicare-made.
11 Davis, Karen and Kristof Stremikis, "The Costs of Failure: Economic Consequences of Failure to Enact Nixon, Carter, and Clinton Health Reforms," *The Commonwealth Fund*, December 21, 2009, http://www.commonwealthfund.org/publications/blog/the-costs-of-failure.
12 Quadagno, Jill, "Interest-Group Influence on the Patient Protection and Affordability Act of 2010: Winners and Losers in the Health Care Reform Debate." *Journal of Health Politics, Policy & Law*, vol. 36, no. 3 (June 2011).
13 "Chronology: Obama's Deal," *Frontline*, http://www.pbs.org/wgbh/pages/frontline/obamasdeal/etc/cron.html.
14 Pear, Robert and Sheryl Gay Stolberg, "Obama Says He Is Open to Altering Health Plan," *New York Times*, March 5, 2009, http://www.nytimes.com/2009/03/06/us/politics/06web-health.html.
15 Cohn, Jonathan, "How They Did It," *New Republic*, May 20, 2010, https://newrepublic.com/article/75077/how-they-did-it.
16 Quadagno, Jill, "Interest-Group Influence on the Patient Protection and Affordability Act of 2010: Winners and Losers in the Health Care Reform Debate," *Journal of Health Politics, Policy & Law*, Vol. 36, No. 3 (June 2011).
17 Cohn, Jonathan, "How They Did It," *New Republic*, May 20, 2010, https://newrepublic.com/article/75077/how-they-did-it.
18 Chaddock, Gail Russell. "Healthcare Reform: Obama Cut Private Deals with Likely Foes," *Christian Science Monitor*, November 6, 2009, http://www.csmonitor.com/USA/Politics/2009/1106/healthcare-reform-obama-cut-private-deals-with-likely-foes.
19 Young, Jeffrey. "AMA Endorses Senate Healthcare Reform Bill," *The Hill*, December 21, 2009, http://thehill.com/homenews/senate/73249-ama-endorses-senate-health-bill.
20 Quadagno, Jill, "Interest-Group Influence on the Patient Protection and Affordability Act of 2010: Winners and Losers in the Health Care Reform Debate," *Journal of Health Politics, Policy & Law*, Vol. 36, No. 3 (June 2011).
21 Palfrey, Judith S. "American Academy of Pediatrics Endorsement of Health Reform Legislations," *American Academy of Pediatrics*, March 19, 2010, https://www.aap.org/en-us/about-the-aap/aap-press-room/pages/American-Academy-of-Pediatrics-Endorsement-of-Health-Reform-Legislations.aspx.
22 Quadagno, Jill, "Interest-Group Influence on the Patient Protection and Affordability Act of 2010: Winners and Losers in the Health Care Reform Debate," *Journal of Health Politics, Policy & Law*, Vol. 36, No. 3 (June 2011).
23 Quadagno, Jill, "Interest-Group Influence on the Patient Protection and Affordability Act of 2010: Winners and Losers in the Health Care Reform Debate," *Journal of Health Politics, Policy & Law*, Vol. 36, No. 3 (June 2011).
24 Connolly, Ceci, "How Obama Revived His Health-Care Bill," *Washington Post*, March 23, 2010, http://www.washingtonpost.com/wp-dyn/content/article/2010/03/22/AR2010032203729_pf.html.
25 Bash, Dana, Lisa Desjardins, and Deirdre Walsh, "AMA, AARP Back House Health Care Bill," *CNN*, November 5, 2009, http://www.cnn.com/2009/POLITICS/11/05/health.care/.

26 Quadagno, Jill, "Interest-Group Influence on the Patient Protection and Affordability Act of 2010: Winners and Losers in the Health Care Reform Debate," *Journal of Health Politics, Policy & Law*, Vol. 36, No. 3 (June 2011).
27 "Chronology: Obama's Deal," *Frontline*, http://www.pbs.org/wgbh/pages/frontline/obamasdeal/etc/cron.html.
28 Zengerle, Patricia. "Obama Signs Order on Abortion and Healthcare," *Reuters*, Wed Mar 24, 2010, http://www.reuters.com/article/us-usa-healthcare-obama-idUSTRE62N61Y20100324.
29 Connolly, Ceci, "How Obama Revived His Health-Care Bill," *Washington Post*, March 23, 2010, http://www.washingtonpost.com/wp-dyn/content/article/2010/03/22/AR2010032203729_pf.html.
30 Klein, Philip. "GOP Cave on Obamacare Repeal is the Biggest Broken Promise in Political History," *Washington Examiner*, March 24, 2017, http://www.washingtonexaminer.com/gop-cave-on-obamacare-repeal-is-the-biggest-broken-promise-in-political-history/article/2618413.

THE SUPREME'S GREATEST HITS

BY DR. LYDIA ANDRADE
The University of the Incarnate Word

LEARNING OBJECTIVES

Students should be able to:

1. Understand how Supreme Court interpretation of the Constitution can be used to influence public policy.
2. Understand the development of Constitutional interpretations over time.

CONSTITUTIONAL UNDERPINNINGS

McCulloch v. Maryland (1819)

Issue of the case: Does the "necessary and proper" clause of Article I, section 8 of the U.S. Constitution allow the Congress to establish a national bank, even if that specific power is not listed among the enumerated powers and can a state (Maryland) use its taxing authority to make it difficult for such a bank to succeed?

Ruling and Significance: The Supreme Court voted unanimously in favor of an expansion of the Federal government's power to include establishing a bank. The court/case established that:

1. Congress has powers not specifically listed in the Constitution under the necessary and proper clause (so it could establish a bank).
2. Laws made by Congress pursuant to the Constitution are supreme over the laws passed by states.
3. Neither the national or state governments had the power to tax each other.

United States v. Lopez (1995)

Issue of the case: What are the limitations (if any) on Congress' ability to pass legislation based upon its power to regulate interstate commerce in Article I, section 8 of the Constitution? The law in question was the 1990 Gun-Free School Zone Act that made it a federal offense for an individual to possess a firearm in a school zone.

Ruling and Significance: In a 5–4 decision the court ruled that the Gun-Free School Zone Act was unconstitutional. The court/case established that:

1. Possession of a firearm was not an economic activity and as such was beyond the scope of the commerce clause.
2. This ruling acts as a limitation on the federal government's ability to regulate individual behavior within states.

Baker v. Carr (1962)

Issue of the case: Does the Supreme Court have jurisdiction over questions of state legislative apportionment?

Ruling and Significance: In a 6–2 decision, the court ruled that apportionment was justiciable issue. The court/case established that:

1. Failure of the State of Tennessee to reapportion their legislative districts in light of substantial population shifts over time, in essence denied equal protection of the laws guaranteed under the Fourteenth Amendment.

Shaw v. Reno (1993)

Issue of the case: Did a North Carolina reapportionment plan raise Fourteenth Amendment issues by creating majority-black congressional districts so usually shaped as to suggest their purpose was to ensure the election of black representatives.

Ruling and Significance: In a 5–4 decision the court held that while North Carolina's reapportionment plan appeared racially neutral, the shape of the districts were so unusual as to suggest they were drawn to separate voter into districts based on race and as such there were questions of equal protection The court/case established that:

1. Lacking some compelling governmental interest for drawing otherwise, districts must not be based solely on the racial makeup of the voters.

McDonald v. Chicago (2010)

Issue of the case: Does the Second Amendment (which was used in a previous case to strike down a Washington D.C. gun ban) apply to states and state gun bans?

Ruling and Significance: In a 5–4 decision the court ruled that the Fourteenth Amendment extends the Second Amendment right to bear arms to the states. The court/case established that:

1. States could not ban handguns.
2. However, states retain their rights to regulate possession of firearms by the mentally ill or felons, of the carrying of firearms in sensitive places such as schools and government buildings, and of conditions and qualifications on the sale of arms.

National Federation of Independent Businesses v. Sebelius (2012)

Issues of the case: Can the Patient Protection and Affordable Care Act mandate that individuals must purchase and maintain a minimum level of health insurance or face a tax penalty under the power to regulate interstate commerce in Article I, section 8 of the U.S. Constitution? Can states be required to accept the expansion of Medicaid which in order to receive any Medicaid funds? Can employers be required to offer for their employees to purchase group insurance?

Ruling and Significance: A divided Supreme Court ruled some parts of the Act Constitutional while striking down other components. The court/case established that:

1. The individual mandate was unconstitutional with respect to the power to regulate interstate commerce, but constitutional under Congress' power to tax.
2. The requirement that states accept the extension of Medicaid in order to receive any Medicaid funds was found to be unconstitutionally coercive and that the Spending Clause did not give Congress the power to threaten states with a complete loss of funding.
3. The Medicaid expansion could be constitutional if it did not include the threat to withhold all federal funds.

CIVIL RIGHTS AND LIBERTIES

Engel v. Vitale (1962)

Issue of the case: What religious activities, if any, are permissible in public ceremonies under the First Amendment's no establishment of religion clause (often simply called the "Establishment" clause)? The state of New York Board of Regents had drafted a nondenominational prayer to be read in state schools in an attempt to take the question of prayer in schools out of individual school districts and comply with the U.S. Constitution.

Ruling and Significance: In a 6–1 decision the court ruled in favor of the plaintiff, Engel. The court/case established that:

1. A state authored prayer violated the Establishment clause.
2. The fact that the prayer was voluntary and nondenominational did not prevent it from violating the establishment clause.
3. This case opened the door for the court to hear a variety of cases concerning religious activities customarily incorporated in public ceremonies. The court would continue to use the establishment clause to prohibit many of these activities.

Lemon v. Kurtzman (1971)

Issue of the case: Did state financial support for nonpublic "church-related educational institutions" violate the establishment clause of the Constitution?

Ruling and Significance: In a unanimous decision the court ruled that such funding was unconstitutional. The court/case established that:

1. A three-part test to determine constitutionality of laws in relation to the establishment clause. To be constitutional any law would need to have "a secular, as opposed to a religious, legislative purpose," its effect should be to neither advance nor hinder religion, and it should not create "excessive government entanglement with religion."
2. The court also warned against the "divisive political potential" of any legislation providing support for church related education.

Wisconsin v. Yoder (1972)

Issue of the case: Did state law requiring all children to attend school until the age of 16 violate the freedom of religion clause of the First Amendment by making it a crime to not to send children to school for religious reasons? The case related to Amish beliefs.

Ruling and Significance: In a unanimous decision the court ruled that the state could not compel a parent to send children to school beyond the 8th grade. The court/case established that:

1. The interest of the state did not outweigh an individual's sincerely held religious beliefs.

Tinker v. Des Moines Independent Community School District (1969)

Issue of the case: Did the school districts actions to prohibition and suspension of students for wearing black arm bands in demonstration of a political position violate the student's freedom of expression in the form of "symbolic speech?"

Ruling and Significance: In a 7–2 decision the court ruled that the district had violated the student's right to freedom of expression. The court/case established that:

1. Limitations on free speech would be justified only through the demonstration that such speech would "materially and substantially interfere" with school operations.
2. Children are not necessarily given the full extent of the First Amendment rights.
3. There is a distinction between communication through symbolic action and that of using words and both have protections under the First Amendment.

New York Times Company v. United States (1971)

Issue of the case: Did the attempt by the Nixon administration to prevent the publication of information taken from a classified Defense Department study violate the First Amendment's freedom of press?

Ruling and Significance: The court ruled that the argument that prior restraint was necessary to ensure national security was unsupported. The court/case established that:

1. There is a "heavy presumption against" the use of prior restraint, that is, using government authority to prevent publication of information.

2. Prior restraint would not be justified unless there was evidence that publication would cause direct, immediate, and inevitable harm to the safety of the U.S. Forces.

Schenck v. United States (1919)

Issue of the case: Did the prosecution of Schenck for violation of the Espionage Act for sending flyers to draftees in the World War I urging them "not to submit to intimidation" violate his First Amendment right of freedom of speech.

Ruling and Significance: In a unanimous decision, the court ruled that the First Amendment does not protect those urging unlawful conduct. The court/case established that:

1. During war certain speech may be considered unlawful which would be legal during times of peace.
2. Speech can be limited if it "were to create a clear and present danger" of bringing about "substantive evils that Congress has a right to prevent."
3. A "clear and present danger" test to be used in future cases concerning the limitations on free speech.

Gideon v. Wainwright (1963)

Issue of the case: Does the right to counsel in criminal cases listed in the Sixth Amendment extend beyond felony cases?

Ruling and Significance: In a unanimous decision the court ruled that when the state of Florida chose to provide counsel for indigent defendants only in capital cases, it denied Gideon (sentenced to 5 years in prison for a misdemeanor under a "repeat offender" law) his rights under the Sixth Amendment. The court/case established that:

1. The importance of a defendant being able to put on a proper defense was integral to the framers' emphasis on due process.
2. States would be required to provide the assistance of counsel for any defendant not able to afford it on their own.

Mapp v. Ohio (1961)

Issue of the case: Is evidence collected as a result of a search conducted without a warrant certifying "probable cause" under Fourth Amendment admissible in state criminal cases?

Ruling and Significance: In a 6-3 ruling the court decided in favor of Mapp. The court/case established that:

1. Any evidence obtained as a result of "searches and seizures in violation of the Constitution is by [the Fourth Amendment] inadmissible in state court."
2. The use of illegally obtained information was prohibited from court proceedings at all levels of government.
3. This came to be known as the exclusionary rule.

Griswold v. Connecticut (1965)

Issue of the case: Did a Connecticut law which made it a crime to provide medical treatment or counseling to married couples for the purpose of preventing conception violate a right to marital privacy? In terms of constitutional issues, was "privacy" protected by the Ninth Amendment to the Constitution?

Ruling and Significance: In a 7–2 decision the court that the Connecticut law was unconstitutional. The court/case established that:

1. While there is no explicit right to privacy listed in the Constitution, the combination of the First, Third, Fourth, and Ninth Amendments create a right to privacy in marital relations. Critical to the finding was that "privacy," though not listed as a specific right in the Constitution, was implied by provisions in the First, Third, and Fourth Amendments. The provision in the Ninth Amendment that a listing of rights in the Constitution did not "deny or disparage others retained by the people" anticipated claims such as the right to privacy.
2. The ruling set a precedent for a right to privacy.

Roe v. Wade (1971)

Issue of the case: Did the constitutional right to privacy extend to a women's choice to terminate a pregnancy by abortion? And if so, when did state interests in protecting the right to life begin?

Ruling and Significance: In a 7–2 decision the court ruled that abortion was covered by the right to privacy and protected by the Fourteenth Amendment. The court/case established that:

1. A woman had the right to seek an abortion in the first trimester of a pregnancy, using the "common law" notion that pregnancy was meaningfully divided into three separate stages, called "trimesters."
2. States were given more leeway in banning abortion in the second trimester when the state was considered to have a greater interest.
3. States could ban abortions in the third trimester, under the common law notion that once a baby had "quickened," that is, once the mother could feel the baby kick, life had begun.

Gitlow v. New York (1925)

Issue of the case: When the state of New York convicted Gitlow for violating a criminal anarchy law for distributing socialist documents calling for the overthrow of the government, did they violate the free speech protection of the U.S. Constitution, even if the Bill of Rights was intended to limit the powers of Congress, and not the states?

Ruling and Significance: The case was argued twice in front of the court. In both instances the court ruled in favor of the state of New York. The court/case established that:

1. The First Amendment does apply to states as well as the national government, and is "incorporated" to the states by way of the intent, expressed in the Fourteenth Amendment, that states must provide citizens the "due process of the law."

2. The Free Speech Clause does not protect all speech.
3. A state may decide a class of speech so dangerous as to be prohibited.
4. An individual may be prosecuted for banned speech even if it does not result in the danger for which it was prohibited.

Miranda v. Arizona (1966)

Issue of the case: Do the constitutional protections against self-incrimination (Fifth Amendment) and the right to counsel (Sixth Amendment) apply to police custody and interrogations? And must those accused of crime be informed about their rights before interrogation can occur?

Ruling and Significance: The court had been asked to hear several cases in which defendants had been questioned in police custody without being informed of their right to counsel. Ruling on the cases jointly, the court ruled that statements made by defendants while in custody could not be used against them unless procedures could be demonstrated "effect to serve the privilege against self-incrimination." The court/case established:

1. A set of warnings police were required to provide defendants upon being taken into custody. These warnings have become known as the Miranda Warnings.

CIVIL RIGHTS

Plessy v. Ferguson (1896)

Issue of the case: Did state racial segregation laws requiring separate compartments on trains violate the equal protection of the Fourteenth Amendment?

Ruling and Significance: In a 7–1 ruling the court upheld the state's segregation laws. The court/case established that:

1. Segregation itself does not constitute unlawful discrimination.
2. It set up a standard of "separate but equal" to determine the constitutionality of segregation laws.

Brown v. Board of Education of Topeka (1) (1954)

Issue of the case: Did racial segregation in public schools violate the equal protection clause of the Fourteenth Amendment?

Ruling and Significance: The court ruled that separate educational facilities were inherently unequal and violated the Fourteenth Amendment's equal protection clause, thus overturning the finding of *Plessy v. Ferguson*. The case established that:

1. Racial segregation was detrimental to minorities and was seen as a sign of inferiority.
2. It forced states to reconfigure public school systems across the United States.

Brown v. Board of Education of Topeka (2) (1955)

Issue of the case: How should states implement the desegregation required under *Brown v. Board* (1)?

Ruling and Significance: In a unanimous decision the court stated that school desegregation should occur "with all deliberate speed." The court/case established that:

1. It was the responsibility of local governments to determine how to implement the desegregation required under *Brown v. Board* but they should move toward full compliance as quickly as possible.
2. If state and local governments did not desegregate under the terms of the ruling, federal district judges would supervise the process.

PARTIES, ELECTIONS, AND INTEREST GROUPS

Buckley v. Valeo (1976)

Issue of the case: Did the limitations on personal contributions to a single campaign and the reporting requirements of the Federal Election Campaign Act violate the protections for Freedom of Speech and Assembly of the First Amendment?

Ruling and Significance: In a 6-2 ruling the court/case established that:

1. Limitations on individual contributions by candidates to their own political campaigns were protected by the First Amendment's freedom of speech.
2. Limitations on independent expenditures would violate the First Amendment's support for freedom of association and right to inform the public regarding political matters.

Citizens United v. Federal Election Commission (2010)

Issue of the case: Did the restrictions on "electioneering communication" entailed in the Bipartisan Campaign Reform Act (BCRA) violate First Amendment?

Ruling and Significance: In a 5–4 split decision the court ruled that the restrictions were unconstitutional. The court/case established that:

1. Political speech cannot be banned based on the speaker's corporate status.
2. The disclosure requirements of the BCRA requiring disclosure of the donors supporting political advertisement/speech were constitutional.
3. It upheld the ban on direct contributions to candidates from corporations or unions.

JUDICIARY

Marbury v. Madison (1803)

Issues of the case: Can the Supreme Court require the U.S. president to deliver political appointments made by the previous president under the Federal Judiciary Act of 1789?

Does the Supreme Court have the authority to review the acts of Congress to determine constitutionality?

Ruling and Significance: In a unanimous decision the court ruled that it is the responsibility of the Judiciary to determine what is constitutional. The court/case established:

1. As the agent of the president, Secretary of State James Madison violated the Judiciary Act's provision to deliver Marbury's appointment to him.
2. However, the Judiciary Act's provision giving authority to hear the case was itself unconstitutional, and therefore the Supreme Court did not have authority to rule in the case.
3. The case established that the Supreme Court had the power of Judicial Review.

Multiple Choice Questions

1. The case in which the Supreme Court ruled that campaign contribution limits placed on candidates contributions to their own campaign were violations of free speech was:
   a. Buckley v. Valeo
   b. Gitlow v. New York
   c. Wisconsin v. Yoder
   d. Smith v. Federal Election Commission
   e. none of the above

   Answer: A

2. The Supreme Court ruled that evidence obtained as a result of unlawful searches and seizures were inadmissible in court in:
   a. Gideon v. Wainwright
   b. Miranda v. Arizona
   c. Mapp v. Ohio
   d. Griswold v. Connecticut
   e. McDonald v. Chicago

   Answer: A

3. The Patient Protection and Affordable Care Act was found to be constitutional due to:
   a. Congress's ability to regulate interstate trade
   b. The power of the President to delegate power to the bureaucracy
   c. The power of the national government to tax
   d. The Fourteenth Amendment.
   e. All of the above

   Answer: C

4. The Supreme Court case which set the precedent for the right to privacy was:
   a. McDonald v. Chicago
   b. Miranda v. Arizona
   c. Griswold v. Connecticut
   d. Gideon V. Wainwright
   e. Buckley V. Valeo

   Answer: C

5. The case which yielded the "clear and present danger" standard for limitations of free speech was:
   a. Schenck v. United States
   b. Brown v. Board of Education of Topeka.
   c. Baker v. Carr
   d. U.S. v. Lopez
   e. none of the above

   Answer: A

Discussion Question

Explain how the Supreme Court has expanded and interpreted the Fourteenth Amendment over time.

CPSIA information can be obtained
at www.ICGtesting.com
Printed in the USA
FFOW05n1431170817